Experimenting with Emerging Media Platforms

Experimenting with Emerging Media Platforms teaches students in media tracks – journalism, advertising, film, and public relations – how to independently field test and evaluate emerging technologies that could impact how media is produced, consumed, and monetized in the future.

Taking a unique trial-and-error approach, the author encourages students to go against their desire for perfection and instead plunge into exercises with the full expectation that they will "fail" many times before they succeed. Through focused assignments, this book provides pointers on how to familiarize oneself with current technology, including extended reality (XR, VR, AR, and MR), open-source coding, photogrammetry, aerial imagery using drones, automation, and artificial intelligence. Readers are invited to create and test their own hypotheses and work outside of their comfort zones to reach conclusions on how a technology could enhance storytelling for a particular audience. Through experimentation guided by workbook exercises, case studies from students and media practitioners, practical tips, and reminders about ethical decision-making, students will learn how to work like explorers and civic hackers to enact change in the media landscape. Readers are invited to share their final field test results online through the book's companion website and social media channels, where the author will post links to further reading, coding templates for simple projects, and short video tutorials.

Built around an established course being taught by the author and informed by over 20 years' experience in media industries, *Experimenting with Emerging Media Platforms* is essential reading for aspiring media professionals and students undertaking courses such as Emerging Media, Media Innovation, and Media Startups.

For additional resources, please see the companion website: www.emergingmedia platforms.com.

Dan Pacheco is Professor of Practice and Peter A. Horvitz Endowed Chair of Journalism Innovation at the S.I. Newhouse School of Public Communications, USA.

Experimenting with Emerging Media Platforms
Field Testing the Future

Dan Pacheco

Routledge
Taylor & Francis Group

NEW YORK AND LONDON

Designed cover image: © Dan Pacheco via Midjourney

First published 2023
by Routledge
605 Third Avenue, New York, NY 10158

and by Routledge
4 Park Square, Milton Park, Abingdon, Oxon, OX14 4RN

Routledge is an imprint of the Taylor & Francis Group, an informa business

© 2023 Dan Pacheco

Library of Congress Cataloging-in-Publication Data
Names: Pacheco, Dan, 1971- author.
Title: Experimenting with emerging media platforms : field testing the future / Dan Pacheco.
Description: New York : Routledge, 2023. | Includes bibliographical references and index.
Identifiers: LCCN 2022056471 (print) | LCCN 2022056472 (ebook) | ISBN 9781032160931 (hardback) | ISBN 9781032160924 (paperback) | ISBN 9781003247012 (ebook)
Subjects: LCSH: Mass media—Technological innovations. | Digital media—Technological innovations. | Online social networks. | Social media.
Classification: LCC P96.T42 P33 2023 (print) | LCC P96.T42 (ebook) | DDC 302.23/1—dc23
LC record available at https://lccn.loc.gov/2022056471
LC ebook record available at https://lccn.loc.gov/2022056472

ISBN: 9781032160931 (hbk)
ISBN: 9781032160924 (pbk)
ISBN: 9781003247012 (ebk)

DOI: 10.4324/9781003247012

Typeset in Goudy
by Apex CoVantage, LLC

Access the companion website: www.emergingmediaplatforms.com

Contents

List of Figures   vii
About the Author   viii
Acknowledgments   ix
Foreword by Gary Kebbel   xi

Introduction: Experimenting with Emerging Media
Platforms: Field Testing the Future   1

1 Who Can Predict the Future?   6

2 Change Theories   18

3 Initiating Your Field Test   27

4 Open-Source Technologies   42

5 XR and the Metaverse   56

6 Augmented Reality   76

7 Conducting Your Field Test   90

8 360 Photography and Video   107

9 Photogrammetry   125

10 Data, AI, Automation, and Bots   143

11 Autonomous Flying Cameras   167

12 Field Testing the Future   185

    Afterword: The Edge of Innovation   193

    Index   196

Figures

0.1 Broadcast student Ryan Baker (left) gets tips from Professor
     Dan Pacheco (right) on how to 3D scan objects using the
     iPhone 12's LiDAR sensors   1
5.1 A scene being created in the Reach.love browser-based editor   66
6.1 The model should appear in your space like this. Just substitute
     your own pet!   82
6.2 Ryan Baker's mobile-friendly site showing how to project 3D
     models of sculptures into a room   85
8.1 A 360 tour of the Newhouse School as rendered in A-Frame   114
9.1 What the Trnio Plus app sees for a typical indoor scene on
     an iPhone 13 Pro. From left to right: the visual picture from
     the phone's camera; the augmented reality capture using AR
     Capture; and the structural data from the phone's LiDAR
     sensors   131
9.2 Sonny Cirasuolo and Amanda Paule using a 60-megapixel
     camera with ring flash to 3D capture the inside of the People's
     AME Church of Zion in Syracuse, New York   137
10.1 How data appear inside a spreadsheet program. This is from
     Google Sheets, but you could just as easily use Excel   146
11.1 An example of a video I captured during a shoot with Syracuse
     University's Otto the Orange mascot   175

About the Author

Dan Pacheco is Professor of Practice and Peter A. Horvitz Endowed Chair of Journalism Innovation at the S.I. Newhouse School of Public Communications, where he teaches courses about virtual reality storytelling, data and digital journalism, and emerging media platforms.

Pacheco is a pioneer in the use of virtual reality for journalism. In 2014, he started and co-produced The Des Moines Register's Harvest of Change VR project for the Oculus Rift, the world's first large-scale use of virtual reality by a commercial news organization. Harvest of Change earned an Edward R. Murrow Award in 2015 for its innovative use of 360 video for virtual reality. He was chosen as a member of the Interactive Board of Jurors for the 2023 Peabody Awards.

Previously, Pacheco spent 20 years in the trenches of digital publishing, everywhere from Fortune 500 companies to startups. He started his career as an online producer for Washingtonpost.com, where he produced Interact, one of the first online news communities. Subsequently, as a principal product manager at America Online, he oversaw some of the Internet's first truly global community products.

In 2005, after pioneering the first implementation of a social networking platform at a US newspaper, he received an NAA "20 Under 40" award. And in 2007, he received a Knight News Challenge grant to build a democratized publishing service that evolved into an eBook platform.

In 2020, he received an Online News Association Journalism 360 grant to work with Newhouse School students to produce "The Racial Divide," a virtual reality piece that explores the African American 15th Ward in Syracuse, whose thousands of residents were displaced in the 1960s in order to create a highway overpass. The resulting project, which can be viewed at Visualizing81.thenewshouse.com, has received numerous awards. Among them are the first place for Immersion Journalism by the Society of Professional Journalists' Mark of Excellence Awards and the first place in Innovation by the Society for Features Journalism Mark of Excellence Awards.

Pacheco gives presentations and seminars about media innovation and XR internationally. He was born on an Air Force base in northwest Florida and grew up in Colorado. He also spent significant parts of his life in Puerto Rico and Holland. He currently lives in the Syracuse University neighborhood with his partner and puppy.

Acknowledgments

There are so many people I wish I could acknowledge here, and I know I will fail to include them all. But I would like to start with the incredible students I have had the pleasure to work with going back over ten years at the Newhouse School of Public Communications. What I learned from watching them run field tests in the Emerging Media Platforms course, both online and in person, especially informed the contents of this book. Thanks to all of them!

I also want to thank the inspiring industry innovators who gave interviews. From the bottom of my heart, thank you to Dan Archer, Bob Bierman, Sonny Cirasuolo, Nonny de la Peña, Bill Frischling, Ken Harper, Mickey Osterreicher, Thomas Seymat, Veda Shastri, Dan Schultz, and Christina Vazquez. I admire you all greatly and also consider each of you friends.

A particular shout-out to Dean Lorraine Branham (now deceased, bless her soul), my previous department chair Steve Davis, and Peter A. Horvitz, who endows my position at the Newhouse School where I do most of the research and development that is explored in this book. The three of them came together to create the Journalism Innovation Chair at the Newhouse School, which afforded me the time and opportunity to continue innovating outside of the media industry while sending students I work with back into the industry to ensure it has a future that embraces change.

I have many colleagues to thank, but especially want to call out Sean Branagan, Corey Takahashi, Makana Chock, Aileen Gallagher, Seth Gitner, Jon Glass, Tula Goenka, Brad Gorham, and Jeff Passetti – each of whom is an innovator in their own right and has done many things to support me and my exploration of emerging media platforms over the years.

Thank you to Jeanette Chavez, for giving me my first writing job as a feature reporter at *The Denver Post*, and Mary Lou Fulton, who as managing editor of *The Washington Post's* Digital Ink gave me my start in digital journalism. Mary Lou later encouraged me to apply for the Knight News Challenge and supported me in my efforts to bring innovation to other newspapers.

Thank you to the Knight Foundation for having faith in me and other innovators in the mid-2000s and setting us on a path of continued exploration. You are one of the modern Medicis of journalism, and I know I speak for many in saying that I would not still be doing what I do if it weren't for Knight's early support and ongoing investment in journalism innovation. In particular, thank you, Gary

Kebbel (now at the University of Nebraska) for starting the Knight News Challenge and continuing to engage with the early winners through the Mobile Me & You conference.

Thank you to my parents, who in addition to making me who I am, held off on visiting for one summer and postponed a family reunion so that I could complete the marathon that this book entailed. And finally, I acknowledge the support of my family, including my partner Jim Costello and my children Elena and Lauren. All three provided the kind of feedback, encouragement, support, and love without which this book wouldn't have been possible.

Foreword

By Gary Kebbel

Dan Pacheco is a perfect person to be teaching students how to think about communication inventions, innovations, and experiments. He brings years of entrepreneurial creativity, daredevil zeal, and solid journalism experience to his position as Professor of Practice and Peter A. Horvitz Endowed Chair of Journalism Innovation at the S.I. Newhouse School of Public Communications.

In his book, *Experimenting with Emerging Media Platforms*, Pacheco shows readers how to prepare for jobs that don't exist yet. In doing that, he also shows us how to tell our stories, or any stories that interest us, in new ways, with new technologies and new power. This book is a wonderful combination of teaching new storytelling technologies, like augmented reality or photogrammetry or artificial intelligence, along with teaching how to think about not-yet-invented technologies. He encourages readers to be that next creator.

The author is teaching us all, from several different directions, not only how to survive in a culture of constant change but also when that culture is inevitable, change is the most fundamental survival tactic we have.

From his past entrepreneurial innovations and his experience at the Bakersfield Californian or washingtonpost.com or AOL, Pacheco has learned that great ideas rarely rise or fall on their own merit. They don't succeed just because the innovator is earnest and works hard and long. They are affected by so many external factors, such as "Is everything right about this idea except the timing?" and "Is it five years too early?"

Surviving in a culture of constant change means you need to learn how to recognize these factors. Pacheco shows us a great way to do it. He discusses a dozen communication technologies that help us tell stories in ways we couldn't 15 years ago. In teaching how to experience the Metaverse, for example, he's not only showing us how to use a new technology but also showing that when we play with a new technology, we learn how to play with future ones. He teaches the mindset we need to thrive in change, and be a change leader.

All teachers know that if they teach their students a skill, and those students are using it a year from now, much less throughout their lives, then the teachers have done their jobs well. *Experimenting with Emerging Media Platforms* teaches skills for now, such as using 360 video and 3D video or drones or bots, as well as the fact that experimenting and just playing around with new technologies is a future life skill.

Pacheco analyzes his innovations that were good enough to receive foundation funding and uses his experience to show what can work and what can go wrong. More importantly, he shows readers how to be honest and turn a critical eye on themselves when analyzing their own ideas. He shows that analyzing an idea that didn't work as intended is still a tremendous learning experience. That's what this book is about: succeeding in the future, not the present. He shows readers how to move out of their comfort zones to learn new technologies, to experiment, succeed and fail, and then to learn from that process before we move on to our next challenge.

The book also walks readers through creating, analyzing, and reporting on field tests of their ideas and experiments. The goal is not to succeed, fail, and learn in private. Help others do the same. Eliminate the need for others to waste time and energy creating what you have already created and learned. Share your work and your knowledge. Become part of the research community.

Pacheco interviews established industry experts and his past students who are rapidly becoming industry experts. They all show that their careers went in directions they never predicted because they were ready and able to take advantage of the cards dealt them. They didn't need the comfort of knowing where they would end up before they started on their journeys. That's another lesson this book teaches.

The author's tone is friendly and patient. Pacheco is just the kind of guide you want when you are uncomfortable and feeling unable to learn a new task or a new way of thinking.

Experimenting with Emerging Media Platforms is a challenge to those embedded in an industry where the believers in the revenue model can't see the way to change, even though revenue keeps falling. As Pacheco says, "What if the changes in an industry are so significant that the only solution is to give up everything old and join the new?" The book urges us to think about that question while imagining our futures. Do we think our best future lies in knowing what people know now, or do we think industry practice now is the baseline from which we must change and be comfortable in a culture of constant change? Future techniques and tools might be unimaginable, but this book shows us that the way to use them and grow with them isn't.

Gary Kebbel is Professor Emeritus at the University of Nebraska-Lincoln, where he was a dean for two years. He has taught journalism for 17 years at Nebraska and Northern Illinois University. He spent four years as the Knight Foundation Journalism Program Director, creating and running the first Knight News Challenge grant program, which provided $25 million in funding for innovative digital journalism projects. He was one of the founding editors of USATODAY.com. While home page editor at washingtonpost.com, he was also on the team that created Newsweek.com. Kebbel was Director of AOL News for four years. Finally, he is a two-time Fulbright Senior Specialist who has taught digital media in South Africa and Ethiopia; and a US State Department social media trainer in Nigeria, Russia, Taiwan, Kenya, Tunisia, and Latvia. He started and runs the Mobile Me & You mobile-first conference which teaches best practices in mobile media technology to students, faculty, and professionals.

Introduction
Experimenting with Emerging Media Platforms: Field Testing the Future

How do you teach the future, and how do you position yourself to thrive during times of constant change? Nobody knows the future, so is this even possible? Those questions are at the heart of this book and the reason that it exists. But to explain, I need to go back ten years to the start of my favorite job.

My Dream Job and Biggest Challenge

Figure 0.1 Broadcast student Ryan Baker (left) gets tips from Professor Dan Pacheco (right) on how to 3D scan objects using the iPhone 12's LiDAR sensors.

(*Source*: Photo/Marilyn Hesler, Syracuse University Magazine. Used with permission.)

In August 2012, I found myself with what can only be described as my dream job as the Peter A. Horvitz Endowed Chair in Journalism Innovation at the S.I. Newhouse School. In what can best be described as a futuristic Star Trek-type job

DOI: 10.4324/9781003247012-1

description, my mission was to "explore the intersection of journalism and technology," preparing students for careers on the digital side of journalism in which they would enthusiastically run toward change rather than cower from it; embrace disruption as a creative force, and use it as a catalyst for careers in which they would be agents of change as opposed to "the changed."

I had done this in my own 20-year career to great fanfare (more on that later), and now I was ready to translate all that knowledge to the next generation. Easy, right? I entered my first class with a glimmer in my eye and a fresh syllabus about creating digital news startups, naively thinking that what worked for me in the past would work for everyone else. I brushed off some PowerPoints about my various travels in the worlds of digital journalism, entrepreneurship, and tech companies and started to engage students, and was met with . . . blank stares.

In that first semester, it became painfully apparent that my initial plan of imparting knowledge based on my own experiences was just not going to cut it. My students studying journalism – and later, every communications field and others like architecture – were interested in their own stories, not mine.

The best just wanted to create some extra sizzle for their portfolios that would help them get better jobs. Their ideas for innovation had more to do with making their content stand out to their audiences, not solving the financial problems of legacy news businesses. And to be honest, by the time I was teaching, most of my examples of innovation from four years prior were already old and stale.

It took me about three years to discover that my job had nothing to do with innovating around the edges or making things 10% better or even improving on what was in the past. And it wasn't going to be my own past innovations that made a difference going forward. I had to completely embrace the idea of constant, unrelenting, fundamental change being the norm. I also had to do what was the hardest thing for a geek like me to do: force myself to look past the shiny objects of what's new today and actually *fall out of love* with technology itself.

And finally, I had to embrace the inherent messiness of innovation and the reality that it must always have a short shelf life. If not, it ain't innovation!

Embrace the Mess

Edward R. Murrow talked about not being distracted by the wires and lights in a box in a medium that was, in his day, innovative: television. But in true innovation, your day-to-day life is often exactly that: a table covered in messy wires and lights and a boneyard of quickly outdated technology that gathers space in a cabinet. For every success, you will have at least 20 failures, and they will inevitably form a long trail of blood-red wires and bolts behind you.

In the Innovation Lab I oversee, we call this space the "Cabinet of Modern Antiquities." It contains so many old headsets, drones, sensors, Arduino shields, 3D printed camera rigs, and other things I can't even identify any more that I feel like I need to call either a recycling center or a technology museum to figure out what to do with the now-useless artifacts stacked up in it.

This book is a culmination of what I have learned in the trenches of teaching innovation and a method of teaching an innovative mindset. It's also a companion for what I consider my best class, Emerging Media Platforms.

It gets into some practical tips for what, in 2022, were cutting-edge innovations. If you're a student, you can use it to brush up on some new digital publishing skills and think about media in ways you may not have considered. If you're a teacher, you can use it for the same or even as a companion for a similar innovation class. And if you're neither, you can use it to start out on a journey toward change.

But what is most important is to keep in mind that the skills you learn here, by definition, have a very short lifespan – at least in how they are described today. I have done my best to pick relatively new technologies that I believe have a five- to ten-year horizon of evolution, but that's just my guess. As you will learn in future chapters, it's easy to guess wrong. What you will learn by trying out some of these technologies is simply that – learning by *doing*. The doing is the part that changes your mindset and helps you spot opportunities that you would never have seen otherwise.

Ultimately, the specific skills themselves won't be as important as the most important skill, which is your ability to evaluate any promising new technology for how it can help you tell better stories today. Also, to project ahead to how it may either fundamentally change how we all produce or consume media or disappear into the boneyard.

Before you get started, I want to warn you that by the end of this book, you aren't going to fall in love with technology. In fact, you may find that you hate some of it and that you become its biggest skeptic. I bet you are a little surprised by that since you just bought a book about technology, right?

Instead, you will be ready to try out a lot of different technologies, some of which scare you, in a never-ending quest to find new ways to enhance your audience's understanding of complex information – which, in my mind, is the whole point of journalism and the best forms of storytelling. If you keep that warning in mind, you won't ever look back at the Cabinet of Modern Antiquities or, worse, end up as an artifact there yourself.

You won't learn any of this by what I tell you but rather by trying it out yourself with your own imperfect project that I call a Field Test. So if you're ready to get your hands dirty, jump into my sandbox.

How to Use This Book

This book is a companion to a course I designed and teach at the S.I. Newhouse School of Public Communications. It can be used as a companion for your own course or as an individual who wants to learn how to innovate on the bleeding edge.

The first two chapters till the soil and get it ready for planting.

In Chapter 1, you'll see some examples of famous predictions that came true and some really bad or mediocre predictions and failed attempts. Through this, you will gain some insights into how to position yourself in your career to notice and take advantage of innovations while remaining skeptical enough not to get dragged down when things inevitably change again.

In Chapter 2, I'll go over some theories for what drives technological change and disruption, how companies and industries respond to change, and what the winners do differently in order to remain relevant in a period of prolonged change.

After that, I'll do some deep dives into media technologies that were on the bleeding edge in 2022. They're broken into these general categories: XR (AR, VR, and MR); open source and coding; 360 photography and video; photogrammetry; data and artificial intelligence; conversational interfaces; and drone technology and regulations.

Workbook Exercises

Throughout the book, you will be invited to participate in workbook exercises. Some involve thinking through concepts, while others involve actually building something – usually with templates I provide – related to the technology covered in that chapter. For any exercise that requires code or a template, you can find them at this book's website: www.emergingmediaplatforms.com. Workbook exercises are organized by chapter.

As you progress, you will be invited to conceptualize and carry out a field test, a controlled experiment where you try to solve a problem for a specific audience using an emerging media platform of your choice. In Chapters 3, 7, and 12, you will work on your own field test, ultimately culminating in a field test report. All of this is buttressed by case studies of field tests done by some of my most innovative students in this course over the past four years and interviews with industry experts who have gone through similar processes throughout their careers.

In order to comply with US Federal privacy laws, students are mentioned by their first name only, and in some cases, I have changed their names. With their permission, some of their field test reports are included with their names on the book's website. Industry experts are always mentioned by name, also with their permission.

While you don't have to actually do a field test to finish the book, I recommend that you still read those sections so that you're prepared to do a field test when you're ready.

Case Studies and Expert Interviews

Finally, I've peppered the book with interviews with industry experts whose careers are defined by innovation. They are presented in a raw conversational style as if you're sitting with them and me at a coffee shop. I present them this way to bring their humanity to the forefront. As you will see, I ask them not just to talk about what they did that worked but also what failed – sometimes spectacularly – and what they learned from those experiences. I also get into some of my own failures.

It's my hope that you see that with just a little bit of work over a long period of time, you can also be like one of those people. What they and I share in common is that we came to be known as innovators by being constantly curious, always plunging ourselves into the unknown. When things didn't work out the way we expected, we examined the data and listened to our intuition, and tried different approaches. The only true constant in innovation is change.

Sharing Your Journey of Innovation

The last aspect of the book happens online. I've created a website and Slack group for everyone who goes through the workbook exercises and field test process so that you can share what you've created. There are also channels in the group for socializing, sharing interesting stories, examples of cool uses of emerging technologies, and places to reach out when you're stuck and need some help. Students who are taking a class with me will also be using the same slack in their own channel. You can find that via a prominent link at https://emergingmediaplatforms.com.

Speaking of Change . . .

When I wrote this book during the summer of 2022, I constantly struggled to keep things up to date. Literally every week, some new update would come about for at least one of the technologies covered in each chapter.

It finally dawned on me that there's no way for a printed book about emerging technology to ever be completely up to date. In 2023 and beyond, you will inevitably read about things here that have changed, evolved, disappeared, or been replaced by something completely different. A good example of that is artificial intelligence and machine learning, which have been evolving at a staggering pace every few months.

I try to address this reality on the website with updates on significant developments in the technologies covered in the book, as well as others that may not be in the book at all. You may also find people talking about these things in the Slack group. But another way to look at it is that what you read about here is a benchmark in time. The important thing is not necessarily to become an expert in any of these technology categories but use them as a springboard for you to become an expert at taking advantage of any new technology when you see an opportunity to use it to solve an information problem or an unmet need.

With that, let's get to the experimentation!

1   Who Can Predict the Future?

One of the most important skills to hone throughout your career is making smart predictions about new technologies and making good guesses about how they might impact the future of media production and consumption. It's also the hardest to get right.

Even the most grounded among us can agree that if we had specific knowledge of the future, we could be rich and successful beyond our wildest dreams. This was humorously explored in Back to the Future II, where Marty McFly's nemesis Biff got his hands on Marty's sports almanac from the year 2020. He returned in time and gave it to his younger self, who went on to make a fortune betting on sports.

Alas, there is no Delorian time machine or Grays Sports Almanac from 50 years in the future, but there are plenty of examples of people who have made predictions. Some came true almost exactly as written by science fiction authors and were even inspired by them. Others came true in part, but not exactly as envisioned or on the same timeframe. And others, well . . . they were too myopic, or just flat out wrong.

As you read through these examples of good and bad predictions, I invite you to contextualize them for yourself today, looking ahead and trying to make intelligent bets for where to position yourself in your career. When you look at technologies that were trends in 2022, like the Metaverse or the DALL·E 2 AI art engine – ask yourself – what might some future almanac say about them in 10 or 20 years?

Arthur C. Clarke's Crystal Ball

We can't see forward in time, but we can look back at the attempts of some prescient people to predict what was coming. My favorite comes from Arthur C. Clarke, the author of the short story that became Stanley Kubrik's movie, 2001: A Space Odyssey, and numerous other sci-fi novels. He's also responsible for this juicy quote: "Any sufficiently advanced technology is indistinguishable from magic," in his essay Profiles of the Future: An Inquiry Into the Limits of the Possible.

One of Clarke's most famous predictions came from an essay he wrote in 1946, suggesting that Nazi rocket technology could be used to place what he called "artificial satellites" in orbit and that microwaves could be bounced off them to send

DOI: 10.4324/9781003247012-2

information across the globe. Not only did this eventually happen but the geosynchronous orbits of such satellites are called Clarke Orbits.

Surely a lot of people looked at this and thought, what a fantastic, expensive, and even magical idea. You can almost imagine their criticism: "That couldn't really work." "It's not practical." "It's too expensive. Who will pay for that?" But a mere 11 years later, the first such satellite (Sputnik) was launched by the Soviet Union in 1957. And today, our entire modern world runs on data, much of which is sent around through communications satellites.

Clarke made other predictions that may seem equally ridiculous today simply because they haven't happened yet. But keep your eye out for these: brain backup technology, cryogenic freezing for long space flights, and deflecting asteroids from the earth by having rockets land on them.

You may think, "I'm a communications student, not a rocket scientist. What does any of this have to do with media?" If so, this next example is for you. Clarke's most prescient prediction was something he called a "newspad." Take a look at this fictional description in 1964:

> When [Floyd] had tired of official reports, memoranda and minutes, he would plug his foolscap-sized Newspad into the ship's information circuit and scan the latest reports from Earth. One by one, he would conjure up the world's major electronic papers. He knew the codes of the more important ones by heart and had no need to consult the list on the back of his pad. Switching to the display's short-term memory, he would hold the front page while he searched the headlines and noted the items that interested him.
>
> Each had its own two-digit reference. When he punched that, a postage-sized rectangle would expand till it neatly filled the screen, and he could read it with comfort. When he finished, he could flash back to the complete page and select a new subject for detailed examination.
>
> Floyd sometimes wondered if the Newspad, and the fantastic technology behind it, was the last word in man's quest for perfect communications. Here he was, far out in space, speeding away from Earth at thousands of miles an hour, yet in a few milliseconds, he could see the headlines of any newspaper he pleased. (That very word "newspaper," of course, was an anachronistic hangover into the age of electronics.) The text was updated automatically every hour; even if one read only the English versions, one could spend an entire lifetime doing nothing but absorbing the ever-changing flow of information from the news satellites.

In 1964, the very idea of automatically, wirelessly updated content on a flat screen was considered magical, but today you may be reading this on a similar device that you rely on daily. In 2010, two years after Clarke's death, Apple launched the iPad – and only three years after launching the iPhone. (Fun fact: Apple had the iPad ready to launch in 2007, but Steve Jobs decided to tackle the mobile phone business first.)

Ten years after that, in 2022, the majority of media is consumed and increasingly produced through iPhones, even though most of our uses are anything but phone calls. And you know what else? There is probably an astronaut zooming above you right now on the International Space Station reading today's news on an iPad that operates exactly the way Clarke described it, tapping on "postage-sized rectangles" of articles that expand and contract.

Looking Forward by Looking Back

We can use this example as a way to look forward by looking back. Put yourself in the shoes of a young newspaper publisher or editor in 1964, reading about how 46 years in the future, all news stories would be available not through paper but on US$1,000 TV screens people carry around in their pockets or backpacks. There are three possible responses.

First, there's the obvious: ignore it because it sounds like fun and magic. There's no way this crazy-sounding Newspad would be created in your lifetime. How could you even make a television screen that thin and light? But assume you were 25 years old back then. You would be in your seventies today, possibly even still responsible for the family newspaper business.

Sadly, many of those newspaper businesses have been sold to larger chains due to digital disruption, or they went out of business entirely. According to the University of North Carolina's ongoing News Deserts study (www.usnewsdeserts.com), 300 US newspapers vanished from 2018 to 2020, causing 6,000 journalists to lose their jobs. The picture is even bleaker if you zoom out 15 years, with 1,800 communities left with no newspaper at all.

Keep in mind that the consumer Internet was just becoming available 15 years before the iPhone was released. During that time, the Internet chipped away at centuries-old consumer behaviors around print, to the detriment of its business model. Suppose you were that young publisher who remained in the "ignore" camp for 46 years. In that case, you might have almost willingly sacrificed your family's namesake business simply because you failed to take technological change seriously and make changes to your approach.

Second, let's say you took the prediction seriously and decided to adopt it full throttle as soon as the first screen-based technology was in ordinary people's hands. Knight Ridder, one of the United States' largest newspaper publishers then, did just that in 1983 with a service called Videotex – and it didn't fare well. Readers would connect their phone lines to a box that, in turn, connected to any television set or personal computer (which themselves were also fairly novel at the time) and receive news, stock prices, and shopping information. It was like an early, proprietary prototype of the Internet.

After putting 50 million into Videotex, the service only generated $16 million in revenue and was determined to be a failure and was shut down. On March 18, 1986, The New York Times quoted Knight Ridder president James Batten as saying, "The time simply was not ripe."

But just because Knight Ridder gave up early doesn't mean there was nothing to this idea. At about the same time, another type of box called a "modem" that was not that different in appearance from Videotex hardware emerged, and other services launched that allowed you to not only get similar information but also talk to people in text chats. Computers would dial each other up over phone lines, and eventually, a decentralized network of computers running software known as Bulletin Board Services (or BBSes) evolved.

I myself, along with many teenagers, had such a system running on the Apple II Plus my parents had gotten for word processing. Using the "Wildcat" software, it would dial a phone number every night and download messages, and send my own messages out to other Wildcat BBS systems. At a snail's pace, these messages would trickle around the world, via one computer at a time that was set up to do the same thing.

Around this same time, a little company called Control Video Corporation launched its own commercial service, which by 1991 was known by another name: America Online, or AOL. Not long after, the open Internet – which had been something only the defense department and some university scholars had used until then – was privatized. AOL tapped into the Internet and made it available to its members. By 1998, the service had attracted 20 million users, each of whom paid around $22 a month to use its services and the Internet at large.

How would you feel if you'd been Knight Ridder's James Batten, knowing that your company could have become what evolved into AOL, but you'd bowed out too early in the game? Probably not so good. But I really relate to Batten because this can happen to anyone and often does. *(Side note: It just so happens that when I worked in the newspaper industry, I won a Knight Batten Award for innovation. I also worked for AOL. And I also often innovated too early but didn't always time things right.)*

The third scenario is the middle way: see the unique value of a new technology and the problems it solves, but acknowledge its inadequacies at the current time.

Look past all of the shiny chrome and candy buttons, and ask yourself: how might the *concept* of this new thing seep into everything that I do and into our society? How do I prepare myself to be able to pivot into that future if I start to see that future take form? And how do I also prevent myself from investing too much of my own personal time and reputation into any one implementation of that concept or trend, just in case that future never materializes – or it appears much later?

The good news is that this middle-way approach is a lot easier for an individual contributor like you to pull off than for a large company to do so. If you're young, you can't afford much anyway, so it's almost impossible to over-invest your cash and resources. But it's completely free to tinker and find little nuggets of insight into what's possible a little earlier than everyone else. This tinkering and, let's just say it, *playing is the way that innovation starts*.

As we will explore later in this book, these days, it's also much less likely that early innovation starts in large companies. It happens through open-source movements and "hackers" (the good kind) messing around for fun. In my experience, even at companies like Knight Ridder or AOL, it's not the companies themselves who do the innovation. It's people like you and me who use them in the same way that the great artists used the Medicis of the Italian Renaissance to sponsor what those artists would have probably been doing anyway. With their help, we can do that work at a higher intensity, or at a greater scale that has more impact on peoples' lives.

I bring up these two companies to illustrate another fact: Knight Ridder imploded in 2006, one year before the launch of the iPhone; and AOL made a huge blunder by buying Time Warner, which eventually resulted in it being sold to Verizon in 2015.

Past is prologue. It's no mistake that we all remember the great Renaissance masters Michelangelo, Leonardo da Vinci, and Botticelli, but not their Medici benefactor Lorenzo the Magnificent. Many of the media innovators you may know of today worked in one of those two companies. While the companies they worked for rose and fell in prominence – or disappeared entirely – the best ideas that lived within them continued. It's been my experience across many companies that people, not brands or sponsors, are the ones who carry the torch of good ideas from one era to the next. That's particularly true in open-source circles.

Predictions Can Also Be Very Wrong

Few of us will ever accurately predict the future, or more to the point, position ourselves to be able to have the ride of a lifetime. The reason is what Batten talked about: timing. But another is that we often fail to understand the problem that people will ultimately want solved.

A great example of this is the Horsey Horseless Carriage, a metaphor I've used in class exercises since I saw a presentation by consultant and former tech industry executive Michael Mace in 2010. The Horsey Horseless Carriage was an invention by Uriah Smith in 1832.

Smith was a bit of a serial inventor, having invented an artificial leg with a moveable ankle and a school desk with a folding seat. He also gets snaps for accurately predicting that the automobile would replace the horse-drawn carriage, but his design had one glaring problem.

In the 1800s, the big problem with getting people to abandon their horse-drawn carriages for something automatic was that horses got spooked by seeing carriages that moved on their own. In addition, the faster-moving carriages would put bystanders in a panic. What well-respecting carriage driver wanted to be responsible for all-out mayhem on the cobblestone streets?

No problem, thought Smith. We'll just make the other horses think these new-fangled carriages are horse-drawn by putting wooden horse heads on their fronts. And thus was born the Horsey Horseless Carriage (HHC), which later earned the title of #1 Worst Car of All Time by Time Magazine in 2007.

What lessons can we derive from the HHC? First, problems demand solutions, but it can be easy to identify the wrong problem. Smith focused on the horses when he should have been paying attention to the drivers. Second, it can be easy to be myopic in our vision. Smith was so focused on not scaring other horses that he failed to see that horses would disappear entirely from the roads.

Another version of this analogy comes from Ben Horowitz, now a superstar venture capitalist investor but once a product manager for the Netscape web browser, and David Weiden, who was a director of product management for AOL.

In instructing other product managers, they pointed out:

> Good product managers listen to customers, but they probe deeper into the underlying problems to get at the compelling value proposition for the customer. *If you had a noisy car, you might ask for a louder stereo, but you would probably be a lot happier with a quieter car.*

The Horsey Horseless Carriage Is Everywhere!

Now that I've put the image of that ridiculous car in your head, look around you, and you will see Horsey Horseless Carriages practically everywhere you go. This is especially true in technology. Here are just a few from the not-so-distant past:

- **Google Glass:** This set of $1,500 wearable augmented reality glasses and cameras launched in 2013. It has a broad variety of features that let the users surf the web, read emails, get information about people and places simply by looking at them, and take photos and videos.

  It stopped shipping to consumers by 2015, partly because of privacy concerns. As cool as it was for the wearers, they came to be known as "glassholes" because nobody could tell when they were being recorded. The glass-less had privacy concerns about what Google was telling the wearer about them when they were looked at. In one case in San Francisco, a Google Glass wearer was even attacked in a bar.

  In 2017, Snapchat creator Snap Inc. launched its much more fashionable Snap Spectacles, which give the wearer nothing but two very visible cameras. Spectacles only record video, and when they do so, a prominent spinning light turns on. Wearers are expected to be transparent about when they are recording.

  In 2022, Google announced it was again moving back into wearables with smart glasses. Will they be better adopted this time? We'll all get to see that story as it happens.
- **The Nintendo Virtual Boy:** This early attempt at consumer virtual reality launched in 1996 with one game: Mario Tennis. A year later, it had only 22 games and was panned by critics who said the 3D graphics were terrible and that it made them feel sick.

  The Virtual Boy was canceled in 1996. A little less than 20 years later, the much better Oculus VR headset was bought by Facebook for $2.3 billion, with users across many different industry sectors, not just video games.
- **WebTV:** This was like Videotex all over again, but for the Internet. In 1990, this set-top box for televisions came out that dialed up to the Internet. It came with a special keyboard designed to let viewers browse the web from their couches.

Microsoft bought the product in 1997 with big plans and renamed it MSN TV, but the service never attracted many users. By 2013, it was abandoned, perhaps because by this time, the Internet had moved into our pockets through touchscreen cell phones. Ironically, streaming services on "smart TVs," Roku, and Apple TV are all the rage in 2022 and are focused on actually watching video on your TV rather than surfing the Web.

What all of these examples share in common is that they were trying to solve the wrong problem, or perhaps the right one, but at the wrong time.

Google Glass thought we needed the Internet on our eyeballs but failed to think about how everyone but the wearer would feel about being examined by an augmented glass-wearing human. And it didn't factor in how adoption evolves organically at its own pace among human beings, for all kinds of reasons that have nothing to do with the technology itself.

Nintendo thought people needed low-quality 3D games when they really wanted a high-quality 3D transportation device. And the technology itself was simply not ready, with poor visuals and sub-par tracking causing people to get motion sick.

WebTV thought we wanted the Internet on our TV when we really wanted the Internet with us everywhere. But later, the Internet allowed our TVs to provide us more control over video and *only* video.

Of course, the larger story is always more complicated. There are other factors at play behind these early failures, which we'll get into in Chapter 2. But the lesson here is that just because something is new, and it excites you and becomes all the rage doesn't mean that it will define the future of everything. When it comes to innovation, the first-mover advantage does not always mean long-term success.

Workbook Exercise 1.1: Find a Current Horsey Horseless Carriage

It's easy to look back decades or even a few years and see products that identified the wrong problem or were too myopic in their vision. It's harder to do it for something that's considered new and shiny right now. But it's essential to do this so that you don't waste too much time on a one-trick pony.

This is especially important when a big company like Google, Facebook, Amazon, or Microsoft comes out with something that gets a lot of press. Everyone wants to be a part of it and do something with these large companies, and that's fine. But it's dangerous to get too embedded in just one solution at the expense of seeing other opportunities from other companies or even no company (like open-source initiatives).

When you find a good example, post it in the channel I've set up for Horsey Horseless Carriages in the Slack group. Anyone teaching this class or one like it can use examples shared there to discuss in class.

Case Study: Printcasting, My Own Horsey Horseless Carriage

Throughout this book, I'll share case studies of field tests from students and professionals related to each chapter. But in this chapter, which is largely about how difficult it is to predict the future, I share with you one of my own failures: the Printcasting service.

Printcasting was a back-of-the-napkin idea that a colleague and I submitted to the Knight News Challenge grant program, a laudable initiative of the John S. and James L. Knight Foundation. In 2007, thousands of mostly journalists and technologists submitted ideas for a chance to get part of a $25 million pot from the foundation to find new, digital approaches to delivering news and information.

When the newspaper industry was starting to really feel the pain brought on by the Internet, the Knight News Challenge asked this question: "Can we deliver the information needed by a Democratic society through something other than the dead-tree newspaper?" I'm paraphrasing there with the dead-tree part, but it's what everyone was thinking at the time.

I had spent the previous three years working as a senior product manager for The Bakersfield Californian, a company that at that time was one of the last family-owned local newspapers in the United States. (It has sadly since been sold to a Canadian newspaper chain that maintains none of its prior mojo.)

Fresh out of AOL, where I had worked for eight years as a community products manager, I helped make the Californian famous in the worldwide newspaper industry by introducing community and social media features into their portfolio. This was in 2005, when Facebook wasn't even available to anyone but certain college students.

We ended up creating multiple niche audience-focused news products. These products were built on the backbone of a user-contributed content platform that I envisioned and managed, which eventually was licensed by The Arizona Republic and several other newspaper companies.

Those social networks, of which the youth-focused Bakotopia is still the most remembered, were highly effective at generating new audiences who didn't engage with the core newspaper brand at all. By the time we had rolled out the final niche site, an external analytics firm had determined that we had built a unique audience of 100,000 people in a town of only 330,000. The Californian at that time had a circulation of about 80,000, so we had essentially doubled the size of the audience for the company in just a few years.

But there was one major problem. All that activity wasn't generating any revenue. Why?

First, it was the very early days of the shift to digital media, and local businesses weren't keen to spend much of their marketing budgets on anything other than print, TV, and radio.

Second, the salespeople at the Californian were understandably most comfortable with print. They didn't know how to package digital audiences for advertisers, but even if they did focus on digital, the numbers were much smaller than their commission-based compensation packages were designed for.

And third, when local businesses did buy digital ads, they did it through Google keywords and highly targeted Facebook ads, which they could sell more effectively on a global scale. With self-serve ads and global reach, Google and Facebook could get away with a business spending only $100 a year because they could draw from the long tail of every business on the planet rather than just businesses in one local community. And thanks to self-serve, there were no commission-hungry salespeople to feed.

When I look back and think about what I would have done differently based on what I know now, I know very clearly. I would have gone to the publisher's office and said:

We need to shut down all these sites immediately if they can't make money. I don't think it's possible for the Californian to make enough money off them because Google and Facebook can continue operating at a global scale forever, while you have no choice but to compete locally at a loss.

Pivoting Back to Print

Who would want to say that to their boss? I couldn't, and I didn't. Neither did anyone working around me. Instead, we all drank the local brand of Kool-Aid and decided to shift to what was more comfortable for the organization: print.

Bakotopia, which had been a grungy youth-oriented digital zine focused on the local music industry, launched a printed version with content that came from what users posted on their Bakotopia blogs. As soon as it hits the scene, our local print-oriented advertising staff was there, ready to sell print display ads. The money was still small, but it fits with their daily workflow and what they knew how to sell.

We soon started to do the same thing with the other six niche products. We launched a magazine for Latinos, a magazine for newcomers, a magazine for the nearby town of Tehachapi, and a few others. Each one made enough money to be sustainable, though looking back, I suspect that a lot of that was built on acts of mercy and borrowed time from the Californian's newspaper staff.

All these years later, I can look back and see that this is where my thinking went wrong, and I became myopic. Tasked with saving the future, I took the available facts in front of me and created a near-term solution that ignored a long-term, systemic shift from physical to digital, for which there still is no answer.

Rather than see reality, my creative mind dreamt up an unscalable solution for a made-up problem. The thinking went something like this:

> We weren't able to get local businesses to buy digital ads, but we were able to get them to buy ads in print magazines. Those magazines in turn got their content from what users posted on their Web sites. Could our answer to the Google and Facebook networks be not just digital networks, but hybrid digital-terrestrial ones? And if we could implement that, could we have stumbled across the new revenue model for local news?

I started brainstorming with my team about how we could scale this crazy idea up. Why stop at just six hybrid website-magazine products? Why not 100? Why not 1,000? Normal people, not the newspaper staff, would create the magazines and we would just turn on the network and the self-serve ad tool.

The idea got bigger and bigger. If we had too many for one city, we thought, why not go national or even global? Could we possibly build a national network of Bakotopias where the audience was all from the long tail, and the revenue came from self-serve print ads? Then, we could be like the Facebook for print magazines.

We put the idea into writing and submitted it to the Knight News Challenge, and the judges liked it enough to put it into the final round. After some tinkering with spreadsheets and a few conversations, we found ourselves with one of about 10 Knight News Challenge grants in 2007. And our grant size was what I now consider to be an embarrassingly large $837,000.

I hope at this point that you're laughing at how ridiculous this all sounds because in retrospect, it is. But at the time, when the newspaper industry was teetering on the edge of disaster, the ideas of "saving the newspaper" and "finding a new business model for local news" were all the rage.

Many people were coming up with ideas like this, and many attempts at launching networks focused on the same problem came and fell. Printcasting was among them, but it was unique in that it still included print as a component. Others, such as AOL's Patch, were purely digital. While history may see Printcasting as one of the goofier experiments in the "save local news" era, I find that print nerds still like it because of its retro quality – kind of like how old vinyl records are suddenly the bee's knees again.

Long before it hits its sustainability wall, Printcasting reached all its metrics. We created and launched a platform that allowed people to feed content from their blogs into print layouts, tweak them, and hit one button to generate a PDF that could be printed anywhere. We called it "People-Powered Publishing," and the people came.

Over the next year, roughly 1,000 new "citizen magazines" were created across multiple countries, and we launched a self-serve ad tool. This tool was designed to make it easy for any local business to type in a few lines of text, add a photo, and instantly have it appear in the magazines people downloaded and printed across multiple publications.

We thought we had a winner. And then . . . the 2008 recession hit, and the party ended.

The ad tool that we'd designed for local businesses failed to foresee one major problem. Local businesses were going out of business right and left. And if they weren't, they certainly were cutting back or reducing or eliminating their marketing budgets. It was like what the world saw in the immediate aftermath of the Coronavirus pandemic, but there was no virus to blame. The world economy itself was sick from the sub-prime mortgage crisis.

Printcasting's sustainability depended on the network keeping a percentage of that ad revenue, and the revenue that came in was pretty non-existent by the end of the next year. By the end of the grant, there was no ad money to sustain operations, and the service stopped.

However, the story didn't end there. In fact, a whole new startup – BookBrewer – emerged from the wreckage. But I won't get into that in this chapter.

How does this relate to the themes covered in this book? Printcasting was one large, expensive field test. Despite all my best intentions and beliefs, my hypothesis was proven spectacularly wrong.

There were a variety of reasons for this, including the economy, but I think the biggest among them is that we were focusing on the wrong problems. Maintaining existing revenue models and consumer behaviors is what almost every business that ever existed has made the priority, but what if the changes in an industry are so significant that the only solution is to give up everything old and join the new?

Who has the courage and practical financial ability to do that? The answer is: very few. But there are some potential solutions to this dilemma. We'll focus more on that in Chapter 2.

Printcasting didn't fail because it didn't work – it actually worked quite well, and it created a lot of buzz in the journalism industry. It also didn't fail for lack of trying. In my opinion, it failed largely because of outside economic forces – the 2008 Great Recession, to be exact – and a rigidity that was placed upon it by what at that point was an inflexible grant management system that didn't allow for change. But the biggest point of failure was that it was trying to solve the wrong problem and suffered from myopia, just like the Horsey Horseless Carriage.

Online Resources for Chapter 1

Find more resources for Chapter 1 online at http://emergingmediaplatforms.com/chapter1.

Sources

Clarke, A. C. (1999). *Profiles of the future*. Weidenfeld & Nicolson.

Mace, M. (n.d.). Why e-books failed in 2000, and what it means for 2010. *Business Insider*. Retrieved August 25, 2022, from www.businessinsider.com/why-ebooks-failed-in-2000-and-what-it-means-for-2010-2010-3

Ridder, K. (1986, March 18). Knight-ridder shuts videotex. *The New York Times*. www.nytimes.com/1986/03/18/business/knight-ridder-shuts-videotex.html

UNC Hussman School of Journalism and Media. (2020, June 21). The news landscape in 2020: Transformed and diminished. *The Expanding News Desert*. www.usnewsdeserts.com/reports/news-deserts-and-ghost-newspapers-will-local-news-survive/the-news-landscape-in-2020-transformed-and-diminished/

2 Change Theories

While it's impossible to predict the future, it is possible to examine trends and use them as a guide. There are a variety of theories and approaches to this problem that come from both academic research and industry. If you use any of these theories or others that you come across, you still have to make guesses about the direction things will go. But going through the thought exercises will deliver insights that you may have otherwise missed.

Technology Acceptance Model

To understand technology-driven change, we first have to look at what's responsible for change. The mere existence of a new technology doesn't mean people will use it – which is why the "If you build it, they will come" approach to anything never works. Acceptance and adoption lie largely in the hands of consumers, not companies or creators of new technologies.

Given that, what factors into people's willingness to use a new technology? In 1989, just as computers were beginning to replace traditional, physical ways of performing work, researcher Fred Davis developed the Technology Acceptance Model (TAM). The theory states that technologies are accepted or rejected by users based on two factors: the users' perception of the technology's *usefulness* for their work, and their perception of the technology's *ease of use*.

Perceived *usefulness* is what people believe that a technology will allow them to do for a particular job. Take writing a book, for example, which I am doing right now. There are many different ways I can choose to write. I can use a computer, an electric typewriter, a manual typewriter, or even a pencil and paper. In my case, I find writing on a computer to be most useful, but I know other writers who find pencil and paper to be more useful for them. TAM states that our individual perceptions and preferences are what drives adoption of these different technologies, not some objective, universal standard of usefulness that everyone magically agrees on.

Perceived *ease of use* is how effortless someone finds a technology to be. For example, I find that writing on a computer takes much less effort than writing on paper, but someone else may find that it takes more effort. Our life experience, education, and training play into this measure quite a bit.

DOI: 10.4324/9781003247012-3

In my case, I took a typing class in high school as well as ten years of piano lessons, so writing on a keyboard is the most effortless way for me to get ideas out into the world. I can close my eyes, put my hands on a keyboard, and accurately write entire paragraphs without a single mistake, and I can do the same with a piano piece I've memorized. But someone who lacks those skills and training may find that a pencil and yellow pad are more efficient than typing with two fingers in a hunt-and-peck method. And it may, in fact, truly be more efficient for them because of their experience writing by hand – a skill I know I have largely been losing over time, thanks to technology, as evidenced by my terrible handwriting.

When Davis was doing his research that resulted in TAM, he discovered that perceived usefulness was 50% more influential on someone's decision to adopt a technology than what they felt about its ease of use. This explains why some people will resist using a technology that is objectively easier to use. They believe that the old way of doing something, even if harder, will have better or more consistent outcomes.

Later versions of TAM explored some of the other factors that influence people's perceptions, and there are many of them. A user's gender, age, experience level, social influence by others, and the extent to which they can choose a technology or are having it forced on them (for example, by an employer) all significantly impact the adoption of a new technology over time.

There is no magic to TAM, and using it won't allow you to definitely determine if a technology is going to be adopted or not. But it does serve as a common-sense warning to technology creators and product developers that influencing peoples' perceptions through marketing and otherwise is as important as developing the technology itself.

Disruption and *The Innovator's Dilemma*

Regardless of its rate of adoption, technological change is inevitable. And when that change arrives, it always looks like it came out of nowhere. But in reality, disruption is all around us – or as I like to think of it, under us – at all times. The seeds are planted decades or even centuries in the past, but a combination of new discoveries, inventions, investment, and social acceptance triggers a fundamental change in how people perform a task.

When I was a kid, one of the houses my parents bought was in a neighborhood on a hill that we learned later was sitting on sandy soil. One day, we woke up to a truly stunning amount of destruction outside. Large parts of the street were cracked and jutting up and out at all angles. It looked like there had been an earthquake. Thankfully nobody was hurt, but some cars did fall to the ground.

What had actually happened was that a water main had been slowly leaking over many years, removing the underlying sandy soil a little bit at a time. What looked like a single disruptive event had been years in the making, with the change happening below our feet. That's how disruption works.

We can thank the late Harvard Business School Professor Clayton Christensen for bringing the term disruption into modern business parlance. His 1997 book,

The Innovator's Dilemma, explored why so many successful companies that seem to be doing everything right often lose their lead as new competitors – which he referred to as "disruptive innovators" – arise.

In the newspaper industry, one such disruptor was Craigslist: a simply designed, unflattering website that allowed people to post events, jobs, and then things for sale online for free. Launched on the web in 1996, it started from even humbler beginnings a year earlier as an email distribution list.

Beginning in the early 2000s, the site began rolling out additional city-based portals. This continued throughout the decade, culminating in a global footprint of hundreds of city portals in 70 countries.

In 2004, when I moved back to working in the newspaper industry, hardly anyone in newspapers was openly talking about Craigslist. If they did, they laughed at it, seeing it as an inferior product to the supposedly higher quality, more effective print + online classified ads newspapers were selling.

But since then, nearly everyone now understands that the entry of Craigslist and its free online ads siphoned money away from newspapers – and newspapers couldn't respond fast enough to that change. One study later put a price tag on the damage: $5 billion from 2000 to 2007. This is apparent when you pick up a typical newspaper today. What was once a veritable book's worth of classified ads is now often just a handful of pages. The loss of ad dollars put newspapers in a crisis in the mid-2000s, and many pointed at Craigslist as the bogeyman.

In fairness, it wasn't really Craigslist that caused this disruption. It was the Internet and its unlimited, less expensive, and highly targetable inventory that was responsible. Craigslist simply was early to the game in creating a simple product that they then scaled worldwide without having to add much staff.

Newspapers could have done the same thing, but doing so would have meant giving up existing revenue, laying people off, and completely changing their business models. Christensen said this is the dilemma that all businesses that are leaders in one era eventually face.

Charting an Innovator's Dilemma Example

Christensen's model is one that you can fairly easily chart for any industry that experienced disruption, and it goes like this. Create a simple X-Y graph, where the horizontal measurement is time, and the vertical measure is performance. Then in the middle, draw a slowly increasing horizontal line that measures the bare minimum level of performance that users need from a product or service.

The key here is that this "good enough" line doesn't mean the highest quality. It's what people in startups often call the Minimum Viable Product, and Christensen called this "performance that customers can use."

The theory states that disruptors begin to have their influence on incumbents when they hit that line, but the legacy companies rarely realize it at the time or take it seriously enough to invest enough resources to compete head to head with the new approach the disruptor has discovered.

When they finally do, the disruptor has done enough damage that the incumbent usually doesn't have the time or resources to respond adequately. And the only possible response, other than going out of business, is often to disrupt itself – which means giving up current revenue for less revenue from the more efficient method of the technologically driven disruptor.

You can go through this exercise with any product category or industry that was pushed out of its leadership role or maybe even went out of business due to external technological innovation. For example, consider traditional film cameras and how they were disrupted by digital cameras.

Plot the major innovations for traditional cameras from the very beginning of film in the 1800s. The quality or performance at this point is going to be fairly low. By the mid-20th century, film resolution was much better, and photographs could be developed in color. Let's call that the "good enough" innovation for legacy camera makers.

Draw a line between those two points, and then extend it further in the future – beyond the "good enough" level. Label this line "Incumbent."

Have you used a camera with film recently? Probably not, because we all know that digital cameras largely replaced film cameras, or at least transformed film from a mass market to a niche category.

The first digital cameras to be made available to regular consumers came out in the mid- to late 1990s, and their quality was pretty awful. Professional photographers rightly laughed at them and didn't see themselves ever abandoning film for digital. And legacy photography companies, like Eastman Kodak, had such a large investment in developing film that they remained primarily focused on that – even while experimenting at a small scale with digital cameras.

For digital photography, you would plot a point on your graph for the "first digital camera" far down on the vertical axis. But over time, the quality of digital cameras got better through what Christensen called "disruptive innovations." This is where the model gets really interesting and calls into question much of the conventional business wisdom that existed before Christensen's theory.

By the time a disruptive innovator gets to that "good enough" line, providing the bare minimum that a customer needs to get a job done, the legacy company is just starting to feel the pain of competition. They most often respond to this by adding bells and whistles to their existing product or approach in an effort to keep their existing customers happy.

Christensen called these "sustaining innovations." But while those innovations do often deliver a higher quality product, the disruptive innovator is exactly meeting customers' core needs in new ways. Quality loses out to increased efficiency, at least initially.

The story of the digital camera and Eastman Kodak's inability to adapt to it, ultimately leading the company to go bankrupt, was one of many examples used by Christensen to illustrate the Innovator's Dilemma. But one thing to note is that Kodak's problem was not that it didn't experiment with digital cameras. It launched a number of them. It's that it didn't invest adequately enough in digital cameras as compared to its continued investment in its bread and butter: film.

And can you blame them? Shifting resources from the lucrative film business, even when it was declining, would have meant leaving money on the table. And that in turn could have meant laying people off who focused on film, which was still generating revenue, in order to hire digital camera staff for whose products wouldn't generate enough revenue to pay them. That right there is the crux of the dilemma for a legacy company.

The same dynamic exists in many, many other incumbent industries – maybe even one in which you work now. Also, lest you think that the newcomers won't find themselves in the same position, just look at what Meta (formerly Facebook) is dealing with now in relation to TikTok. Yesterday's disruptors can later be disrupted in a heartbeat.

Christensen did have a recommended solution to the Innovator's Dilemma. He advised incumbent businesses to create small disruptive companies specifically designed to compete with and eventually replace them.

In reality, what many media companies do is create innovation units that make great products – like the unit I was in at The Bakersfield Californian. But that investment tends to go away as soon as economic storm clouds emerge, as happened in the 2008 recession and some economists believe started to happen again in 2022.

One company that many believed solved the Innovator's Dilemma in a unique way is Apple, in particular after Steve Jobs returned. He slashed staff and completely killed many existing product lines, and focused the company on Mac desktops and laptops, with only one consumer version and one pro version. Later, the iPad openly competed with both the laptop and iPhone. Many suspect Apple will do this further with its answer to smart glasses.

Gartner's Hype Cycle

Everything changes, driven by innovation. But how do you know how seriously to take a new technology or trend? What takes it from being nascent to something that fundamentally changes entire consumer behaviors or entire industries?

Take the Internet itself, for example. People my age remember well the many discussions in the hallway, at the water cooler, and even in company meetings about the value of the Internet. Who would prefer reading on a computer screen to reading the newspaper? Could it be just another version of the CD-ROM that would come and go? And then, when the hyped-up economy of overfunded Internet startups collapsed in what was soon called the "Dot-Bomb," plenty of Luddites jumped on the bandwagon to declare the Internet age to be over.

Of course, we all know what happened after that. The shakeout removed the weakest businesses from the system, and Web 2.0 came on with a fury. Google, YouTube, Facebook, and Twitter quickly grew into what are now essentially technology-driven media companies. The Internet as a disruptive technology didn't change society in a straight line but in more of an S-curve.

The technology research and consulting firm Gartner has a name for this: the Gartner Hype Cycle. They believe every new technology goes through this cycle in five distinct phases, and it can be expressed in another X-Y graph. The horizontal axis is time, and the vertical axis is expectations.

When a technology first appears on the scene – an event Gartner calls the Technology Trigger – expectations for it are typically very low. But early adopters and dreamers start talking excitedly about the possibilities for this new break-through. Some even begin to experiment with it and make predictions on where it will lead. I will admit to you right now that I am one of those people, and maybe you will be too after completing this book.

If there's any true potential for innovation, more and more attention from media and early adopters drive the expectations through the roof. This is the second phase: the Peak of Inflated Expectations. And that is usually exactly when the air comes out of the hype.

This inevitably leads to a fall in expectations, especially when more than just the early adopters get their hands on the innovation. While in the Peak, everyone focused on successes, in this phase, the stories of failures dominate the narrative. Phase 3 is, therefore, the Trough of Disillusionment. Technologies can be stuck in the trough for a few years or a few decades. Some may never emerge from the trough at all. It all depends on the rate of improvement, solid use cases, and most importantly, adoption.

But just like in your favorite action movie, just when things seem to be at their worst, that's when things get real. Thanks to more realistic, targeted initiatives and improvements in the technology or approach, the technology may enter its fifth phase: the Plateau of Productivity. Over a longer, slower, and sometimes even boring period of time, the expectations gradually increase. This is the phase at which a technological innovation potentially changes entire markets and consumer behavior.

Workbook Exercise 2.1: Chart an Innovation

Now that you understand how Gartner Hype Cycles work, chart the cycle for a disruptive technology, service, or company. Then, in another chart show how that disruptor displaced an incumbent technology, service, or company. You can even string multiple cycles together and show how a one-time disruptor later got disrupted itself.

Here are some fun topics to examine:

- Traditional movies and VCRs.
- Blockbuster and streaming.
- Dial-up Internet and broadband.
- Vinyl records and compact discs.
- Compact discs and MP3s.
- MP3s and streaming music.
- Radio shows and Podcasts.
- Hardbound books and paperbacks.
- Printed books and eBooks.
- Printed newspapers and newspaper sites.
- Desktop computers and mobile phones.

Axes of Uncertainty

At the start of the COVID-19 pandemic, Amy Webb of the Future Today Institute sent out an email to the firm's clients, and fans about a tool FTI had developed called the Axes of Uncertainty. It's a thought exercise they had been using with their clients to help them not predict the future but use uncertain outcomes themselves to develop insights to help them plan for various contingencies.

COVID was probably one of the most uncertain times any of us had dealt with, so it was a perfect time for people to reflect. If you go through the exercise, what you see is that even in the most tumultuous of times, where everything seems topsy-turvy, it is possible to predict at least four potential futures that are dependent on two possible opposing outcomes. It can help you visualize where things might head depending on choices you or your company make, as well as choices that are completely out of your control.

I've been having my students perform this exercise every semester since, and I find that it really helps spark more effective conversations about the future and gets them unstuck when they're paralyzed and indecisive.

Here's how the tool works. You start by writing two completely opposite scenarios for something that involves any of the following: economics; social factors; technology; and regulation, politics, or activism.

Here's one of my examples. As education moved largely online during the pandemic, I wanted to know what the impacts might be for comparing the two factors.

The first pair of opposites was universities hiring more people. The opposite of that would be universities significantly laying off staff and closing programs. During the pandemic, we saw both scenarios happen at universities across the country, with some even closing their doors while others doubled down on hiring faculty and staff.

The second pair of opposites I imagined was universities adopting more immersive and interactive online learning platforms – essentially moving beyond what you can do in Zoom and having students meet as avatars in virtual reality. The opposite of that would be that universities did not adopt more immersive techniques and stuck with Zoom. (And sadly, this is largely what happened.)

It's important to make the two polar opposites starkly different from each other. Whatever the first scenario is, make its opposite the antithesis of that.

Once you have those pairs, draw a horizontal line that intersects with a vertical line so that your drawing looks like one large plus sign and it has four quadrants. Write the opposites for the first pair on the horizontal line and the opposites for the second pair on the vertical line.

The last thing you do is imagine what will happen in each quadrant. You will end up with four equally plausible stories – four possible futures, with a very clear understanding of what factors influence those futures. When you read and consider the headlines for each possibility, you should also categorize them as long-term opportunities, long-term risks, or existential threats.

For my example earlier, the following are the four possible futures I imagined for online education using this Axes of Uncertainty exercise.

- Prediction 1: If universities adopted more immersive online platforms and they hired more faculty and staff, online college education could transform into Virtual Reality (VR) with small, intimate classes. This is a long-term opportunity and could be a new golden age of online education.
- Prediction 2: If universities adopted more immersive online platforms, and also significantly reduced their number of faculty and staff, online college education in VR would be unmanageable with large virtual lecture halls and a low amount of interaction. This is a long-term risk.
- Prediction 3: If universities failed to adopt more immersive online platforms and hired more faculty and staff, online education would be stuck in its current state of asynchronous videos and Zoom Hell. This is also a long-term risk.
- Prediction 4: If universities failed to adopt more immersive online platforms and significantly reduced their number of faculty and staff, online college education would decline in quality, fewer students would enroll, and programs may close. This is an existential threat.

The Axes of Uncertainty exercise is, by itself, uncertain to work for every scenario. I think of it as a way not to predict the future but as a way to focus. It gets my brain thinking about the interconnectedness of multiple factors, and I imagine many possible futures.

That, after all, is the nature of reality and the number one tenet of Quantum theory, where multiple paths always exist in superposition. We will never be able to change that, but we can map out paths so that when two possibilities collapse into one, we get to cross out at least one quadrant.

Workbook Exercise 2.2: Imagine Four Possible Futures

Think of two sets of possibilities that you believe may impact media in some way. One of them should have to do with a particular technology that interests you, with the other having to do with economic, social, or regulation/policy/activism. Put them on two intersecting axes, and write a short headline for what those futures mean.

Here are some pairs of opposites you can start with:

Technology:

- The Metaverse replaces the Internet as we know it / The Internet remains two-dimensional.

Economic:

- The world economy enters a recession / The world economy is vibrant.

Social:

- Pandemic lockdowns end indefinitely / Pandemic lockdowns continue indefinitely.

Regulation/politics/activism:

- Drone regulation increases / Drone regulation decreases.

Online Resources for Chapter 2

Find more resources for Chapter 2 line at http://emergingmediaplatforms.com/chapter2.

Sources

Allworth, J. (2011, October 24). Steve jobs solved the innovator's dilemma. *Harvard Business Review*. https://hbr.org/2011/10/steve-jobs-solved-the-innovato

Axes of uncertainty. (n.d.). *The Future Today Institute*. https://futuretodayinstitute.com/mu_uploads/2019/08/FTI_Axes.pdf

Davis, F. D. (1993). User acceptance of information technology: System characteristics, user perceptions and behavioral impacts. *International Journal of Man-Machine Studies*, 38(3), 475–487. https://doi.org/10.1006/imms.1993.1022

Gartner. (n.d.). Gartner hype cycle research methodology. *Gartner*. Retrieved August 25, 2022, from www.gartner.com/en/research/methodologies/gartner-hype-cycle

Seamans, R., & Zhu, F. (2022, July 1). Responses to entry in multi-sided markets: The impact of craigslist on local newspapers. *Management Science*. https://pubsonline.informs.org/doi/abs/10.1287/mnsc.2013.1785

Webb, A. (2020, March 16). How futurists cope with uncertainty. *Medium*. https://medium.com/swlh/how-futurists-cope-with-uncertainty-a4fbdff4b8c6

3 Initiating Your Field Test

Throughout this book, you will be exposed to a number of emerging media platforms, and you will get a sense of how they work. The workbook exercises will give you a basic understanding of how to create a piece of media using one or two of them. But at the end of the process, you want to create something innovative and new.

So, where do you start? Contrary to what you may think, you don't start with the technology you want to use. You start by finding a big, thorny problem.

Find a Problem or Unmet Need

Years ago, when I was struggling with BookBrewer, my own eBook startup that emerged from Printcasting, I attended an entrepreneurial event where venture capitalists shared their advice for getting funded. I will never forget what one of the VCs said:

> I'm tired of people pitching solutions in search of problems. You need to start with a real problem and demonstrate that it exists, and *then* build a solution for it.

You could see every entrepreneur in the audience shift nervously in their seats, because pretty much all of us had been guilty at some point of taking the shiny new object that we were so proud of, and in order to make it relevant, tried to match it with a problem.

In fact, this is exactly what I had done with my Printcasting project. Instead of abandoning it and moving on to something else, we took the bones of the blog-to-PDF method and refocused it on blog-to-eBook. And after we had built that, we started fishing around for audiences.

In the startup world, they call this a pivot, and it's inevitable that you will need to pivot at some point. But it's a terrible place to start. Ideally, you do the hard work first to identify where things are imperfect, missing, or just plain broken in the world. After you've done that, then you come up with an idea for how to fix it.

DOI: 10.4324/9781003247012-4

This simple advice should be true for every product or service you design, and even for a story that you may write. And it doesn't apply just to serious, heavy topics. Even something fun and enjoyable, like a video game or a good movie, is ultimately solving the problem of boredom.

Another way to look at it is through the lens of pain. Think of the last time you had a truly splitting headache and the relief you got from having the pain removed through a painkiller. If you can find a true pain that exists in the world for any audience, and your product or service can remove that pain, you have the potential to do much more than just provide a service. You may even have a new business.

The problem you find can be very big, applying universally to everyone, or it can be a problem unique to a niche audience. In *some cases*, it can even be your own personal problem, as long as you can extrapolate that to others. But be careful with solving your own personal problem, because it is easy to fall into the logical fallacy of projecting it onto others without basis just to confirm your own selfish biases.

Also, even if you do identify a problem that scales to everyone, try to think about a specific audience to which you can point your solution so that you can test its effectiveness. While you're not building a business with a field test, picking a specific target audience is generally a good idea for marketing purposes. And you will need to do a bit of market research, and even marketing outreach, in order to test out your hypothesis.

Here are just a few examples of problems my students have tried to solve using an emerging media technology:

- Long, dense indoor lines at food vendors during the COVID-19 pandemic put students' health at risk at peak times, such as lunch.
- A local shelter has trouble getting people to adopt older dogs, even with photos and videos of the dogs on its website.
- A city planning board doesn't believe wider bicycle lanes are necessary on a busy bridge, but more cyclists keep getting hit by cars during rush hour.
- A media relations department at a university is frequently overwhelmed with journalists often asking the same questions and looking for expert sources.

Identify Failures

For every problem, there are many different solutions, but in the case of an Emerging Media field test, you want to pick a technology that you think can solve it in a completely new way that is better than traditional methods. And that is the key: the problem still exists despite a traditional method being available.

Ask yourself: how can a new technology or approach solve it in a better way than what's already out there? It can be helpful to list out those existing solutions and broken experiences first. For example:

Problem or Unmet Need	Existing Solutions (What's Broken)
Long indoor lines are exposing students to pathogens	• Fill out a paper menu that patrons fill out with a pencil before ordering • Choose a less busy time to eat • Skip lunch
Older dogs aren't getting adopted	• Put photos and videos of the dogs online • Send the dogs to other shelters • Euthanize the dogs • Stop sheltering older dogs
Cyclers are threatened by bicycle lanes that are too small	• Traditional journalistic stories with photos of the problem areas • Increase ticketing of cars that put cyclists' lives at risk • Encourage cyclists to switch back to cars
Media relations are overwhelmed with inquiries	• Post long FAQs on the media relations website • Receive inquiries by email to review in the order they're received • Prioritize the largest media outlets first

You know that you can design a better solution when the existing solutions are as bad as the ones I've outlined earlier. We'll get to solutions soon, but before that let's look at another type of field test that happened not too long ago.

Lessons From Newspaper Next

Before delving into your own field test, I'd like to take a divergence into another massive field test in the newspaper industry that almost nobody on the outside ever knew existed. It directly challenges the mythology that newspapers didn't try to make themselves relevant in the digital age. In fact, there were thousands of digital experiments – real-life field tests – going on within newspapers in the mid-2000s, but they were caught up in *The Innovator's Dilemma*.

The guiding principle that many of those experiments utilized was an initiative called Newspaper Next, or N^2. This was a project launched in 2005 that was run out of the American Press Institute (API), a research and training organization for the newspaper industry. And one of the main minds working on it was none other than Clayton Christensen, author of *The Innovator's Dilemma*.

The API worked with Christensen to adapt and modify his methods specifically for the newspaper industry, which at that time was going through its first major downturn. For over a year, 26 individuals in key roles at newspaper or digital media companies provided input into the N^2 model, and it was tested out with seven demonstration projects.

We won't delve into those tests here, but you can read about them in the final N^2 report, which is still available online through the API website. The unique lessons of those projects perhaps don't apply so much in 2022 as they did in 2005, but in my opinion the N^2 process is still extremely valuable. In many ways, it served as a blueprint for the field test approach that I have used in my Emerging Media Platforms class.

It also isn't unique to just newspapers. Having come out of the Christensen work, which was based on studies of hundreds of companies across all sectors, this same methodology is also used in the startup world. The Agile Development Framework and Eric Ries' *The Lean Startup* share much in common with N^2.

The N^2 model is divided into two primary phases. Phase 1 is initial product development, and Phase 2 is evaluation and improvement.

In Phase 1, individuals are invited to spot opportunities and then develop solutions for them. Spotting an opportunity starts with identifying nonconsumers: people who are not using your particular product or service (remember, this model was developed to help newspapers turn their fortunes around). So, for example, if you ran a classified advertising section and only 30% of car buyers were using your auto classifieds to make a car purchasing decision, you should focus on how to serve the 70% you're not getting, ideally with a different type of product or service.

N^2 went on to redefine the customer relationship by flipping it around. Instead of assuming that customers choose or don't choose your solution, you should think of the customer as someone who has a job to do, and that they either hire you or hire someone else to do that job. Just like a candidate who wants to get a fancy new job, you as the service provider need to freshen up your skills and maybe even change your outward appearance in order to get hired by this more discriminating customer-turned-hiring manager.

It's important to note how fundamentally different this mindset is for a legacy business, especially one as old and set in its ways as newspapers. What it says is that instead of continually beating people over the head about why they should subscribe to your service, you sometimes need to acknowledge that your service will never meet the needs of particular audiences. Solving their problems requires something entirely new – a disruptive innovation from within.

The ideas of jobs to be done can be written out as if someone is writing an ad or putting up a Help Wanted sign. Here are a few examples from the N^2 report:

- **Enlighten Me:** Help me stay informed on issues that are relevant to me.
- **Educate Me:** Help me make better decisions to increase my value as a parent, employee, or student.
- **Enrich Me:** Give me information that will give me a material benefit, such as making or having money or time. Help me build a deeper connection with my customer base.

These are essentially the same things as an unmet need, or a pain, that I mentioned before. They're just redefined as jobs to be done.

The last step of Phase 1 is to conceptualize potential solutions. Phase 2 is a long process of testing and assessing those solutions through prototypes, focus groups, and sometimes even launching small tests that are targeted to specific audiences. Only after analyzing the data were you encouraged to publicly launch and market to your audience.

Applying N^2 at the Scale of You

Thankfully, your field test is not a full-blown product with revenue responsibilities and peoples' jobs on the line. You're just trying to test a single idea. If you find something truly unique, it *could* potentially evolve into a large product with business potential – a startup, essentially – but your goal is just to create and assess a new way of doing things.

That said, having this skill and methodical focus is incredibly valuable as an employee in any organization. If you can refine the ability to identify, build, and run small field tests that result in data that indicate that the approach is worth real investment, you may find yourself as the "idea factory" wherever you work. When a new technology comes along in the Hype Cycle, the bosses will come to you asking you to try it out, knowing that you will be able to inexpensively evaluate it with real data.

And also keep in mind that no matter what the results are that you come back with – either finding that a new solution based on your hypothesis is worth more investment or determining that a technology isn't yet ready for adoption – you are adding value in both cases. If your field test identifies new market potential, you are growing the audience and hopefully also revenue for your employer. If you find the technology isn't worth investing in right now, you're saving your employer money by avoiding a costly mistake.

Finalizing Your Field Test Idea

OK, let's get back to your field test. After identifying all of that pain, you're finally ready to think about how a new approach can address it better.

This is where having even a cursory knowledge of what different emerging technologies can do becomes helpful. If you also have some basic experience creating something simple with them, such as with the workbook exercises throughout this book, then you can start to dream up new approaches.

But conceptualizing is only half of it. Think of it more like practical brainstorming: you want to dream up an innovative solution that you also think you can build with minimal time and investment. It doesn't need to be perfect or even a complete product experience, but it does need to be good enough to test your hypothesis.

Let's focus on just one of the examples explored earlier in this chapter: the long lines at restaurants. Write out the problem and current, broken solutions in a paragraph:

> Long indoor lines at the student center's food court are putting students' health at risk during the COVID-19 pandemic. The restaurants are trying

to address this by having students fill out paper menus that they hand to the cooks, but this isn't solving the problem. The only choices students have are to leave and come back at a less busy time, or simply skip a meal.

Now is when you want to think of technology-driven solutions to these problems. For example, here are a few ideas (your list should be a lot longer):

- A website or app that allows students to order in advance and pick up the order at a specific time.
- Text to order, and receive a text when your food is ready.
- Chat with an AI order bot, and get a response for when to pick up your food.

During your brainstorming, ask yourself: which ideas are both compelling, and feasible for me to build? You don't need to have all the skills right now to build it, but you do need to know enough about the technology to know what you still need to learn.

By the end, you will be making a guess about what you choose to execute. As you go through the discovery process, you may find that you bit off more than you could chew, and that's fine because you can always gracefully degrade your plans. You don't have to test the exact idea that you came up with. You just need to test something with a target audience to see if it solves their problem.

Workbook Exercise 3.1: Propose a Field Test

Look at the world around you and identify a problem or broken experience for a specific audience. List out the existing approaches to the problem that aren't working well, or that aren't working for everyone. Then, conceptualize a better way to solve that problem using one of the emerging media platforms in this book, or another that you come across. You can use this template as a guide:

Problem (2–3 sentences):	
Target Audience:	
Emerging Technology Opportunity:	
Your Hypothesis:	

Workbook Exercise 3.2: Create an Independent Learning Plan

Once you have your concept, you need to spend some time familiarizing yourself with the technology you're wanting to use. Feel free to skip ahead to the chapter in this book that covers the technology you want to use, and go through the workbook exercises for that particular technology. You will likely also need to do some of your own independent learning. This is particularly true for a technology not covered in this book.

There are fortunately many places online where you can learn the basics for almost any technology tool or program. Sometimes they are free, while others have a marginal cost. Here are just a few resources you may want to peruse:

LinkedIn Learning: https://linkedin.com/learning
Formerly Lynda.com, LinkedIn Learning has hundreds of video-driven short courses. Just type in a technology (for example, artificial intelligence) and you will likely find a basic course about it. If you are enrolled at a university, it's possible that your access will be available for free by logging in with your student ID. In some cases, your library will give you access with a library card.

Udemy: http://udemy.com
Udemy offers many similar courses to LinkedIn Learning but has a subscription fee. It's a good alternative for someone who isn't enrolled in a university, or whose university doesn't subscribe to LinkedIn Learning.

CodeAcademy: http://codeacademy.com
Learn to code in various languages with guidance from an AI robot. HTML and CSS courses are free. Others are available via a subscription.

W3Schools: www.w3schools.com/
This site offers free, text-driven courses on HTML, CSS, and a few programming languages used for web development. After going through tutorials, you can practice the skills in an emulator.

YouTube: http://youtube.com
Yes, YouTube! If you search specifically on YouTube for how-to videos, you will find a number of people and even companies with channels dedicated specifically to teaching people how to build, create, code, and fix almost anything.

You'll have to hunt and peck a lot, and the production quality is sometimes low, but it gets the job done. One of my favorite instructional YouTubes of all time was from a fifth grader who was sick at home, and made a video tutorial for how to create a Nadir patch in a 360 video. Between sniffles and sneezes, he did a better job showing all the steps than anyone else. By the end of it, my students and I wanted to send him a care package.

Expert Interview: Bob Bierman

DAN PACHECO (DP): *Bob Bierman is a former student in the Emerging Media Platforms course and now a good friend of mine. But Bob has also done a whole of things in his career that definitely fit the definition of innovation.*

Bob, I think you've even had Innovation in your job title at some place, and you do innovative things now. Tell us a little bit about yourself and your career path, and what you're doing today.

BOB BIERMAN (BB): Sure. I actually started my career in the technology trade show business in 1992. There weren't pictures on the Internet, and I didn't have an email address for another year or two.

DP: *Can I just say, I love that phrase, "When there were no pictures on the Internet." Because for those who aren't old enough to remember that, that was a thing!*

BB: Yeah, I remember downloading my first picture on the Internet. It was a cartoon of some sort and it took about 20 minutes. I actually literally went in and made myself a sandwich and ate it, and then came back to see if the picture had downloaded over my dial-up.

DP: *I remember those days, too. In particular newsgroups. You would actually download the portions of pictures, and then they would stitch together.*

BB: Yeah! So from there, I moved to Fortune Magazine, where I ran a group called Fortune Multimedia, which had a variety of assets. There weren't really organized digital teams at that point. But there was a weekly TV show, and there was a global conference business. We actually even launched a blog as part of that in 2004.

From there, I launched a multimedia business at Bloomberg and ran that, and grew it around the world. I then spent two years at The Washington Post in the era just after Amazon founder Jeff Bezos had bought the company, which was an interesting time, and I worked with quite a few startups.

I'm currently the Chief Product Officer for a company called Everest, which is for companies that all have membership models. We deliver everything from in-person meetings, to research, to content, to all kinds of other assets that help people connect with each other and be better informed at the top of the business world.

DP: *Wow! That's a whole lot of innovation there, over a long period of time. And it sounds like you're working with pretty large companies who are doing really cool, innovative things. You sort of have early advanced warning of things that will be coming along.*

BB: I spend a lot of time talking to people who are very senior in very large companies. And one of the things that's interesting is that there is still not 100% certainty as to what the right and wrong answers are or how to measure success.

Everyone has different ways of doing that. I just had a head corporate venture capital leader remind me a couple of weeks ago that this entire industry of commerce and content being available on the Internet is really only about 30 years old. So people who are just getting into the [digital media] field aren't going into a 100-year-old industry with all kinds of practices there. This makes testing and the ability to come up with your own answers really important.

DP: *Do you think there's a lot more change coming in digital media?*

BB: There's a huge amount of change on the way. Just to give you an example, in my current company we are going through a rebranding. As part of that, one of the things you would see today is a website that has the company name on it, and very little else. But if you look at the tech stack behind it, there's a tremendous amount of technology already running behind that site that helps us to understand and analyze who's going to the site, and how to better optimize content and how we target it.

As we curate the content that we create, that is for our members only. But we find pieces that they are willing to share externally. That back-end technology is all there to help us make those decisions and help figure out how to be efficient about what we share so we don't share too much and we understand what's actually resonating with people.

The analytics and data science side of content has come an awfully long way in just a few short years.

DP: *But part of that is because there are entities out there that already know so much about all of us, right? If you're running a digital business of any type, if you're not using that aggregated data, you aren't operating like a modern media site. And you aren't able to compete with those that do.*

This all comes at the expense of our privacy, which is important – much more so in the European Union, where privacy laws are particularly policed.

BB: In the past five or six years, the demand of the information consumer to have things personalized to them has been very, very high. And if you're not able to have good data and know what to do with it, and as a content creator, know what gifts that technology offers you, then it's very hard for you to deliver on that kind of personalization at scale. It's really important for people to understand that, whether they're a creator or whether they're in the media business or a technologist.

DP: *But aren't we consumers the ones that made that happen? We're handing over our personal data because we want that personal experience.*

BB: The popular wisdom is that we traded our online privacy long ago in exchange for the ability to post cat photos for free. But I do think that the unwinding right now of some of that data collection comes down to being transparent about what's collected, and giving the user more control.

Almost any time you have a difficult situation like this online, the default is now, "How much control can I give the user over this? And how much can I let them know what I'm collecting and what I'm using it for?" I think those are the biggest ways to deal with this challenge of consumer trust when it comes to data online.

DP: *There are specific circumstances where people see what's collected and say, "Oh, this could put me at risk. Maybe I shouldn't use that."*

For example, in the United States where abortion is now being made illegal in some states after the US Supreme Court overturned the Roe vs. Wade ruling, women are looking at period-tracking apps and thinking, OK, maybe I should delete that. In that case, the cost of surrendering private data isn't just annoyance. It's potentially being charged with a crime in that state for

*somebody even suspecting you may have conducted a medication abortion.
Which is really disturbing.*

BB: I know we both like dystopian stories. We just don't like to think we might live in one. I'm thinking of things even as simple as the Lyft ride-sharing service. They recently received a letter from one state representative delegation telling them that whether they're operating in that state or not, they could be tried for criminally aiding and abetting if they take someone to an abortion clinic. If that data like that gets requisitioned by the government, what happens? We don't know.

DP: *Well, we're going in a lot of dark directions. Let's pull the conversation back to some of the positive things about emerging media platforms.*

Can you talk about some of the digital products that you worked on that were innovative in their time, and what you learned through the process of launching them? It's not like you wake up one morning and a light bulb appears over your head, and go build what you imagined and perfectly execute it and everybody instantly loves it. That never happens, right?

BB: I'll give three examples, starting very long ago and moving into the present.

A long time ago in the trade show world of the company I worked for, we invested heavily in a piece of software to help match-make businesses with each other, connecting buyers and sellers to help them find each other. It was a native piece of software. We would enter exhibitors into it, enter the participant list, and people would be able to find each other and find partners, customers, and that sort of thing.

Today, there are dozens if not hundreds of applications like that in the Cloud to help people find each other, to ask and answer questions, and to connect. But at that time, it was a great idea that nobody used. Hundreds of thousands of dollars were invested into it, and it failed. It was too early.

DP: *In this book, we touch on the Technology Acceptance Model theory, which is all about how people accept technology only if they believe it will be useful to them in their jobs at that moment. They have to believe that it will solve their problems and be easy to use. Acceptance depends on the time, and all kinds of other factors, right?*

BB: That's right. And in fact, that sort of painful failure of a project softened the ground so that when there were tools that were available from third parties, all parties involved were ready for it. I'm not sure they would have been ready for it if we hadn't spent a lot of time, effort, and of course money to try to encourage them to use such a tool that just ended up being a little too hard to use because it was first.

People couldn't quite wrap their heads around why they would go up to a kiosk at a conference and type things in to try to find a buyer or seller. But then just four years later, when Internet-based tools made it a much easier process, people actually asked for services like this.

DP: *It's funny, because a lot of us experience FOMO, the Fear of Missing Out. We lament being four years too late to a trend, but in this case you were four years too early. Shame on you for innovating too fast!*

BB: Yeah, exactly. Also shame on us for not convincing people they wanted something that they didn't know they wanted yet.

DP: *What's failure number 2?*

BB: So one of my favorites, because it seems like such a simple thing now, was at a major business magazine. We launched a blog in the early 2000s at a time when we didn't even have a fully resourced website. At the time, doing this required a third-party service provider to do the coding and create the blog and build some fairly rudimentary CMS behind it.

We hired a couple of tech-savvy writers who were very expensive at the time because they knew how to use technology and how to write articles on innovation. We built this great blog but what we didn't understand was how audience development worked for that type of a product. It seems so simple now when you can create a blog in 60 seconds, but back then it was a monumental effort to launch something like that . . .

It gave us the opportunity to look at what type of content we should create, and in what format. We did eventually start understanding what people actually spend the time to read online so when the time came, and we had a big, splashy, fully resourced website, the writers had already been trained to write for that format. The blog was an experiment that was challenging at the time. It's all part of a continuum.

DP: *If you think about it, there's no such thing as a failure. Everything is an ongoing test, and the series of tests are the process of innovation.*

BB: I recently talked to the co-founder of Snap and asked him, "What was your biggest failure?" And he replied, "There's no such thing. We take experiments and we put them in front of our consumers and they tell us what we need to do with the next version."

I think just about any sort of innovation ends up being somewhere along that continuum.

DP: **Right. Everyone's field testing their own future. OK, so what's the third?**

BB: Most recently at The Washington Post, we and many others in the newspaper business thought that the whole world wanted to have immersive content, because that's what advertisers told us.

There were quite a few really beautiful, immersive projects that still exist, and are actually more consumed now than they were then. They were proofs of concept of everything from a trip to Mars to war zones and all kinds of things that had not been available in the emotional way that immersive technology can make possible.

One of the big learnings was that the hardware (headsets) was behind the quality of the content. But as the content ecosystem grew, we assumed there would be more headsets out there in consumers' hands, but that didn't happen fast enough.

DP: **And now, even as many news organizations have dialed back on VR, brands that used to be their advertisers are spending billions in the Metaverse.**

BB: A good example of that is Nike, which has been experimenting with the Metaverse for a while. I've heard that they now have a Chief Metaverse Officer. And one of the major sports leagues has been doing experimentation in this space for quite a while in both AR and VR. When you see something like that, you can bet that there are partnerships coming.

DP: *Well, there's finally a word for it, right?*

BB: Yeah, it's like it's a construct for something that everybody has already been doing. And now it's packaged neatly into something that they're ready to run with. Without that early experimentation, they would be years away from being able to even play in this new Metaverse marketplace and future.

DP: *The Metaverse as currently envisioned could also not work the way that companies are saying it will. True validation, or rejection, of various visions of the Metaverse depends on all kinds of other factors, including the economy, whether people are ready to invest time and money in a new technology, and if they're really ready for it.*

Let's switch track a little bit and talk about the field test you did when you were in my class. I have to admit that when I first saw your proposal, I laughed because it sounded so ridiculous. And then I thought, it sounds so crazy that it just might work.

BB: I'm still very proud of it. When I was taking the class in 2016, there had been an incident in Dallas of a shooter who was in a standoff with the police. News organizations were trying all these different ways to get video or other images of the situation, including drones.

It occurred to me that if we can use drones for a story like this, maybe it's cheaper and easier for a smaller local news organization to use a little ground-level robot that could go and capture images. Robot Journalism.

The idea was to be able to roll a little robot into a scene that was too small or dangerous for humans to enter, in the same way that SWAT teams had already been doing in other scenarios.

I thought it would be easy. There are kits available to build a robot that has small tank wheels, and it had a platform to which I thought I could attach an iPhone and light. And it had an infrared remote and Arduino computer to which you could attach other sensors.

DP: *And was it as easy as you thought?*

BB: It turned out to be a series of problem-solving exercises through every stage of the project, which was actually what made it so much fun.

My view of a field test is that you have to keep trying things that scare you until you fail. And then you keep failing and fixing, failing and fixing until you either have everything perfect or you run out of time. Most of the time, you're just going to run out of time, and that's fine.

It turned out that building the robot was the easiest part. But figuring out how to take one iPhone and make it the lens, with another iPhone being the viewfinder, was harder. I eventually found a little $1 app that did this. But then I realized I had to light it. I used rubber bands to put a photo LED light on it. And that worked great.

DP: **What else did you have to learn?**

BB: The infrared remote required me to learn some programming code in a language that Arduinos use. I found this amazing open-source place online that had snippets of code that people had already written for the exact remote control I was using, so I just had to download and install them.

Once the whole thing was working, I took it to a protest in Washington Square Park in New York City. I decided that I'd just drive this thing all the way up to the front, right in the middle of the protests, but it only got into the second layer of people. Someone kicked it because they didn't know what it was, and it looked dangerous.

DP: **Yeah, right! They probably thought, "What is this, a bomb?"**

BB: Yeah. I realized that even little things like putting a smiley face flag on it were important to overcome that. These are the lessons that I had to learn that I never would have thought of if I hadn't tried using the robot for a story.

DP: **I also remember seeing pictures the robot took of the police kind of giving it the side eye.**

BB: There must have been 60 officers, so I decided to go take a little picture of them. I didn't ask first, which was part of the problem. But then as I rolled it up to them, I could watch the heads turn in, and officers were looking at this thing that was coming at them.

You don't know these things until you try it. Nothing bad happened. I didn't get a ticket. I didn't get thrown in jail. They actually thought it was funny.

After it got kicked, I had to take some model glue and repair a couple of things, and it was actually invigorating to have new problems to solve.

DP: **This reminds me of the very early 360 camera rigs, which were a bunch of GoPro cameras stuck together. You would control them with one controller. You'd then leave and hide and hit the remote button and it would beep six times and all of the cameras' lights were flashing. It also scared people. They acted like they were afraid you were setting off a bomb.**

Those human factors are key, and there is no way to know how people will interact with something new until you just put it out there.

BB: One of the things I've learned is that it's really important to find something that you can simplify. If you're using an easy technology, find a way to use it in a complicated way so you can have more fun with it. If you're using something that's a little bit complex from a technology standpoint, the test doesn't have to be something that's going to change the world.

The ultimate test I did, which actually ended up giving this project its name, was "The Rat." In New York City there was a garbage worker's strike, and garbage was piling up. On the morning of garbage day in New York City, I went to various places and experimented with sending the robot – now renamed The Rat – into garbage heaps.

It was silly and very simple. It was not a story that anybody would publish necessarily, but it managed to show me things like how the motor noise was a little too loud to be able to capture sound. I also learned that the robot itself was a little bit too light, so if there were bumps in the sidewalk the speed was difficult to control. All these insights came from running these types of small tests.

DP: *I always encourage people to publish their field tests online because I think it just shows that you're somebody who can be trusted to go out and try new things. Do the companies you consult with value employees like that?*

BB: Yes. It has helped me work better with my own technology team. When I was in this class, I was actually working at The Washington Post at a time when it went from four engineers working for the entire company to 70.

Our philosophy was that you can teach a journalist about technology, but you can't teach a technologist to write. But if you put both groups together in a room, they can do amazing things that nobody thought were possible.

I don't think that without doing field testing, I would have had the courage to dive into an environment like that because it can be embarrassing to fail in a workplace, or to not be able to talk to engineers.

Now, I work very closely with the Chief Digital Officer at my current company. We're building a content strategy with technology behind it, and experimenting with different ways to tell stories. It's a very smooth process because we know how to talk to each other and are willing to try new things even if we fear they might fail.

The second thing is it gives the team that works for you the courage to fail. I can tell them about my robot, and they feel safe trying their own crazy experiments . . .

DP: *When you eventually started teaching the class, are there any field tests your students did that stood out?*

BB: One of the student projects that was a real standout was from someone using Unity voluntarily. Before moving into communication, she had been a K-12 teacher. She surmised that Unity would allow her to create better educational tools for kids. She created some very simple walk-throughs of a jungle and annotated the objects with facts about the jungle animals. It was a fascinating application of a gaming engine based on what she was passionate about: teaching kids.

DP: *What's your advice for people who are just starting out, and want to have a career focused on the digital edge like you've had?*

BB: First, it's important to have the perspective that you're looking at a digital/online industry that is not that old. This means you're not as far behind as you think you are.

Second is that it's the imperfections and the unpredictability of humans, combined with the technology tools that make amazing things. Being able to put those things together without fear ends up being that one thing that's your greatest protection in a world where others are worried about technology or are wondering if it's going to take their jobs away.

If you're willing to learn about it, understand how you can take your humanity and the gifts of technology, and implement great ideas, you have a bright future.

DP: *What's one technology on the horizon that excites you?*

BB: The technology that excites me right now is mixed reality. I think we've just started figuring out what it can be. What's great about almost every technology now is that it's become very easy to implement it.

For example, think about 360 photography, what it used to take to stitch. Think of how much work it used to take, and now how simple it's become. This means you can focus more on the idea and the story rather than having to spend all your time fighting with the technology.

This is starting to happen with all of these immersive technologies. It's freeing people up to start thinking about what sort of amazing things they can do in this new medium, versus being focused on just being able to use it.

DP: ***What's something on the horizon that scares you?***

BB: Artificial intelligence, which is really a collection of a lot of different technologies and issues. It is the greatest, most exciting, most incredible promise, but not in the things that people are talking about right now.

I don't confuse intelligence with sentience, and I'm not necessarily concerned about AI coming alive. What I am concerned about is what humans, unchecked, might be able to do with that sort of access to data and that sort of predictive capability and the analytic capability that AI can bring.

No technology by itself is good or bad. It's all about how we use it. I think AI is one that has a lot of power, but it can go the other way depending on who's using it and what they're using it for.

Online Resources for Chapter 3

Find more resources for Chapter 3 line at http://emergingmediaplatforms.com/chapter3.

Sources

American Press Institute. (2006, January 1). *American Press Institute*. www.americanpress institute.org/wp-content/uploads/2013/09/N2_Blueprint-for-Transformation.pdf

4   Open-Source Technologies

Have you ever worked on a creative project – whether it be a piece of art, a home construction project, or a recipe – and you spent hours alone writing out all the steps, only to find out that the end result didn't meet your expectations? And if it was something you made for other people, like a dinner entree, maybe they politely told you it was good – but you could tell from their expressions that it was mediocre or bad.

To extend the cooking metaphor, think of every season of The Great British Baking Show (Bake Off in the United Kingdom) and the beautiful, idealized drawings of cake show stoppers. Then compare to how many were derided by the judges as stodgy, underbaked, or a total disaster. This was so common on the show that Netflix created an entire parody series called "Nailed It!" With every individual working alone, and in secret, baking disasters are almost guaranteed to occur.

This method of working alone – or if you extend it to a company, a team working in a closed room with no outside input or help – is how most software was built for decades. If you think back to any piece of software you used before around the year 2000, it was pretty bad and buggy – just like those bad cakes. The "blue screen of death" crashes on PCs were a regular occurrence largely because only a small group of individuals (the coding team and maybe some beta testers who signed non-disclosure agreements) were finding and fixing bugs. How could they catch them all?

The Cathedral and the Bazaar

In 1997, a Linux programmer named Eric Raymond wrote an essay in which he gave this approach a name: "the cathedral." He suggested another approach, "the bazaar," in which software was built in public view, with all of the code posted on the Internet as it was being written. The essay was later published as a book, "The Cathedral and the Bazaar." This came to be known as the open-source approach, and it changed the way every company that creates software today operates.

If you were to apply this more open, chaotic bazaar approach to Bake Off, it would be a very different show. Contestants wouldn't work individually, but together like a mob. One baker might throw out ideas for ten different cake recipes for a show stopper. Two others who specialize in buttercream and jellies would sign up to build the top layer, while the architect-turned-baker would offer to build several different bases.

DOI: 10.4324/9781003247012-5

The tent walls would come down, and the families of the bakers would be invited to try different pieces of cake while it was being constructed. Sponges would be thrown out and rebaked several different times. The recipes would also be there for anyone – including members of the audience – to try themselves, and they would be invited to bring their modifications to the recipe back to the bakers in the tent to be considered for the final show stopper. Anyone – not just judge Paul Hollywood – would be free to call a sponge stodgy or flavorless at any point, right there on live TV.

Why would anyone want to subject their project to all that chaos, scrutiny, and mess? Because it prioritizes the final product – the cake, if you will – over the pride of the creators. Individuals and teams alike tend to fall in love with their ideas and naturally want to work on things in secret until offering them up to the world. But if you want the best end product, open source offers a better path to eventual quality thanks to the collective work of the crowd.

Open Source and Coding for Media

Nearly 25 years after Raymond wrote his essay, the vast majority of digital tools you use every day incorporate at least some open-source code. Even Apple, one of the most secretive tech companies around, uses open-source code, and it publicly shares its code on the Internet for those who want to try to see it (see opensource. apple.com).

This is a great thing for you as a media creator. A lot of open-source code is available for you to use for free, with just two stipulations: give credit for the code you're using if you publish something with it, and provide any changes or improvements to the source code back to the developers so that they can incorporate them and share with everyone else.

Even better, most of the cool, interactive stuff you see on the Web – like data visualizations on the New York Times or Washington Post – is built using open-source code that you can find and use for your own work. But to understand what to look for, you first need some basic knowledge of how the modern Internet works.

I like to think of open-source code like the mythical (or not?) flying saucer that crashed in Roswell, New Mexico, in 1947. We all know the story: a UFO crashes in the desert, broken pieces are strewn all over the place and, with the exception of the dead alien bodies, a lot of those pieces still seem to work. The military scientists start plugging things together and voila, something levitates.

They didn't need to know how any of those pieces were built, and they just needed to understand what they are and how they fit together. If you know just a few things about how the Internet works, you too can reverse-engineer UFOs to make your media content look great and do cool things.

A Web Server Is Like a Short-Order Cook

Let's start from the very beginning of the process of how you access a website. When you type a website URL and hit enter, content and interactivity magically appear on your browser. But what's happening behind the scenes?

You may have heard of the term "web server," thinking that this is some kind of fancy tech wizardry. It's actually quite boring, and you are likely using one right now. The content that shows up on your browser when you type in that web address is in a publicly visible folder on a computer not that different from your laptop. The "web server" is just a piece of software that runs on that computer and looks for requests from people like you, and then serves them what they ask for.

You can think of the web server as a short-order cook for files. Someone comes to my diner and asks for a slice of apple pie, but they also ask for it based on where they see it in the glass cooler. They may say, "Can I have the slice of apple pie on the top shelf of the cooler, above the banana cream pie?" The web server goes to that specific cooler and shelf and serves that piece of apple pie to the customer.

On the computer, the diner would be the domain name, and the cooler and shelf would be the folder. The piece of pie would be the file – mostly likely an HTML file, which we'll get into next. You could write it like this:

```
http://diner8234.com/cooler1/shelf1/pie.html
```

Looking Under the Hood

The next few sections get a little technical, and if it's new to you, you may experience a little anxiety wondering: do I need to know how to write all this code? And the answer is no, you don't (though you may want to learn that separately later). But just like it's important to be able to pop up the hood of your car and identify where to put the oil and windshield washer fluid, it's important to be able to identify the parts of a web page and how they fit together.

HTML, CSS, and JavaScript are the three types of files that create most of what you see on the Internet. This book won't teach you how to code (there are many others you can find to learn how to code in them, as well as websites), but you'll know how to identify these files in open-source libraries you want to use.

HTML: The Content

HTML, which stands for Hypertext Markup Language, is what delivers every headline, paragraph, and image you have ever seen on a web page. An HTML file ends in .htm or .html, so if you made a page about your apple pie it might be named, pie.html.

You can see the HTML behind the website you're looking at by choosing the View > Developer > View Source menu (in Chrome). Scroll through the massive amount of code you see on a site, and hit Command-F (Control-F on Windows) to search. Type in any headline you saw on the page and you will see something like this:

```
<h1>Hello, world</h1>
<p>What's up?</p>
```

That's the HTML for that headline, and the h1 / h1 are "tags" that say, hey user's web browser, this is a headline so make it bigger. Pretty easy! Don't worry about all the other codes or tags that you see for now. Just know that content is delivered inside tags.

CSS: The Look and Feel

These files, which end in. css, control most aspects of how content appears on a web page. That includes the fonts, colors, lines and widths of lines, margins around elements, and a whole host of other things. They're like instruction books for your HTML to determine how to make things look.

Inside a CSS file is a list of styles for certain tags, and each one is called out by a name referred to as a class. So, let's say you want your H1 to be large, green, and bold, and you want your paragraph text to be small, black, and italic. You would give each class a name that can be anything you want.

Let's call the large bold class "bigtitle" and the small paragraph class "small-text." The CSS might look like this:

```
.bigtitle {color: green; font-family: Arial; font-
    style: normal; font-weight: bold; font-size: 100px;
    margin: 0;}
.smalltext {color: black; font-family: Arial; font-
    style: normal; font-weight: normal; font-size: 25px;}
```

Those styles would then be applied in the HTML by adding the class names to the tags, like this:

```
<h1 class="bigtitle">Hello, world</h1>
<p class="smalltext">What's up?</p>
```

Finally, the HTML file would be told where the CSS file is near the top of the HTML file before the closing of the </body> tag:

```
<link rel="stylesheet" href="style.css" />
```

JavaScript: The Pizzazz

When something moves, flashes, or allows you to interact in any way, the chances are it's written in JavaScript. And unlike the HTML and CSS we just talked about, JavaScript is the only file that is actually computer code. (The other two are markup languages.)

You can think of JavaScript files as similar to apps on your smartphone. When you want to use it, you just reference it in your HTML file – and you almost never modify the actual JavaScript file unless you have studied computer programming languages. So we're not going to get into the mechanics of JavaScript at all here.

Just know that if you see something like this on a web page, it's "downloading an app" that will make the page do cool interactive stuff:

```
<script src="script.js"></script>
```

GitHub: Where Open-Source Lives

I mentioned that open source changed the way every company handles code, with large portions of software code being shared publicly for other developers to experiment with. What I didn't tell you is how they do that: through "code repositories" or "repos" for short.

A repo is a place for professional coders to share their code in a way that makes it easy for others to download it and then share improvements back with the developer. GitHub is one of the most popular. We will get into more details about how GitHub works, but for now all you need to know is that once you identify the name of some code that does something cool, you can usually find its "repo" on GitHub.

As just one example, you may notice that a lot of your favorite websites share similar design styles. It turns out that many come from an open-source design library called Bootstrap. You can download the basic templates from Bootstrap on their GitHub repo:

```
https://github.com/twbs/bootstrap
```

If you click the green Code button and then Download Zip, you'll have all of the code (mostly CSS) to design sites that look just like the professionals' sites. You can also add two lines of code to your web pages to allow them to use Bootstrap design elements. At http://getbootstrap.com there are clear directions on how to do that.

Workbook Exercise 4.1: Learn HTML With Help From a Robot

If you are new to HTML, I'll tell you right up front that you aren't going to learn it by just reading a book, or by reading anything. You learn it by writing HTML. But how do you start writing HTML if you know nothing about it?

Fortunately, there are a number of ways to do this online that are completely free – and they utilize AI to check your progress. Think of them like Duolingo, but for HTML and CSS.

W3Schools is one such site. It has detailed tutorials on different tags, followed by a "Try it Yourself" mode where you can modify HTML in a template with your own content. The code you modify appears on the left, and the resulting change in the website appears on the right after you click a Run button.

If you have never coded a bit of HTML in your life, spend some time going through each section in the W3Schools HTML tutorial: www.w3schools.com/html/.

After you do that, you can continue on to its CSS tutorial: www.w3schools.com/css/.

The site has other tutorials, such as JavaScript and Python, for more advanced users. But do yourself a favor and just avoid those for now, because without a basic understanding of HTML you won't be able to effectively use true programming languages. But you will be able to make your digital stories look better!

Another site worth trying is Codeacademy. This site is more of a true AI/robot approach. At each step, you read a little about the tag you're trying to master, and then it tells you to modify that code in a template in a specific way. When you click Run, it will try to detect errors in your code and give you pointers. You can't progress to the next step until you master the one you're on, which forces you to stick with that step until you figure it out.

As you're learning HTML and CSS code, you're bound to get frustrated at times and even want to give up. When you feel that way, just remember that every other person who ever learned these markup languages experienced the same types of moments when they started. Just like any human language, learning a coding language takes time and practice.

Workbook Exercise 4.2: Glitch

Glitch is a free service that lets you mess around with HTML, CSS, and JavaScript code and see what it would look like when published. It's also a great way to overcome your fear of code and start messing around – just like those military scientists who reverse engineered the Roswell UFO.

Go to Glitch.com and create an account. Then, click New Project and choose Glitch-Hello-Website. Once it loads, click on the index.html file. Then, click the Show button at the top (the one with a sunglasses icon) and choose Next to the Code.

Change the text of Hello World to anything you like, and you will see it change.

After that line, add <p> </p> for Paragraph, and type some words for a paragraph like this:

```
<p>This is my amazing paragraph.</p>
```

You will see your paragraph text appear immediately below the headline.

Finally, go to the. css file and change the color for the .title class to blue, like this:

```
title {color: blue;}
```

You'll see the headline change to blue. See how simple this HTML and CSS are.

Workbook Exercise 4.3: Open-Source Code Library Hunt

Find a site you respect that does something cool and interactive, such as a data visualization. View the source code (View > Developer > View Source in Chrome) and then hit Command-S to search. Type in ".js" and start reading the names of the JavaScript files you see.

Eventually, if you see something that sounds like it may create the effect you like on the site, you can go to http://github.com and type in that JavaScript file. You will be surprised how many come up as code repos that you can download and apply to your own web pages.

Case Study: Using AI to Identify Fake News

Before taking my class, Ben had never touched code in his life other than changing a few headline styles in WordPress. Upon learning that anyone can search for and use open-source code libraries, he sought to find and test code that could help address one of the biggest problems in our society: fake news.

His hypothesis was that if AI and machine learning could accurately track and sort news articles by their levels of bias and accuracy, then fake news could be stopped in its tracks before spreading like wildfire across social media. He also felt that an impartial, AI-driven truthfulness score could help people decide on which news providers to trust. But there were a lot of "ifs" in his hypothesis for what still proves to be a thorny problem. If even human beings have trouble distinguishing between real and fake news, sometimes even preferring the misinformation, could AI really solve the problem?

After some digging around, he stumbled across an open-source library on GitHub called Fakebox (https://machinebox.io/docs/fakebox). This software uses two methods to identify fake news. First, it uses human-assigned categorization of web domains to tag them on various measures of truthfulness, such as bias, clickbait, conspiracy, fake, parody, and satire. It then scores the headline and content as being either biased or impartial.

He fed 113 articles into the system. There were an equal number of biased articles to impartial articles. Bloomberg News, The New York Times, The Washington Post, the Wall Street Journal, Politico, and Slate.com were all categorized as trusted domains; The Daily Beast, Fox News, and Breitbart were categorized as political domains; and Huzlers and the Onion were categorized as satirical domains.

Across these articles, he found that Fakebox correctly identified real news, but it completely failed to identify stories from sites known to contain misleading or false information: Infowars, Newsbusters, and Breitbart. In those cases, the best the algorithm could do is to mark the stories as "unsure."

He concluded that:

> artificial intelligence is able to detect bias and whether or not an article comes from an authentic source, but human intelligence remains the best way to detect fact of content and discern real news from fake. In the framework of our hypothesis this would be considered failure. The experiment highlights several potential uses for this emerging media technology, however.

His French fry moment came from noticing that every single article sent through Fakebox tested positive for at least some bias. And that makes sense, given that stories are researched and reported by human beings who have biases. But being biased and being outright fake are two different things. The AI could not identify content that Ben knew to be completely inaccurate or made up.

"This is a branch of computer science, and as in any scientific field there will be more experiments, higher rates of success, and impactful breakthroughs," he wrote.

I don't doubt that machine learning will be able to fact-check articles in the next few years. In this future scenario, there is a real opportunity to rebuild public trust in news by showing which publications are performing their functions and which ones aren't.

Expert Interview: Dan Schultz, Civic Hacker

I recently caught up with Dan Shultz, an open-source civic coder who I met when he was a programmer-journalist through the Knight-Mozilla Open News program (now spun off as just OpenNews). He went on to do some interesting interactive work for the Boston Globe as an embedded coder. Later, we invited him to the Newhouse School for a semester to show students and faculty alike how to code interactive sites in HTML, CSS, and JavaScript. I personally learned a lot from him during that period, much of which is reflected in this very chapter.

DAN PACHECO (DP): **Welcome, Dan! Can you tell us a little bit about yourself?**

DAN SCHULTZ (DS): Sure. I grew up in the Philly area. My mom was in the journalism space as an executive director of a nonprofit, and I was very much in the nerdy space. But my dad was a musician, which I think adds to my creative elements too.

I was the kid who carried around a laptop, before kids carried around laptops. And then I got a degree in Information Systems from Carnegie Mellon University, where I also studied some computer science. That's when I got really involved in how technology and community can work together.

I went to grad school at the MIT Media Lab as part of their Center for Civic Media, which really hones in on that question of how technology can help our civics. After graduating from MIT, I went through another program that was a collaboration between the Knight Foundation – which is all about journalism – and the Mozilla Foundation – which is all about applying technology to community. In that group, we focused on how to make sure the control of the web remains in the hands of the people. Also, what we as developers can build to help people stay in control of the web.

From there, I met a whole bunch of amazing creators like yourself and others. We'd been in touch and started a lot of freelance work on open-source projects. We started a group called The Bad Idea Factory, which is a little bit whimsical. It's a chance for people who may have full-time jobs or grant-funded projects but can cooperatively work on open-source tech. A lot of us have roots in journalism and technology, which is sometimes called civic technology.

DP: **When you talk about open source, what do you mean by it, and why is it important to journalism and civic democracy?**

DS: For a consumer, the value of using open-source tools is that they're transparent about what's going on. That's especially important in a world where people believe the information they're consuming. If that information is driven by algorithms that are closed, and we don't know how they're being used, that gets concerning.

Openness is a really critical piece of a long-term free society where you're not totally beholden to any entity. If a change is made that feels unethical or doesn't align with your personal principles, you have the ability to keep using the old software, or you have the ability to find something else. It means that we don't have to be locked into this world where the platforms we use are controlled by the Bezos and Zuckerbergs of the world. At the end of the day, even their technologies are built upon open standards.

But this isn't always true. We all use cell phones, which are generally not open. Let's say that Apple decides that they want to track something. A lot of your life is already built around that phone. You have a choice to switch to Android, but what if both Apple and Google decide to do it? Then you have no choice but to be tracked.

This is why way back, Mozilla leaned in with Firefox. It stopped Microsoft from being able to say, "Hey, this HTML thing is pretty cool, but we want to add these proprietary features that only work on our platforms." When it's open more people are able to innovate on it instead of it just being one company's vision.

Our quality of life and our ability to do things very much relies on the technology we're using. When it's open, it allows the community to be in control of what's possible – a very democratic principle.

DP: **What does open source make possible for coding?**

DS: As a developer, it makes me more efficient. For example, I'm glad that I can create something without having to write the software that knows how to send messages over a network, for instance. I can just build on top of something someone else wrote, whether it's open code that's doing that, or an open protocol that's been defined by a bunch of people where everyone agrees to follow the same protocol. Without those kinds of open systems, we wouldn't have the Internet we have today.

DP: **Do you encounter resistance from media companies to open source their code?**

DS: First, I will just say that open source does not mean you cannot fit into a business model.

A lot of news organizations say, "Well, you know, it's just antithetical to open source our platform that we're spending a lot of money to build. Why would we give that away?" And the reality is that technology has never been the thing that's earning news organizations money, right? It's their content and their support of community.

And yes, that also includes the tools that enable that, but it's not like the Boston Globe is suddenly going to disappear because they open source the code for their mobile app, right? Or that suddenly they're going to have a competitor who has this major advantage by having access to that code, and it allows them to overtake the Boston Globe.

The promise of open source is that it actually can provide a way of interacting with your users that is much more accountable, and much more respectful.

DP: **Just like with democracy, you could easily teeter into rule by the crowd and go in all kinds of crazy directions. How do open-source communities deal with that?**

DS: The kinds of projects I've been involved in are usually sponsored by an organization, or it is the project of an organization. It is open source, but at the end of the day they have an engineering team with product milestones, and they have determined that they want to build it as an open-source project.

Their strategy is that we're building it, and we believe it should be open, so we're going to do it in a way that is well documented and following best engineering practices such as making sure that things are well tested. All of that makes it easier for an open-source developer down the line to pick it up and maybe add a feature they want, and that has the potential to be available to everybody who uses the code.

Projects like this usually have a weekly meeting of their code "maintainers," a sort of half hour to check in on what features you're looking to add, what bugs need fixing, and that sort of thing. That translates to a roadmap that is treated just like for any other software. This allows them to keep track of what their goals are and make sure they're collecting feedback from the people who are using it so that the changes are aligned with the needs of their core users.

DP: *A lot of people who read this book have mostly only used a little HTML and CSS but are discovering that they can go to GitHub and see if there are code libraries they can use to make their sites better. Do you still see value in that for the average digital journalist?*

DS: I think the most important thing to know is that if you're not interested in it, it is not a requirement. If somebody loves journalism and is anemic to computers and programming, they do not need to eat their spinach and learn how to code.

But if somebody is interested in it, I think it can be very empowering. For a person who enjoys making things, knowing how to find and use open-source code can unlock new types of things that you can do. The most important thing to learn is to understand what's possible, and that you don't need to go out and code something yourself.

We're still in the Golden Age of computing and being able to make digital content that other people can see. Hopefully, that will be true forever, where if you have an idea and you want to throw something together and put it on the Internet, you can just do it.

It's just like how, if you work for a newspaper, knowing that on mobile devices things work this way, versus how they work on a desktop, will help you create more engaging content. Knowing the nuances of how a phone reading experience works versus a browser reading experience is going to help you design your content better. This also goes for knowing what's possible in the code, and what the coders actually do and how they work together.

DP: *If you don't know all that and you ask a developer to build something, it's going to come across as asking for magic, right?*

DS: Exactly. You'll be asking for things that can't exist instead of things that can actually happen. It's always better for you to ask for the thing that can happen, and to have a vision that leads to an actual creation.

But if you're somebody who wants to actually learn to build things that people are able to click on, read, and scroll through, you need to learn HTML, CSS, and JavaScript. Those are the baseline three technologies that you're going to want to be able to pick up.

DP: *What are some of your favorite open-source projects that you've worked on?*

DS: I made a thing called Internet Noise. Congress had just passed legislation that made it more legal for Internet Service Providers to track your activity, and in anger and frustration, I made it in about four hours. That's not because I'm some amazing coder. It was just a very simple idea.

Internet Noise would randomly create a new browser tab every ten seconds with a random search term. It would send it to a Google URL called "I'm Feeling Lucky" that would automatically go to the first page that matches the first page of search results for a term. I looked up 5,000 common English words and wrote a little script that combined two random words, and just opened a new tab with those random words and sent them to Google.

Suddenly, my browser was generating a bunch of random web traffic. The ISP doesn't care to find out what's random and what's intentional. All that random Internet noise made it harder for them to track other things that I'm doing over my Internet connection.

It went viral, and I even got profiled in the New Yorker because of it. It was ridiculous. But it was also just a piece of performance protest art with technology. That kind of programming is within the grasp of anybody.

DP: *I know you've also done some work with archiving and analyzing video during political campaigns. Can you talk about that?*

Sure. My other favorite project is one that I'm still working on that started at the Internet Archive, where I was working for a little while.

The Internet Archive is the world's largest digital library. The idea of the archive is that digital media is ephemeral, and it will disappear. A server that's on today may not be on in a week, and whatever content was on that server will no longer be accessible.

The Internet Archive is trying to prevent a future scenario when all of human knowledge could be lost because the servers aren't there anymore. They have tons of robots that are crawling the web, scraping it, and storing copies of it. You can go to https://archive.org and type in a URL, and it will show you what it looked like over the years.

I joined the Internet Archive to specifically work on a project that was less about archiving the Internet, and more about archiving TV. You can go to their TV Archive to find recordings of the past – roughly ten years of Fox News, CNN, MSNBC, and other cable news programming. For the 2016 election, I helped them build a thing called the Political Ad Archive. We expanded beyond just cable news and started looking at a lot of local stations. We could then figure out which political ads were being aired in different parts of the country.

DP: *What's an example of a project you worked on that failed, or didn't do what you thought it would do?*

DS: I worked on a project called Truth Goggles that came out of my thesis at MIT. I was trying to create interfaces that help people think more carefully about the content they're reading.

The first interface we built helped people read content through the lens of somebody else. I know how I'm reacting to an article, but what would jump out for somebody totally unlike me? What phrases would trigger my defense mechanisms? What would jump out as credible?

After that, I leaned in on the fact-checking space. I wanted to see if I could detect phrases in news articles that have been fact-checked, and surface that right on the article. The idea was that if something has been fact-checked, that means it is popular enough and potentially questionable enough that people should think carefully before they just take it at face value.

Through that, I learned a lot about cognitive bias, which is what causes somebody to just inherently trust or distrust something. I wanted to see if it was possible to create an interface that cuts through those biases – not necessarily tells you what to think but helps you reach better, more critical conclusions.

Here's where it fell short. Natural Language Processing was not where it is today, and frankly even now it's still not good enough. Finding variations of the same phrase and accurately mapping them to fact-checked phrases is not an easy thing to do. If you get it wrong, you don't want to highlight something that's completely unrelated to a fact-check and then confuse the reader further.

The other challenge was that there were way more claims of things that should be fact-checked than actually should be. Most stories out there contain information that is not a strict matter of true and false. Truth Goggles wasn't the right metaphor for them, but "Hey, think about this more deeply. Here are a bunch of resources to consider" was better. And that's where the project ended up.

My whole experience with Truth Goggles is a reflection of how dangerous it is to consume information online without a certain level of critical thinking. I think we as a society have all failed on that lately, and hopefully we will get a second chance.

DP: ***If a journalist or storyteller wants to work with civic hackers like yourself, what are some practical ways they can go about doing that?***

DS: The OpenNews organization (https://opennews.org/) is a great group for networking, but you may also have civic hackers where you live. There are a lot of co-working hubs and spaces with community events. They're not just full of coders but also people interested in civics and journalism. You'll find plenty of people there who don't know how to code or don't have an interest in actually coding, but they all want to understand what's possible.

You can also just find a tool that you think is interesting or read about, and go see if it's on GitHub. It's not just the code that you will find there. You can also get access to the makers of these tools.

In GitHub you can open an issue with a question, and there's usually a discussion forum for a given tool. These are people there who probably would love to hear from you. It's going to make their day that somebody reached out saying that you love their tool, and you'd love to know more or are interested in a collaboration.

DP: **What else can you do with Git and GitHub besides code?**

DS: Git is useful for anything where you want to be able to track versions over time. For example, I use it for accounting. We use it for bylaws at Bad Idea Factory, so that anyone can see how the bylaws have changed over time. By the way, GitHub is not the only way to use Git. There's also Gitlab (https://about.gitlab.com/) which is pretty good. You can even spin your own copy of Gitlab on your own server.

The idea of tracking issues while also having discussions alongside the work product, and being able to review a change before it's added in, is really useful for teams. I think it's important for people to understand how the teams that build these kinds of projects work in an open way and how that factors into how the Internet works.

DP: **What ethical concerns come up with code?**

DS: The biggest ethical challenge I'm seeing right now for toolmakers is ensuring that you're thinking about the people who are going to be impacted by a system – especially for people who are different from you. If you don't do that with AI in particular, and you use data that has been generated on the Internet by a society that has misogynistic, racist, homophobic, and transphobic tendencies, then that AI is going to create systems that perpetuate those same biases.

The data on the Internet are being trained by a largely white male culture. Maybe instead of saying, "The vast majority of our system is driven by this type of data, so we're going to add a veneer on top to sort of hide that fact." What if instead we figured out a way to build systems that are inclusive and include all cultures and imagery?

I understand it's an uphill battle because the source of the data is the Internet, right? The source of the data is the dominant society that has all these problems. And so asking a toolmaker to solve all of those problems is a heavy lift. But the toolmaker does need to understand the limitations of their tool. It's a big conversation.

DP: **Do you think the lack of openness of algorithms can create the potential for certain biases to be inserted that people don't know are there?**

DS: In any technology, there is a chance for a reflection, or lack thereof, on your user and therefore on the system and group of people that are going to be interacting with it and are therefore most affected by it.

That's not just about computers, it can be about anything. When a car is designed, who's going to be able to open its door? Or if you design a bench, is it something that anyone can sit on?

In the world of technology, those types of design decisions are amplified because things happen so fast. There's so much power because so many more minutes of a given person's day are spent on it. And that's triple-charged when you're talking about things like machine learning, artificial intelligence, and the sort of stuff where we're giving up our control to the math and just hoping that the math comes out with an outcome we want.

Online Resources for Chapter 4

Find more resources for Chapter 4 online at http://emergingmediaplatforms.com/chapter4.

Sources

Raymond, E. S. (1998). The cathedral and the bazaar. *First Monday, 3*(2). https://doi.org/10.5210/fm.v3i2.578

5   XR and the Metaverse

In 1992, just as the consumer Internet was barely starting to creep out of government offices and universities, a little-known author named Neal Stephenson published the novel *Snow Crash*. Set in the cyberpunk genre, it quickly spread among young and old techies alike to emerge as a shared vision for what the then-nascent World Wide Web could be if it were able to be experienced in three dimensions using headsets.

While Stephenson didn't invent the idea of virtual reality or even coin the term, his vision of how it might ultimately replace text, images, and links with fully embodied virtual experiences in a simulated environment called "The Metaverse" (a term he did invent) took hold. Thirty years later, the idea of a Metaverse where people virtually live, work, and love is not just an idea – it's here. From Second Life to Roblox to Decentraland, there are multiple companies and movements underway to make the Metaverse mainstream. Most notably, in late 2021, the company formerly known as Facebook rebranded itself as "Meta" as a sign of its investment in creating what its Oculus headset's founder Palmer Luckey once called "the final compute platform."

But as a media professional, what is the Metaverse really to you, and why should you care about it? Where does it fit on a Gartner Hype Cycle graph? Is it a trigger, is it at the peak of inflated expectations, or maybe even in the trough of disillusionment? One thing everyone can agree on is that the term itself is definitely hype – as witnessed by me as an author even using it in this chapter's title. But the concepts behind it and what they allow you as a storyteller to do for your audience in new and exciting ways are very real.

Extended Reality Technologies – or XR

While Metaverse is casually thrown around in marketing circles, there is a better term for the underlying technologies that make Stephenson's vision possible: Extended Reality, or XR for short. It's used for a very practical reason: it encompasses all of the ways that reality can be simulated: VR, AR, MR, and other "R's" that may surface in the future. Here's what they each are, and how to think about them.

DOI: 10.4324/9781003247012-6

Virtual Reality (VR) uses headsets to transport peoples' consciousness elsewhere. When you put on a headset, in most cases, you lose touch with the world that you're in, and you see other spaces instead. Good VR tricks the brain into believing it's somewhere that it's not. As of this writing, the most popular VR headsets were made by Oculus, Vive, or PlayStation.

Augmented Reality (AR) typically uses the camera on a mobile phone or tablet to make it look like other content is in the room with you, but it can only be seen on that screen. You can think of mobile AR as a magical window that adds information and context to your environment. In addition, the 3D nature of the content you see in mobile AR is still 2D, just like the content of Pixar movies as seen on a typical television screen.

Mixed Reality (MR) typically uses a headset to place 3D objects in your current environment. Unlike mobile AR, which limits the augmentation to the phone or tablet screen, MR lets you see these objects in full 3D with proper depth perception.

I mentioned other Rs that may come, and as of this writing, there was a fourth: Simulated Reality (SR). (*Are your eyeballs beginning to bleed with all these R's? Now maybe you can see why people who work with these technologies all adopted XR as a single term?*) SR uses hidden cameras on screens to tell what each one of your eyes is watching and then sends slightly different content to each eye. The result is that in about three seconds, 3D content quickly looks like it's jumping out of the screen – all without the user having to wear glasses or a headset. In addition, some SR screens make it possible for two people who are looking at a screen to see different content. Of all the XR technologies earlier, I personally think that SR could have the biggest near-term impact because of how well it would fit into how people already use screens.

Forget the Lingo – It's About Immersion

What all of these technologies do for storytelling is put the person formerly known as the viewer or reader into the story itself. This is a real superpower for journalists in particular. If done right, it's more than just immersing someone in content. It's about transporting someone's consciousness into another place, person, or even animal or object.

Why would a journalist want to do that? If you're a journalist, I want you to sit back and think of a situation or place that you reported on or filmed, and no matter how hard you tried, you were either at a loss for words or couldn't capture the *feeling* of what it was like to be there. Your reporting ultimately fell short because of the limitations of your chosen medium. When describing the experience to others, you may have even stopped short and said something like, "I guess you had to be there."

With XR, you no longer have to stop at that point because *you can take people there!* The fundamentals of your newsgathering, writing, and production remain the same, but your role as a storyteller can evolve into something more like an experienced guide – not unlike being a docent at a museum. Imagine yourself standing next to your reader or viewer and reading your story, then reaching out your hand and saying: "Here, let me take you into the scene I just described."

The Origins of VR Journalism

I have the distinction of being one of the early journalists to experiment with XR in a journalistic way, starting with a project I managed for USA TODAY and The Des Moines Register in 2014 called *Harvest of Change*. This piece, which ultimately won an Edward R. Murrow Award, used CGI-based environments, 3D modeling, and 360 video to transport peoples' consciousness to a working farm in Western Iowa.

We debuted *Harvest of Change* at the 2014 Online News Association conference in Chicago, introducing thousands of digital journalists to the idea of immersing people in stories using virtual reality headsets.

But I don't deserve credit for creating this new storytelling form. That goes to Nonny de la Peña, who in 2012 published *Hunger in Los Angeles* which used virtual reality to transport people into a food shelter line that was struggling to meet demand. In this groundbreaking piece, "viewers" become experiencers who feel they are physically standing in a food line when an elderly, diabetic man collapses into a coma. The audio is real, but the buildings and people are all digital avatars that were painstakingly animated by Nonny and her volunteer friends, acting out every character's movements in a motion capture suit.

I had known Nonny previously, and when I ran into her at a conference that year, she ecstatically told me that I needed to try out the virtual reality experience that she was exhibiting at the conference. I will admit that I wasn't convinced, and the idea sounded a little kooky to me. I also had never had good experiences with VR, which had several false starts in the 1990s, and I told her that I even get sick watching 3D movies.

She grabbed me by the lapels, stared intensely into my eyes, and practically yelled, "No, you need to try this. VR is going to change everything!" So I did, and she was right. That winter, with some tips from Nonny, I learned how to use the Unity gaming engine, and a year later, I was producing a VR project as a summer consultant at USA TODAY.

Incidentally, *Hunger in Los Angeles* also changed the world in another way. In order to exhibit it at the 2012 Sundance Film Festival – which marked the first-ever VR "film" to be shown at the festival, or really anywhere – Nonny needed a headset. She wasn't allowed to take the very expensive set of goggles she had been borrowing from the University of Southern California's Mixed Reality Lab on the road. Palmer Luckey, who was a part-time lab manager, had been experimenting with his own, less expensive VR headset, and he agreed to let it be used for the showing. And thus, the world's first example of VR journalism was also the first demonstration piece for what nine months later became the Oculus Rift.

Thought Exercise 5.1: Your First Immersive Story

Whether experienced in a full VR headset, or through your phone via augmented reality, it's important to think about why a story should be told immersive instead of through an existing form. Here's a checklist I use in my Virtual Reality Storytelling class before students create their first immersive stories.

- What specific experience do you hope to transfer to someone else? Why is immersion the best medium to achieve that?
- What specifically is compelling about the experience people will have?
- How might it feel physically to be in this particular place and time? What sensations might people experience in their bodies, and in which parts of their bodies?
- Why might some people want to avoid this particular type of experience, and why?
- What do you hope people will understand or know better by "being there" that they couldn't by reading a story or watching a video?

Using Gaming Engines to Create Immersive Experiences

Some of the most dynamic immersive stories are essentially created as apps using a type of software known as a "gaming engine." The two gaming engines most relevant to XR are Unity and Unreal Engine. For XR, pieces developed for journalism or Unity have traditionally been the most common. For purposes of explanation, I'll focus on Unity, but many of the same features are available in Unreal. You can download a free version of Unity at https://unity.com/ and Unreal at www.unrealengine.com/.

In William Shakespeare's play *As You Like It*, the character Jaques says, "All the world's a stage, and all the men and women merely players." As it pertains to XR, you can think of a gaming engine as a stage for creating virtual worlds.

In the Unity gaming engine, you start off by adding a ground known as your terrain. You then add a 360 photo or "skybox" (a set of six images designed to create the illusion of a seamless sky) and add 3D models to the terrain. After you have your basic scene (or stage set?) setup, you use something called a state manager to create interactivity.

When the first Oculus headset came out, gaming engines were the only way to create XR experiences. While most of the functionality was free, it was also extremely buggy and often required learning C# or JavaScript. But things have evolved, and there are now much easier ways to create immersive story experiences. For this reason, I won't get into Unity much at all in this book, but on this book's website there are some video tutorials you can follow to learn how to get around in Unity should you choose to go down that path.

What I think requires much more attention by journalists and storytellers are the Metaverse and the 3D Web.

Experimenting With the Metaverse

The idea of "the Metaverse" is all-encompassing, and even companies like Meta say it's probably ten years away. But in the meantime, there are a variety of tools sometimes referred to as "Social VR" that let you experiment with Metaverse approaches.

The key difference between a standard VR story and a story in a Metaverse platform is that other people can meet as avatars in the scene or story that you build. In this way, the story can be potentially collectively explored along with other people being in the same "room" – not unlike the way museum exhibits work. A Metaverse story allows you to meet people "in person" and guide them through a seemingly physical space, or use the scene as a springboard for a larger discussion. And just like in a museum, when you go will determine if you are the only one in the room, or are surrounded by others.

I first started to get interested in Metaverse platforms at the start of COVID-19 during that awful period where two-week isolation at home stretched into weeks and then months before vaccines were available. AltspaceVR, which had started in 2015 and was purchased by Microsoft in 2017, had already been available for a while through Oculus headsets, but during the pandemic, the service began to promote its virtual events calendar. Some were purely fun and social, such as concerts where real musicians would play their music with real instruments while wearing VR headsets. Fans' avatars would bob to the music, and there were even virtual bars in the back where you could grab a virtual drink.

Obviously, none of that has any application to storytelling, but I soon discovered that it had a lot of implications for information. Another Metaverse platform by Mozilla – the creator of the Firefox web browser – called Mozilla Hubs (http://hubs.mozilla.com) was also starting to pick up steam. Unlike Altspace, Hubs is completely open source, and it even has its own world-building tool called Spoke. Best of all, it's completely free to use.

Through one Hub promoted in one of Mozilla's Slack channels, I soon found myself in a COVID-19 event where people were meeting to share 3D models of face masks and face shield visors they had designed for 3D printing. I observed their avatars "walking" around different designs they had uploaded, looking closely at every detail and discussing how well things like clips and fasteners held up after being printed. Some of those printable models ended up being used in the field and arguably saved lives.

Workbook Exercise 5.2: Create a Mozilla Hubs Scene

Hubs has an editor called Spoke (https://hubs.mozilla.com/spoke) that makes it incredibly easy for anyone to make a scene. Once the scene is created, you can open a room with that scene, post, or send a link to others and participate in an event in the Metaverse environment you set up.

Click the big, blue Get Started button, then New Project and New Empty Project. Mozilla has very good and easy-to-follow documentation for how to use Spoke in its Docs area (https://hubs.mozilla.com/docs/), but here are a few tips for the type of hub you may use for a story.

The "Viewport" shows your world as you build it. You can click anything in the viewport to move it, which you do by clicking and dragging the arrows that surround the object you've selected. By default, the selector is set to "translate," which means the arrows will move it forward, left, right, up, or down. You can change the selector to rotate or scale.

At the lower right of the screen are properties of whatever you've clicked on. Play around with those features, and you will see that you can also resize and move things by changing the numbers in X, Y, and Z.

If you're not sure what you clicked on, look at the upper right under Hierarchy, and it will highlight the name of the asset that you're currently modifying. To delete something, click on it or its name, and then click Delete.

You can add other objects – which are called Assets – in the Assets area at the lower left. The Rock Kit is a simple way to add some depth to your terrain, and Sketchfab is a way to add royalty-free assets and get comfortable with using the Spoke editor. Assets can be everything from 3D models and 3D scans to 360 photos and videos you find on YouTube. If you pull in a 360 video, be sure to change the projection from flat to 360 video in the properties panel.

One of the more useful assets is the Spawn Point, which is a place where the people you invite into your hub will first materialize. You can add multiple Spawn Points and move them around the scene. This will cause each person to materialize in a different part of the scene. So, for example, if you want your experiencers to start off around a table, find a table in Sketchfab and then add four Spawn Points around that table.

When you're done setting up your scene, click Publish to Hubs and wait for it to upload everything. You can then view the scene and create a room with the scene. Once the scene loads, you can use the arrow keys and mouse on your computer to move and look around. (Not sure how to navigate using WASD keys? Ask your favorite teenager or other game-playing nerd and they'll show you.)

The last step is to invite a friend to join you in your scene, which you can do by clicking the Invite button at the lower left.

As I mentioned, Hubs isn't the only Metaverse tool like this. Some other commercial alternatives are FrameVR (framevr.io) and Spatial (spatial.io). These commercial platforms typically employ a "freemium" business model, with basic features available for free and more advanced features – or support for larger file sizes and projects – available for an additional fee.

Thought Exercise 5.3: Building a Story as a Group Exploration

Now that you know how a Metaverse scene works with Mozilla Hubs, think about what kind of story makes sense for people to experience in a social setting with others. Many of the same types of topics that museums use for exhibits, or local issues that people in your community regularly meet about, can also make for good Metaverse-based stories.

Some examples are as follows: exploring the complexities of an urban planning project along with the city planners there in the room as guides; hosting a virtual meeting with an artist along with their 3D-scanned sculptures; or taking readers on a walking tour of a crime scene in which you lay out using simple architectural recreations. In each case, the scene needs to be able to stand alone if someone explores it individually but comes alive if a journalist or subject matter expert is available to guide people through the scene at a set time.

Here are some questions to think through as you plan out a story experience in the Metaverse:

- What types of stories are happening in your community that could benefit from having people experience the story together in a spatial narrative, guided by you, the storyteller?
- What will the scene look like, and what are the assets you need to find or have created?
- What's the first thing someone sees when they enter the space you created? How will they know what they can do? Do you need to prepare them for what they will experience or give them instructions – perhaps through signage or an audio greeting?
- Where will people appear in the scene in relation to the other assets in the room, and in relation to each other? How will the different Spawn Points affect how they interact with each other, and with the information you have provided?
- Can this story be experienced alone without a guide, or do you need to have someone present to guide people through it, and maybe even a Master of Ceremonies?

If you publicize an event through Hubs or any other Metaverse platform, make sure you know the limitations of the platform. Each one will usually have a maximum attendee limit, just as with Zoom. And have a plan for how you will manage the discussion, just as you would do in a live chat. If someone is getting disruptive, don't hesitate to remove them. Just as in other online community interactions, events in Metaverse platforms must be moderated.

The 3D Web and A-Frame

Not every story will be suitable to be experienced with others. In fact, probably most won't. But almost any story that you may publish online today can be enhanced with interactive 3D elements using "Web graphics library" (WebGL for short) functionality that has been built into most web browsers since the mid-2000s.

WebGL is incredibly complex to write at the code level. For that reason, for several years it was only startups with serious coders or large companies like Google that were experimenting with it. You can see some of their early examples at ThreeJS (threejs.org). But since then, another layer of code has been added to the stack, which is more accessible to people who know basic HTML and CSS. A current fan favorite is A-Frame (aframe.io).

A-Frame was started in 2015 as an open-source web framework for building virtual reality experiences that could be published on any web page. At that time, the Oculus Quest and HTC Vive headsets had just launched, and the only way to create immersive experiences for it was to use a gaming engine (more on that later) and then publish an app to the Oculus store or to Steam. Just as with smartphones, apps require a user to go to the app store and perform a download and install.

While apps make sense for things like games, they rarely make sense for individual stories. Think about it: how often have you learned about an interactive story from your favorite news site and clicked a link to download an app that is specific to just that story? Apps don't fit within the paradigm of discovery for news and information, but clicking on a link does.

With A-Frame, any web page can be dressed up with immersive 3D features that can be explored with a keyboard and mouse, on a smartphone or tablet, or in a VR headset. The entry point for all these different methods of experience is the same link, and the code used in A-Frame determines what the experience will be like from each type of device.

You can see many examples of projects built with A-Frame on the left rail of its home page, and you can learn about the basics of A-Frame in the Docs area at the top right. While it's impossible to explain every feature of A-Frame in this chapter (that would literally take an entire book of its own), three specific features can be applicable to almost any story. They are:

- 360 photos that you can click or tap and drag to see the entire scene.
- 3D models – either artistically created or 3D scanned from real objects.
- Simple 3D objects, such as squares, spheres, and planes.

To see examples of how each of these immersive elements can be used in a story, I will direct you to Visualizing 81 (visualizing81.thenewshouse.com). This is a six-part piece of enterprise journalism that I oversaw with a group of students at the S.I. Newhouse School in 2020, with funding support from the Online News Association's Journalism 360 grant. The piece explores the past, present, and future of a Black neighborhood in Syracuse known as the 15th Ward that was demolished in the 1960s in order to make room for Interstate 81.

As you go through it, you eventually will come across 360 photos of children playing on the street in the Pioneer Homes public housing project. Our objective was to connect people who know the current state of that neighborhood with the past, and to see that it was a thriving community. Incidentally, it was also one of the few places where Black families displaced by the highway could move in the segregated 1960s.

In later sections, we used A-Frame to surface several 3D scans of structures mentioned in the story: The crumbling underside of the Interstate 81 overpass, which will be demolished and replaced with a ground-level street; a copy of *Freedom Train: The Story of Harriet Tubman* which holds the signatures of the last congregation to meet at the People's AME Zion Church; and then the Zion church itself, including both the outside and inside.

In later chapters of this book, I'll explain how to shoot 360 photos and videos, and 3D image objects and buildings. For now, all you need to know is that if you have a 3D model saved in the right format, you can use A-Frame to embed it into your story.

Workbook Exercise 5.4: Create a Simple A-Frame Scene in Glitch

Like many open-source frameworks, A-Frame has some simple templates on the Glitch website. Glitch sets up your browser with two panes. The left lets you mess around with code, and the right shows you what you changed.

To get started, go to Glitch.com and create an account. Then go to Hello WebVR Glitch project (https://glitch.com/edit/#!/aframe), and click the "Remix to Edit" button at the upper right.

You will see a simple scene with four primitive objects: a square, a cylinder, a sphere, and a plane that serves as the ground. Click the index.html file, and you will see code like this. (Note, you can find this code online in a Glitch I prepared for you at this link: www.emergingmediaplatforms.com/chapter5/.)

```
<script
src="https://aframe.io/releases/1.3.0/aframe.min.js"></
script>
  <a-scene>
    <a-box  position="-1  0.5  -3"  rotation="  0   45
      0"></a-box>
    <a-sphere position="0 1.25 -5" radius="1.25"
    color="#EF2D5E"></a-sphere>
    <a-cylinder position="1 0.75 -3"radius="0.5"
    height="1.5" color="#FFC65D"></a-cylinder>
```

```
    <a-plane position="0 0 -4" rotation="-90 0 0"
      width="4"
    height="4" color="#7BC8A4"></a-plane>
    <a-sky color="#ECECEC"></a-sky>
  </a-scene>
```

The first piece of code is a line inside the header area with a script that points to the A-Frame server. Whenever you want to include a-Frame code on a web page, just include that line in your own header tags and it will be super-charged to show magical A-Frame elements.

After that are elements for "a box," "a sphere," "a cylinder," and "a plane." There's also "a sky." Some of them have three numbers for position. Just like in Mozilla Spoke, those numbers stand for X, Y, and Z coordinates. Change some of the numbers to be bigger and smaller and you will see the shapes move accordingly. The same is true for rotation.

Finally, you can modify the colors of the objects or even of the sky. The colors you see are represented as HTML Hexadecimal colors. To find new colors, go to Google and search on "Hexadecimal Colors" and you will see numerous sites that let you find a color and grab the six characters that make up that color in HTML.

When you have something you like you can just copy and paste that code into your own HTML pages and voila – the scene will be in there.

A challenge I often give my students is to see if they can use primitive objects to virtually recreate something that exists in the real world – such as a snowman, which would be three spheres of different sizes that are colored white and positioned on top of each other. The snowman's eyes would be small black circles. The nose would be a cone that's colored orange.

Workbook Exercise 5.5: Create a WebXR Scene With Reach.love

It's long been my hunch that the tools for creating WebXR will be getting easier. While I still believe it's vitally important to understand the underlying code – such as A-Frame – and specifically how it works, the rush to the Metaverse will result in the publishing tools for Internet content will evolve to include immersive.

One of these early initiatives is Reach.love, another initiative of Nonny de la Peña's Emblematic Group. (For full disclosure, I am an official advisor for Reach.)

Reach is geared toward storytellers, and it focuses on the most basic build-ing blocks that are necessary to tell immersive stories. Much like Spoke, you start out with a blank canvas. Then you click the buttons on the left to add the following:

- **Video:** Any video can be imported, and Reach specifically supports videos of people in front of green screens. The green screen creates the illusion of a person standing inside an immersive scene. While it's not a full volumetric video, the effect is similar because you see them projected inside a 3D space.
- **Audio:** Upload MP3 files to play in the scene when users click or tap on them.
- **Objects:** 3D objects in the GLTF format can be uploaded and placed in a scene.
- **Terrains:** Terrains are typically GLTF files of the ground, occasionally with buildings.
- **Skies:** Any 360 photo can be included as a skybox.

You change the positions of objects by adjusting their X, Y, and Z coordi-nates. To publish a Reach, you just click a button and receive a link that you can send to anyone. If that link is opened on a VR headset such as the Oculus Quest, the recipient can jump inside the scene.

Reach was in beta during the writing of this book but was slated for a full launch in 2023. Go to https://emergingmediaplatforms/chapter5/reachexample to see a world I've created. You can also scan the QR code below. You can find a link there to create your Reach own world without any coding.

Figure 5.1 A scene being created in the Reach.love browser-based editor.

(*Source:* Screen capture/Pacheco. Used with permission.)

Case Study: Matthew's Pandemic Classroom

The best field tests solve clear information problems for an audience. Matthew, a grad student who also teaches sixth-grade history, was solving one of the biggest problems during the COVID-19 pandemic: young students bored to death at home in Zoom classrooms. While this is technically an educational context, the goals for media are the same: engaging an audience through an emerging technology to process information.

As he put it in his report, "Zoom fatigue has taken its toll on everyone who is expected to engage with the platform for numerous hours each day. This is particularly true for students who spend the entirety of their school days on Zoom."

Matthew was in the middle of teaching a course on Ancient Greece when the entire grade had to go into extended quarantine and remote learning. His solution was to use Mozilla Hubs to create a virtual reality environment with open-source 3D models of scanned statues from Ancient Greece. He also hypothesized that his students would use the interactive features in the virtual room to share objects and drawings with each other.

He created his hub and invited his class into it from their laptops. He immediately noticed that students who typically were hunched over with their eyes cast down were suddenly propping their heads up, with eyes fixed on the screen. The experiment seemed to be working!

Then it hit a wall. After five minutes, he realized that half of the class was engaged in the virtual room, but the other half was silent. He began receiving messages and emails from students who were using the school-provided Chromebooks, which were overheating and unable to process the complex graphics required by Hubs. He terminated the exercise and returned the class to zoom. His hypothesis had failed!

But not quite. In the ensuing class discussion, he learned that the students were very interested in using the virtual room for the class. They just couldn't all access it due to varying types of computers. The Digital Divide threw a wrench in the machine.

Matthew's French fry moment came from discovering that students were equally engaged by simply watching a screen share of him moving his avatar through the room, and he also had more control over the lesson. The entire class could participate together, telling the teacher where they wanted him to go, and he then had the opportunity to teach them about different objects that his avatar was visiting.

As you think of Matthew's experience as a teacher in a virtual reality classroom, consider how your media company might combine screen views of virtual explorations in Zoom meetings or webinars. What could you 3D scan, or obtain a scan of from elsewhere, and explore with a live audience in an online event? Perhaps you could collectively explore a crime scene, take your audience to Mars with the Perseverance rover, or take them on a tour of Assisi or Machu Picchu? Thanks to Matthew's field test you know that not everyone needs to be in the VR environment to benefit from the visualizations.

Expert Interview: Nonny de la Peña

Nonny de la Peña is the CEO of Emblematic Group and founding Director of ASU's new center for narrative and emerging media in Los Angeles. I caught up with her to talk about what the center will be doing, and what she's focused on next.

DAN PACHECO (DP): **Welcome, Nonny! Can you tell us a little about your background in journalism and film?**

NONNY DE LA PEÑA (ND): I grew up in Venice, California, and went to Venice high school. I got into Harvard when I was 17. I'd never been to the East Coast, and I showed up at school with no coat, no boots, and had to figure it all out.

One of the things that we all had to do in freshman year was take basic programming, kind of like an extra-curricular thing you had to pass. It turned out that I was really good at it. I figured it out really fast. My friends were saying that their other computer science classes were really hard and they didn't know if they could do it. I ended up teaching three-quarters of the kids in my class. It was pretty funny.

Other than that, I was very unprepared. I certainly caught up, and by the end, I was a straight A student. But at the beginning, I struggled for many reasons. I was afraid to continue the programming courses and ended up always doing photography and writing and creative stuff.

For my senior thesis at Harvard, I went back and forth to LA and hung out with a Chicano gang, and I wrote about and photographed them. The piece was published by the Pacific News Service after I graduated. That's how my journalism career started.

I ended up in New York and was trying to get a job in journalism, and I convinced my roommate to let me turn the closet into a dark room. Print was the thing to survive off. I eventually ended up getting a job as a correspondent for Newsweek magazine for four years.

I left that because the visual part of my brain wasn't being satisfied and I ended up as a staff writer for TV shows and making documentary films. And then, HTML came around and I taught myself HTML. I really wanted to get back into coding. I felt like that was a missed opportunity for me, and that I could use it for storytelling.

DP **When did you start thinking about what we now call immersive journalism, a term you coined?**

ND: I read Howard Rheingold's book about Virtual Reality in the 1990s, and I thought: If I could put people on scene, maybe they would have more empathy for people in my stories.

My films were often about that, especially Post 9/11, with the destruction of civil liberties in America and people being locked up unnecessarily. I really felt that if I could get people to be on scene with somebody, they might have a better connection to the story and the people in the story.

DP: *So just to be clear, you originally had the idea for virtual reality journalism in the 1990s before it was even possible?*

ND: Yeah, just based on Howard Rheingold saying, "Hey, this is coming." So fast forward about a decade later, and I had done a film that had a big segment on Guantanamo Bay prison. There was a place there that was off limits to most citizens, and the press and people were forgetting about it. It was such an extrajudicial place, and what was happening there was against everything that I believed was the way that our court, politics, and society are supposed to work.

I felt like we still needed to call attention to it, and I saw that there was a grant from the MacArthur Foundation to take a documentary and bring it into the digital field. I contacted a wonderful digital artist friend and said, do you want to do this with me? She said yes, and suggested we do it in Second Life.

I was like, "What is Second Life?" I tried it out and became immediately engaged in Second Life and created a community of friends there. So with a lot of help and donated virtual land, we built a virtual Guantanamo Bay prison. Suddenly we found that there were tourists going there from universities, and it got a lot of attention.

DP: *Second Life was ahead of its time, and it wasn't even connected to a VR headset because there were no VR headsets. When did you start experimenting with true head-mounted VR, like what Rheingold had predicted?*

ND: After Gone Gitmo was finished, I registered the Immersive Journalism domain name and began to really pursue full VR. By luck, I ended up in the lab of Mel Slater in Barcelona. We built a piece on what it means to be put into a stress position in VR, like the detainees in Gitmo.

It was surprisingly effective, with people sitting straight up in their chairs while reporting feeling like they were hunched over as a detainee. That was my first real, six degrees of freedom experience. We based a journalism paper on that which is still one of the most downloaded articles in the history of the MIT Journal, Presence.

DP: *Is that when you started working on Hunger in Los Angeles?*

ND: I made Hunger in Los Angeles a couple of years later. I had to learn to be a better C-sharp coder, and I had to beg and borrow and get a lot of favors.

I had avatars donated to me, and I just put in the amount of work that it took. I put in $700 of my own money. I look back on it now and just think, "How the heck did I pull it off?"

The idea for Hunger was that I knew that food banks were running out of food at that time. The idea of fully immersive VR was becoming more dominant in labs, and there were no 360-degree cameras back then to shoot with. I recruited an intern named Michaela Kobsa Mark, who was a recent high school graduate who was just going off to college. I had to find a high school student for help because nobody at the University of Southern California journalism school wanted to do this with me.

DP: *I bet a lot of them are regretting that decision now!*

ND: Right. So Michaela and I were recording audio at food banks because I thought we'd have this moment where the food would run out, and a parent would have to turn to their kid and help them deal with that. I thought, that's gotta be heart-rendering, and people would respond to it.

And one day Michaela came running back to my office, and she was crying. She just had experienced a situation where a man with diabetes didn't get food in time, and he dropped into a diabetic coma. It was incredibly chaotic, and then it took forever for the EMTs to come.

In the chaos, somebody tried to steal food and the woman who was running the food bank was overwhelmed, saying, "There's too many people!" The audio was extraordinary. That was a moment when I decided I would work with it, and that became Hunger.

This wonderful guy, John Brennan, knew how to do motion capture, and he wore the mocap suit and played every character. Another guy named Bradley Newman was really instrumental in helping with the coding and the creation process.

DP: *How was it received by the public? And how were they able to see it? Consumer VR wasn't a thing just yet, right?*

ND: It ended up premiering at the Sundance Film Festival, the very first VR piece ever exhibited there. We had people waiting in lines that went on for hours. We stayed open every day way past closing time.

The goggles we used were crafted by Palmer Luckey. At the time, USC had a $50,000 pair of goggles in the USC lab, but they thought what I was doing was too weird so we couldn't use them. Fortunately, Palmer let us use his.

DP: *What was it like creating this project in the middle of the last big recession?*

ND: It was an interim year for me because it was financially just terrible. It was during the last economic downturn, and my husband had his salary cut. We basically ran out of money. There was a moment when my kids were play testing at Activision and they'd get these $50 checks that I would buy food with. It was bad.

DP: *Wait, you were working on Hunger in Los Angeles while you and your family were hungry in Los Angeles?*

ND: My husband had a professor job, so it wasn't like we were going to die, but we ran out of money. We were renting a house and I always thought I'd have a good job, and I couldn't get a job. I couldn't really even apply for a job because I was about to start my PhD. It was a tough period of time.

There was one night where he was getting paid the next day, and I'd used every nickel and dime and credit cards were maxed out. I had a friend come over one day and she asked if her kids could have my leftover food, and after that, there was no more money to buy food. When you're in that position you just feel embarrassed to ask anybody to help. It was a brutal moment. For the first time in my life, I was like, "Oh my God, I don't have any money for food."

DP: *That must have had some impact on how this piece came together though. You and your family found yourself right on the edge.*

ND: I did get right to the edge. Anyway, making stuff is hard! I had a vision, but I remember saying to my husband, "I've got to just stop. I can't keep doing this. I need to get a real job." And I remember him just looking at me and saying, "No, hold the line, you can do this. Hang on."

DP: *I'm glad he did that, and that you listened!*

ND: Yeah. Hunger ended up becoming a huge hit. I went on to make Use of Force around the same period of time. Use of Force ended up being the very first VR piece ever shown at the Tribeca Film Festival. I later learned that it was used by the Department of Homeland Security for training.

Since then I've done an immersive piece on Syrian refugees which went to the World Economic Forum, to LGBTQ, homelessness, domestic gun violence, Japanese-American concentration camps, and Lyme disease. I even did the first multiplayer piece with hydraulic cars at the site of Formula One in Singapore.

We did a live AR data visualization feed from the stock market data visualization. I showed it to Google, and they gave me a standing ovation. You have to give the credit to my engineers who were working for me. They're a group that has come and gone and come and gone, but with them I've continued to be able to push the envelope for new kinds of work.

DP: *Well thank you also to those engineers who keep coming back to work with you! Can you talk a little bit about what you do now, your position with ASU and this new program that you're starting?*

ND: I'm now the Founding Director for a new center for narrative and emerging media based in downtown Los Angeles. The point of this center is to house a graduate program and a research institute that explores policies and hosts events with a goal of inclusivity. We want to focus on who we include versus who we exclude. This new center is thinking about the body in every aspect of what we do, particularly around narrative storytelling.

DP: *I hear you use the term "body" a lot when you describe immersive media. How important is the body to immersion? I think that's a really important thing for people to understand.*

ND: We live our lives through our bodies. People have always had this idea that there's a dichotomy of a body-mind split, that you see things with your eyes and hear things with your ears. But nobody thinks about how much we experience the world through our bodies as well.

I think what these immersive practices do is return the body to its proper place in the context of how we experience the world, and therefore the way that we can experience a story.

DP: *What does it mean to use the body as a foundation of storytelling?*

ND: In the next few years I think we're going to see all kinds of interesting innovations in haptics. We can also use the haptics for inclusion. I once had a woman who was deaf go through my Project Syria story wearing a haptic vest. We all thought that the audio was the crucial thing in that piece, but when she went through it, she was pinging me about it for weeks afterward. It was that powerful for her.

What does it mean for a deaf person to feel a story that others hear with their ears? This is something that I think that we need to really explore more deeply. I'm really excited to be able to have a place where I can pursue this in a more significant way.

DP: *This idea of "embodiment" might be a new concept to people reading this book, especially if they haven't tried full-body immersive VR before. But it really is pretty central to the whole field of XR and immersion, right?*

I also did some experimentation in Second Life, and people in journalism circles publicly called me out as being crazy for even taking it seriously. And yet here we are in 2022, with the future Metaverse sounding like Second Life on steroids. Do you see that, or do you think the Metaverse is something different?

ND: Well first off, there's a lot more money involved with the Metaverse. A lot of people have come back into shared immersive experiences, but we can look back and see where people made their errors.

I think it's kind of interesting to see the same kinds of things with NFTs as we saw in Second Life. You want certain objects in your digital world, but the digital objects also need to have value for the experience. If it's just a digital object with no experience associated with it, it's unlikely to have any kind of staying power.

I remember Coca-Cola just dropping in its digital Coca-Cola's into Second Life and expecting people to buy them, instead of thinking, "Oh gee, we can let people become bubbles in a Coke bottle and float to the top." It's really important to be thinking about the experience in these spaces.

But a lot of us felt very alone out there in Second Life. We were like the original VR weirdos.

DP: *I think we saw something though, and it's now starting to move. I mean, as you said, the money is coming in. You can now put on an Oculus Quest or Vive Focus without a computer, go to a web page in a virtual browser, and then literally jump inside the 3D world in that web page.*

ND: One of the things I'm doing this fall is prototyping an immersive journalism publication in WebXR. I have a little bit of funding, and I have some people who will be dedicated to building it with me.

A journalist from New Zealand got a fellowship to come work with me on this. But then, of course, COVID hit. We didn't even get to know each other before he had to leave. But now he's going to spearhead this immersive journalism publication this fall. I also have a BBC reporter coming in from Nigeria who will be working five hours a week on immersive journalism projects.

DP: *Can you talk a little about your Reach.love startup, and its goals?*

ND: Early on when I started seeing the power of WebXR, I started thinking about how we could get away from the complications of learning how to code in order to tell a story in an immersive way. I never became a great coder, but I certainly had to learn how to code in C-Sharp in order to start doing the Unity piece of Hunger in Los Angeles.

Before it launched at Tribeca, I was up all night trying to keep the code working. Immersive interactive projects are always hard to make. Creatively, if we really want this medium to grow, it's gotta be more akin to Photoshop or Premiere. . . . Reach is all about making the tools more accessible. It's finally coming out of beta, funded by the Knight Foundation.

DP: *Others have tried to do this, but focused on different audiences. Unity definitely focused on the game development space. Mozilla has its Spoke system for Hubs that's tied into creating worlds that you can experience with others. Meta has its own immersive creation tools. And even back in the early days of Second Life, it had creator tools baked in.*

Would you say that Reach is focused primarily on journalistic storytellers, or is it broader than that?

ND: I remember what it was like trying to learn the Second Life tools, and I certainly know what it's like to use the Unity tools. One of the biggest differences between them and what I'm trying to provide with Reach is that it's literally a storytelling tool. It doesn't have the complications of the game physics.

There's a lot more complexity when you get into Unity, but it's not necessary for a lot of storytelling. Look at the tools for creating stories on TikTok or Instagram. They don't need the extra complicated stuff.

I mean, if you're gonna do a big immersive feature film, you're going to want Unity, right? You're going to want much more complex special effects. But for the average person and for educators, they often just want to show you something and talk about it without necessarily having it come alive. I think for these kinds of spaces, Reach is a really good tool. I can't wait to see how it evolves.

DP: *What do you think of the growth of Social VR? Now it's often referred to as the Metaverse, but a lot of these ideas are not new. Do you think people will want to experience stories together in a collective way, and if so, how does that work?*

ND: I think we've seen successful ways that people can mingle through Minecraft and Fortnight. We've also seen gatherings where women have been harassed. The Metaverse is a reflection of our real world. So just like in the real world, we need to start thinking about how to protect women.

DP: *Maybe we'll all need to go through some kind of safety training, just like we do in the real world. I remember back when my kids were really young, going to a seminar about how to keep them safe from predators. The trainer said to tell your kids early on, "You are the boss of your body, and nobody gets to make decisions about your body other than you."*

ND: I agree with you. I mean, we, you know, we don't know what that kind of policing looks like.

It goes across genders. I did a study once where we were looking at sexual harassment in Second Life. We asked for the gender of their avatars, and they self-reported. We got some very interesting data from female avatars who reported their real-world gender as being male. They reported feeling more harassed than the woman did! It was a small sample size but easily can be repeatable in a bigger way.

That to me is the kind of thing we have to look at. How do we know we're creating compassion and empathy, which has always been one of my goals as a journalist? It's why I did stories such as one of a father falsely accused of child abuse in a small town in Michigan. So much of my work throughout my traditional journalism career carried into my Virtual Reality career, from Hunger in Los Angeles to LGBTQ homelessness, to Syrian refugees, to Lyme disease.

DP: *What are you doing in the area of immersive training, which is a growing category for VR?*

ND: Early on, Google Jigsaw asked us to do an early prototype that would train police to de-escalate situations. There are a lot of training documents about this topic, but in VR you can really see what officers do.

You can track the timbre of their voice or the volume of their yelling. Are they talking calmly? Where are their hands? Are they reaching for their guns? These are the kind of methodologies that flat video or text is inadequate for in terms of training.

How close are you standing to the suspect or the person of interest? There's so much that is possible to track and study that's just not possible in the two-dimensional environment. Real in-person training can also be successful, but the in-person character has to be a very good actor. In VR, we can use real audio from real scenarios.

Later, we made a much more robust version, and I think they're going to release it to help police officers de-escalate situations.

DP: *I still show the piece you did with PBS Frontline and NOVA on Greenland Melting because it utilized so many different, truly cutting-edge immersive technologies in a way that I haven't seen anything really approach since. It had everything from photogrammetry to volumetric video to interactive animations.*

Is there a new immersive superpower or trend that you plan to explore next?

ND: Well, I love the fact that most people now have a photogrammetry device in their pockets (their phones). How are we going to start telling stories with that? And at the other end of the spectrum, I have a Leica camera on back-order that you can put out on the street, and in three minutes you've got the whole street corner captured. How can more journalists use these tools?

DP: *Last question: how do you deal with the inevitable setbacks when things don't work the way you thought they would? Because we both know, that's kinda the norm when it comes to innovation.*

ND: I think that's true with any creative process. I'm working on a really huge piece now with the National Center for Human Rights. But as we go through that process, we have to ask: how do you build a story like that which includes the truth without traumatizing people?

I've been working on it for a year. I came to the realization this weekend that one aspect of it isn't working. But if we do it a slightly different way, it will work. And that's just the way it goes.

It's what sometimes makes production expensive. You think you have a concept of how something is going to come out, and then your vision doesn't always work out the way you thought it would and you have to do some new iteration.

Online Resources for Chapter 5

Find more resources for Chapter 5 line at http://emergingmediaplatforms.com/chapter5.

Sources

de la Peña, N. (2015). *The future of news? Virtual reality.* www.ted.com/talks/nonny_de_la_pena_the_future_of_news_virtual_reality

de la Peña, N., Weil, P., Llobera, J., Spanlang, B., Friedman, D., Sanchez-Vives, M. V., & Slater, M. (n.d.). Immersive virtual reality for the first-person experience of news. *Presence.* https://ieeexplore.ieee.org/abstract/document/6797389

Emblematic. (n.d.). *Emblematic.* http://emblematicgroup.com

Volpe, J. (2015, January 24). The godmother of virtual reality: Nonny De La Peña. *Engadget.* www.engadget.com/2015-01-24-the-godmother-of-virtual-reality-nonny-de-la-pena.html

6 Augmented Reality

Now that you have a good understanding of XR let's take a deep dive into AR.

Of the various types of XR, Augmented Reality has had the fastest growth in terms of audience engagement. Part of that has to do with the fact that anyone with a relatively new phone from Apple or Google already has the equipment needed to access AR. In 2022, VR headset sales were still measured in the low tens of millions, but smartphone sales were in the billions per year.

But as with XR in general, it's important to think of AR stories being experienced on an ever-evolving spectrum of immersion.

What Makes AR Possible

Augmented reality brings information and objects into your world by turning your phone into a magical window that adds information to a scene – like a magnifying glass that provides more information about what the camera sees. As you examine things through your phone's camera, you can see other things or characters who may even interact with the environment. Or, you can learn what an object is – such as identifying a plant, animal, or iconic building.

To understand what AR can do, it's important to break down how the sensors and cameras in your phone are used in concert to create seemingly magical AR effects.

- **Cameras:** The input from either the phone's front-facing camera or selfie camera is used to create the scene upon which the action occurs. The front-facing camera sets up the room you're in as the stage, while the selfie camera modifies your face or appearance. If a phone has more than one camera, the software on your phone will be able to see depth – just as we do with our two eyes.
- **Computer Vision:** This type of artificial intelligence is the most essential technology for AR, as simply placing images or text on top of photos doesn't create the level of immersion necessary to make your brain believe the augmented content is physically there. The software on your phone uses artificial intelligence to identify and distinguish between what's a floor, a wall, a tabletop, a chair, a couch, and so forth. Increasingly, services tied to apps on your phone or the phone itself are also using computer vision to identify other things – such as plants, animals, products, and so forth.

DOI: 10.4324/9781003247012-7

- **LiDAR (Light Detection and Ranging):** On newer iPhone Pro phones, the LiDAR sensor sends out pulsed light waves which bounce off objects. When they return, the sensor can tell how far the light traveled. In this way, LiDAR scans the 3D environment you're in and captures its structure. LiDAR is not absolutely necessary for AR to work, as computer vision also interpolates objects' structures when it has seen them from enough angles. But LiDAR allows it to interpret structure more quickly and accurately.

ARKit and ARCore

As of this time, there are two main frameworks for AR, and they depend on the type of phone the user has. iOS devices use Apple's ARKit, and Android devices use Google's ARCore.

As an AR content creator, you don't need to know much about how these platforms work, as they're built into the devices themselves and their companies' cloud processing infrastructures. But to practically develop content that works for anyone with either an iPhone or Android device, you typically do need to do some extra work to make sure that your experiences work for both types of users.

Sometimes you can have the same experience that works for people regardless of which phone they're using, while at other times, you need to branch them off – iPhone users at this link, Android users at that link. And unfortunately, there are cases where something is available on only one company's device. (Sorry, Android users, but unfortunately at this time that will more often than not affect you. I know how you feel!)

It's also important to keep in mind that while people currently use their iPhones and Android phones to experience content, many experts – myself included – are betting that both Apple and Google will make content created with their frameworks operate seamlessly through their upcoming augmented reality glasses. It doesn't matter when each company launches its version of smart glasses. Just assume that your stories will soon probably be able to be experienced by someone using either immersive glasses or a phone.

Examples of AR Storytelling

What many people who experimented in the early days of VR will tell you is that despite all the hype from Oculus, Facebook (now Meta), and Google, the audience they promised didn't materialize fast enough. It was a good six years between the launch of the first Oculus developer kit, which required a high-end Windows gaming computer, and the standalone Oculus Quest.

Despite the incredible and meaningful work done by VR Journalists, the high cost and complicated setups of the early headset systems severely limited the number of people they could reach. It was too difficult to attract the scale of audience needed by advertising and subscription-dependent news organizations.

But just as those types of projects slowed down, a side door opened that allowed many projects to continue in another form. In 2017, Apple launched its ARKit framework for iPhones, and Google followed with its ARCore framework for Android phones. Immersive storytelling teams saw an opportunity to refocus their work on mobile.

- A good example of this was **Ecosystem AR, from Sarah Hill's XR studio, StoryUp:** https://apps.apple.com/app/id1486109864.

It took 360 video projects previously built for VR headsets into an AR wrapper. Upon launching the app, the experiencer points the camera at the floor and an elevator rises up in their environment. When the elevator door opens, a 360 video is revealed on the other side and the user naturally walks through it to experience the video. Different videos can be viewed by tapping "teleport" icons.

USA TODAY, which had earlier created the first large-scale commercial VR project with *Harvest of Change*, made a similar pivot. It added an augmented reality section to its mobile app which had some of the best AR experiences available around a variety of topics, including

- Viewing 3D-scanned costumes from top Oscar-nominated films for 2019.
- A virtual look at the January 6 insurrection in Washington, DC.
- A visualization about how far germs can travel wearing a face mask or no mask; and a larger production called Flatten the Curve, which led the user through different scenarios during the COVID-19 pandemic to understand CDC guidelines.

The New York Times' R&D department began producing AR pieces using Instagram's platform SparkAR Studio. Their projects were promoted through the NYTimes Instagram account but have since been removed. Among the more impressive were:

- **The Bronx Fire:** This helps you visualize what it would have been like to be inside a massive fire that destroyed a building. Using visibility estimates, the user experiences how difficult it is to navigate through a space, as previously clear areas look like a gray wall.
- **The California Megastorm:** This piece visualizes what future climate change-driven rainstorms in California will be like, based on interviews with climate scientists. The storms appear inside your living room, and when you walk into them the screen on your phone appears wet.

The Evolution of AR Content Authoring

Just a few years ago, the only way to create AR content was to pay an app developer a good chunk of change to build an app for you. And you would have to have them build two apps – one for iPhone, the other for Android – which most companies didn't want to do. It wasn't common to see the few media companies experimenting with apps choose just one platform for cost reasons, which would cut off at least half of their audience. This was a major hindrance to adoption.

But then, three things happened that resulted in an explosion of creative AR content.

- First: Companies that serve digital ad agencies started to introduce their own AR app-creation tools. Two of the main ones, Vuforia and 8th Wall, initially had prices so high that only the largest ad agencies could afford them. But their fees slowly came down to lower, indie-creator-friendly levels.
- Second: The 3D web started to support AR. A-Frame, which we explored in the last chapter, introduced some augmented reality features, and Google followed with a web service called Model-Viewer.
- Third: Companies like Snap and Meta (through Instagram) launched their own consumer-focused, free AR applications to create experiences targeted to their own platforms. Adobe also introduced its own free Adobe Aero AR creator for iPhone, quickly followed by Apple launching its Reality Composer app.

Because we're just experimenting with minimum viable products, I like to focus on the free tools. But if you find yourself wanting to make AR a career focus – which based on the adoption is a good bet in my opinion – you may want to try at least some of the commercial tools that have free trials or low monthly fees. I don't get into them much in this book, but don't limit yourself.

Thought Exercise 6.1: Crafting an AR Story

Before you start down the rabbit hole of any particular AR technology approach, it's important to think about how an AR story will be experienced through someone's phone (today), as well as through glasses. With AR, you have the unique challenge of designing something that needs to work in many types of spaces, and you don't get to choose what they are. One person may be in a hotel room, another in an office with a desk, another in their living room with other people watching TV and moving around, and still another outside. Here's a checklist to go through as you design your AR story.

- Why is AR the best medium for this particular story? What will someone learn, understand, or feel that is difficult or even impossible to do so without using AR?
- Describe the various environments someone is likely to be in when they encounter your story. What types of objects (furniture, walls, etc.) are likely to be in it?

- What are the likely sizes of these spaces? Will the experiencer need to be told to move to a specific type of space or avoid certain spaces?
- Will the experiencer use your AR story alone, or can there be other people in the same space?
- What is the trigger for the experience to happen? Does it happen instantly, require a tap, require scanning of a code or image on a poster or flier, or does it get triggered by a specific movement of the user?
- On what "canvas" do the AR elements do their thing? On the floor, floating in the air, on top of a desk or table, or on the wall?
- How will people discover your AR story? Is it standalone, or is it embedded into a larger story?

Workbook Exercise 6.2: Adobe Aero

Adobe Aero offers a relatively easy and free way to experiment with augmented reality. While the experiences can currently only be created from either an iOS device (phone or iPad) or in a desktop app (Mac or Windows), Adobe has finally released a beta version of Adobe Aero Player. It's safe to assume that an Android creator app is around the corner.

The most natural way to create an Aero experience is in the app itself (iOS only for now). Just open the app and click the blue + icon. As you move your phone around, Aero will identify floor and wall surfaces.

Select *any* floor or wall and click the + again to set it as the anchor, then tap the + again and choose Starter Assets. Select any asset and then place it in your space with another tap, and you'll see that object in the room with you. You can keep placing starter assets to create a scene that fits your story.

Click the Share icon at the upper right to create a link. You can send that link to anyone or include it as a hyperlink in a web story. The person who clicks on the link will be prompted to download either Adobe Aero or, on Android, the Adobe Aero Viewer software for desktop computers. They will be able to see the scene you created in their own environment. Phone users will see it in their physical space, and desktop users will see it on their computers.

After you've created a simple static scene, you can add interactivity through what Adobe calls Behaviors. Simply tap any of the objects you added, and then click the Behaviors button at the bottom of the screen. Behaviors require a trigger – which can be a tap of the object, getting close to it, or moving away from it. After that, you choose an action – such as playing an audio clip, bouncing, moving, or animating. Not every object has an animation with it, but if it does, you will see a list of possible animations.

With assets, triggers, and actions, you can create some pretty interactive and fun scenes, and the assets can be your own rather than just using Adobe's starter assets. Just make sure any supported file type that you want to use is uploaded to either your Adobe Creative Cloud account or that it's in your iPhone's local file storage if you don't subscribe to Creative Cloud.

Try this: Create a scene and add it from one of the Directable Characters assets. Then, add a trigger for Tap, and choose Play Animation for an action. Most characters will have a Wave animation, but you can choose any of the behaviors that work for your story. After adding a wave, add another action for Play Audio. Choose Whoosh for now. When you hit the Play button, you should see the character appear in your room, and when you tap them, they wave and you will hear a Whoosh.

To complete your scene, all you need to do is to record or acquire some audio in WAV or MP3 format. Transfer to your phone's storage or iCloud Drive, and you should be able to select it when adding an audio action.

See an example of a finished Aero scene I created for you at this link: www.emergingmediaplatforms.com/chapter6/.

NOTE: If you don't have an iPhone, you can download a desktop version of Aero creator from Adobe's site here: www.adobe.com.

Workbook Exercise 6.3: WebAR With Google Model-Viewer (iPhone and Android)

As mentioned earlier, most modern browsers are now 3D capable, and some are beginning to include support for augmented reality. Google has been pushing forward in this area in its search engine. You can see an example by searching for "Tiger" in Google on an iPhone or Android. On the first page of the results, you should see an invitation to meet a life-sized Bengal tiger up close.

This is a powerful feature of modern smartphones because, just as with A-Frame, it's not absolutely necessary for someone to download an app in order to see immersive AR content. They already have the app – it's called a web browser. So how do you as a storyteller let your readers interact with AR tigers, characters, or objects?

What's going on behind the scenes is that some code on the Web page you're viewing is telling the phone to download an animated 3D model, and the phone's own software takes care of displaying it in AR. The 3D format for iPhone is USDZ, and the format for Android is GLB (the same as GLTF, but just renamed to GLB).

Figure 6.1 The model should appear in your space like this. Just substitute your own pet! (*Source:* Photo/Dan Pacheco)

We will get into how to create these kinds of files in a future chapter, but for now, you can super-charge your story with AR code using an open-source library from Google called Model-Viewer.

The code for Model-Viewer is easy to construct through Google's own Model-Viewer editor: https://modelviewer.dev/editor/.

You simply drag and drop a GLTF or GLB file into the screen, click some buttons on the right, and grab the code that it wrote for you. You can try this with the GLTF file you got for Sketchfab in Exercise 4.6. Hotspots can be added by clicking into the pencil tab, and then looking for Hotspots. Double-click places on the model you want to annotate and write in a few words, and the code to display the hotspot will show up in your model.

The code you get will need to be embedded on a web page, and the 3D files that you reference in the HTML will also need to be uploaded some-where with the links pointing to that specific location. If you go through the HTML and GitHub Pages exercises in the Open-Source chapter, you will have the skills you need to do both of these things.

There is one important cross-platform thing to be aware of with Google's Editor. It will only write the code necessary for an Android phone to view the AR content. Google's code *does* work for iPhones, though, so how do you add that functionality? You need to add code for the object's USDZ file, too. Google's documentation explains how to do this; they just don't make it easy for newbies in the editor.

But no worries! In this Google Model-Viewer template, I've made for you, you can change the GLB and USDZ links to add 3D scanned objects to a web page that displays in AR. Go to this link to find the template, and then remix it to create your own copy: www.emergingmediaplatforms.com/chapter6/.

If you play around with your own files enough, you will see that you only need to add one extra line of code to whatever the editor writes, and it will then work on iPhones too.

Workbook Exercise 6.4: Creating Snap Filters With Snap AR Lens Studio

With its 322 million active daily users, the majority under 30, Snapchat is emerging as a powerful way to reach younger audiences. And because of its early adoption of filters that it calls Lenses, it's also a great way to experiment with augmented reality.

The first lenses to catch on were what I think of as "AR on your face" – filters that modify how you look in your Selfie camera so that you appear to have a dog's ears, devil's horns, or even breathe fire. Face filters have since been adopted by both Instagram and TikTok. To be honest, in my opinion, the face filters don't really have a lot of application to media and storytelling beyond branding and marketing, with a few exceptions.

What does have storytelling application is lenses that modify what the phone's standard, or rear, camera sees.

To get started, go to http://ar.snap.com and click Download to install Lens Studio. You will also need a Snapchat account. If you don't have one, you can create it during the install process.

The easiest way to get started with Lens Studio is to use a template. You can do this by going to the File > New Project from Template menu. For rear-facing camera templates, choose World. You will see a number of templates for different types of scenes that will take place in the user's room.

For example, try opening the Simple World Mesh. After you select it, assets will download and you will see several panes. The upper left pane lists what's in your scene. The middle pane shows what will be in the Snapchat app's camera. If you click any of the objects in the left or middle pane, a new Inspector pane will appear that lets you modify properties.

You can see what the default settings will look like in Snapchat by clicking the Preview in Snapchat button at the upper right. A "Snapcode" graphic will appear. Open Snapchat and tap the Scan button, and then choose Pair with Lens Studio. This will connect Lens Studio with your Snapchat account, after which the button's name will change to "Send to Snapchat." After a few moments, you will be able to select that lens in your Snapchat app.

The Simple World Mesh is a little whimsical. You move the phone around a room to scan the floor and furniture in it. Then you tap in certain places, and a silly dancing mushroom appears wherever you tap. So how exactly might a scene like this work for news or information, or even an advertisement? For that, you would need to replace the 3D objects in the Lens Studio software.

With some time and tinkering, you will be able to figure out how to make a simple scene – but I'll be honest. It's not as easy to master as other platforms I've covered in this book. Creating good Snap lenses requires collaboration with 3D designers and possibly even programmers. But by trying out the different templates and pushing them to your phone, you can get a good idea of what's possible, and you will have a baseline from which to collaborate with people who have technical game design skills.

Case Study: Using AR to Build an Everywhere Museum

Ryan Baker took Emerging Media Platforms in the spring of 2022, right as the world was starting to reopen from the pandemic. He knew he wanted to do more with photogrammetry, but what problem could photogrammetry solve in a way nothing else could? He settled on art museums.

Like most public spaces, the Syracuse University Art Museum was closed for a good part of the pandemic. When it became safe to reopen, they had a hard time getting people back into the habit of visiting the museum.

Ryan's hypothesis, inspired partly by what the Smithsonian was doing, was that art museums could engage with patrons in a unique way using photogrammetry and augmented reality. He believed that giving an augmented reality experience of a collection to potential visitors to interact with in their own homes would drive them to want to visit the museum to see the collection in person.

But there was also the possibility that the second part of his hypothesis would be false, and that people would like the AR experience so much that they would feel they didn't need to go to the physical museum. This has been a long-standing argument for both museums and arts venues: that making too much content available online or now, in XR, can cannibalize the terrestrial business.

Ryan set off to create his test. He worked with one of the museum's curators to identify a collection of ten statues that he could scan using the Trnio Plus app. He processed the models, set them up with the Google Model-Viewer AR code, and embedded each model into a website. You can find a link to his site here: www.emergingmediaplatforms. com/chapter6/.

The site also included very clear visual instructions on what to click in order to project the models into a space.

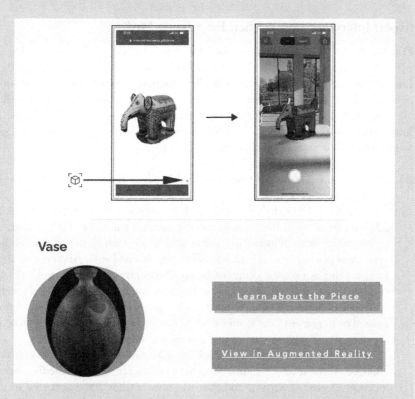

Figure 6.2 Ryan Baker's mobile-friendly site showing how to project 3D models of sculptures into a room.

(*Source*: Photo/Ryan Baker)

He found 20 students to test out his Everywhere Museum and gave them a survey that asked, among other things, if they felt they were more or less interested in visiting the physical museum after using the AR museum. The vast majority reported that the AR experience would be a good add-on to a physical exhibit but not as a replacement for actually visiting the museum.

Ryan's conclusion was that rather than just a marketing tool, the Everywhere Museum would work better as a way for the museum to display more of its collections inside its actual museum than it could without AR. He postulated that the museum could put plaques with QR codes in and around existing exhibits as a way for visitors to explore more of the artifacts than the collection could display in physical space.

Expert Interview: Dan Archer, Empathetic Media

Dan Archer is the founder and Chief Executive Officer of Empathetic Media with offices in London, England, and New York in the United States. Since 2015, Empathetic Media has produced multiple immersive interactive pieces for journalism, media, and health clients, including augmented reality and virtual reality. He was a fellow at the Tow Center at Columbia University (2016), a Reynolds Journalism Institute Fellow at the University of Missouri (2014), and a Knight Journalism Fellow at Stanford University (2011).

DAN PACHECO (DP): **How did you get into this whole space of the metaverse or whatever we call it now?**

DAN ARCHER (DA): I founded Empathetic Media, which is an immersive studio, in 2015 as part of an RJ Reynolds Journalism Institute fellowship. Prior to that, I'd been working more in interactive journalism, largely with Flash animation rollovers. I was playing around with JavaScript pop-ups and stuff. And prior to that, I was working as a graphic journalist. So my whole entry point into journalistic storytelling was using visual communications to try and scratch that particular itch.

My goal has always been to use technologies that readers might not know existed or to present new stories in different, unfamiliar ways in order to create more of a lasting impact in and among audiences.

In 2014, obviously, when Facebook (now Meta) bought Oculus, everything changed. I saw it as a big sort of turning point. Through 3D media, there's a certain degree of agency, and that was always what really appealed to me about the form in terms of the audience being able to choose where they went or the perspective that they might take. The new VR medium borrows paradigms from video games, but it was really creating a three-dimensional spatialized story. That really continues to fascinate me.

Since then, we've made over 50 stories for clients – cinematic experiences as well as about a dozen room-scale VR experiences for the Vive, Index, and Quest headsets.

Now, people are saying that VR is passé and augmented reality is the glistening future. We've also played with mixed reality. I see XR as a broader jumping-off point to an immersive extended reality Metaverse, where there is no prescriptive way of pigeon-holing it to one technology. A lot of people tend to like to think of things in terms of categories instead of potentials.

DP: *It sounds like what you're saying is that XR is about the immersive impact of media in space, regardless of the specific platform – VR, AR, MR?*

DA: I definitely think I'm agnostic when it comes to the platform. I mean, I still think that in terms of the potential and affordances, VR still has so much baggage because its biggest hurdle is the onboarding. It's getting the headset and putting it on, and once you're in it, providing the experience.

Good VR is like a conversion experience. People love it, and you can do all sorts of crazy stuff that harnesses their attention. But the problem is that even headset owners don't often go into VR for casual experiences. Until we get to a point where the versatility of onboarding is just like pulling out your glasses and putting them on, and they automatically sync to your phone, there won't be a major VR inflection point for media. I think it's going to be hard to create this sort of mass medium until we have that.

DP: *What are you working on now that excites you?*

DA: I'm currently in a fourth-year PhD in Computer Science at University College London. I'm looking at embodiment and biosignals, specifically as quantifiable metrics for measuring impact inside immersive experiences . . .

I'm incorporating Bluetooth wearables to measure heart rate, galvanic skin response, temperature changes, and looking at stress while people are inside immersive experiences and how that relates to engagement, sense of presence, and therefore impact.

DP: *How critical is it to be comfortable working with code in order to innovate with XR?*

DA: To be a storyteller with any of these technologies, you have to be able to get in there and work with code. I remember when I went to RJI, I had the privilege and opportunity to take any course that I wanted. Some of the journalism courses did offer things like Bootstrap, a framework that is widely reusable and applicable.

Everyone who works with code remembers that first phase of discomfort and frustration and banging your head against the wall. But then, once you somehow pierce through that, it slowly crystallizes.

I still do everything in Unity largely. I'm sort of dancing around a bit now in Unreal Engine just because I feel like it's time to branch out. Occasionally I try other stuff, like VVVV.

DP: *What are one or two projects that you worked on that are front of mind for you?*

DA: I would always say my favorite is the next one. My current project for my PhD is a crystallization of everything I've done, and the beauty of what I'm trying to achieve with it is to change the story according to the user's biosignatures.

This project is focused on Islamophobia in London in the wake of Brexit. It's trying to embody you into a Muslim man or woman essentially, and you're at the center of their experience. It is using biosignals as users are immersed in the first-hand experience of an Islamophobic incident, and it looks at where people's stress levels are and how that affects their ability to remember information and also feel present.

I'm using that to moderate essentially how much we can impact them in the longer run and generate more pro-social attitudes toward out-groups. The story kind of adapts the intensity of the experience to how well the sensors can tell that you are processing information.

The question is now, can you change the intensity of a story, and how do you do that without taking too much liberty with the story? Of course, we still have to deal with people saying, "This isn't journalism."

DP: *That's a truly emerging media approach that you're taking, having the story adapt to how someone feels. I'm sure you're going to get a lot of criticism about this, but it will also be a really interesting experiment to see what it means for peoples' understanding of the story to adapt to their mental state.*

DA: One of our findings in a Columbia study was that there is definitely an intensity threshold. When people reach a certain level of discomfort, they essentially will disengage. And if you lose engagement, you're just throwing stuff at the wall and seeing what sticks. So it's sort of like how can we find that sweet spot?

Part of our struggle in these platforms is trying to push the form in new directions, but with the ever-diminishing attention span of audiences. In the age of TikTok, how can we become immersive storytellers when you're competing with a 15-second sizzle reel?

DP: *So what has to happen for XR to be as mainstream as TikTok?*

DA: I think the power will be in its seamless integration into our reality. The reason TikTok is so successful is that we've all become zombies and slaves to our handheld devices. TikTok has a seamless integration into our daily experience because we're always on our phones. XR is harder because you have to have that device ready and charged, the light conditions have to be perfect, and no one can stand in your proximity.

I can fully imagine a Minority Report future where people have things like a contact lens instead of a headset.

DP: *Do you think we will even have phones in the future, or will everything around us become our "phones" through AR glasses or contacts?*

DA: Yeah, I think it will . . . but there is still the physics question of how you can put it all in the active area of a display for AR glasses. Even the HoloLens 2 is pretty limited in that regard.

We need to be careful that we don't oversell expectations. I remember thinking, "Oh, I'll just go to newsrooms and give some Unity workshops, and next thing you know, there'll be all these VR experiences." But then I went into newsrooms and would speak to an actual journalist, and they'd say they're drowning under deadlines. How can they learn a new skill as complex as VR?

I think it will always be the evangelists that are already seated within the organizations who have the technical skills to be able to make decent experiences and then get the hierarchy to pay attention.

DP: *How do you feel about social Metaverse-like experiences like Mozilla Hubs?*

DA: [Social VR] is escapist by definition because it's happening in a virtual space, and therefore, it gives me almost carte blanche to be able to behave exactly how I would if there were no repercussions. We're still in his Wild West, where our virtual avatars aren't quite linked to real identities. So I think there is a lot of malfeasance happening.

I do think there's something powerful about it. VR Chat has a huge community. It's very, very niche, but the mods and stuff that are happening in there are interesting. And obviously, there are games like Fortnite. I think the beauty of something like Fortnite is that it's so cross-platform, onboarding is no problem. You can just jump in wherever you want to.

The fundamental difference between something like Fortnight and an immersive story is that a story requires attention and time. You need to be in a contemplative, meditative space, which is hard if you're always sprinting to the next colorful, shiny bright thing.

DP: *Yeah. It's almost like we're all little kids in a science museum pushing the buttons, but not actually reading the content in the exhibits.*

DA: 100%. I do think we will get there. There are kids who are digital natives or whatever you wanna call them, and [the Metaverse] won't seem so weird to them. But I do think that attention is probably the biggest problem that needs to be solved to get people away from screens . . .

Can you imagine if people tried to read Shakespeare by just scrolling a wheel, and they're like "I'm about the witches, right? Yeah, yeah, speech, yeah, dialogue. . . . Battle scene, wicked! Oh, that was fun." Did they really absorb Shakespeare? You know what I mean?

DP: *What scares you about technology today?*

DA: I think the thing that people seem to constantly forget is that in a free service, you are the product. What all these companies are doing is scraping our analytics and selling them to third parties. So, much like attention, I think people devalue their own behaviors inside these experiences. That's the nefarious shadow side to all this. I think we're all quite careless with our digital identities and where our information goes, and how it's processed.

Online Resources for Chapter 6

Find more resources for Chapter 6 line at http://emergingmediaplatforms.com/ chapter6.

Sources

Hopperton, J. (2022, March). The opportunities and blueprint of XR for media. *International News Media Association*. Retrieved October 24, 2022, from www.inma.org/report/ the-opportunities-and-blueprint-of-xr-for-media

Smartphone sales value in the United States 2005–2022. (2022, August 11). *Statista.com*. www.statista.com/statistics/191985/sales-of-smartphones-in-the-us-since-2005

Storytelling in new dimensions. (2022, August 16). *Syracuse.Edu*. www.syracuse.edu/stories/ sonny-cirasuolo-newhouse-virtual-reality/

7 Conducting Your Field Test

By this time, you have hopefully already done many workbook exercises and tinkered around with a technology you're interested in. Maybe you even took some free courses online or followed some tutorials on YouTube. You're ready to go and build what you will test. Let's go!

Prototyping and Wireframing

Before spending a significant amount of time building or coding something, it's a good idea to sketch out what the user experience will be. In product development, this is called prototyping.

A prototype is typically a visual representation of the key functionality that a user will go through when interacting with a digital product. It can take many forms, including just pencil on paper, but the key thing to focus on is how your audience will interact with the product. This helps you get into the mindset of your target audience and make sure that the experience is truly solving the problem you set out to solve. Also, it helps you make sure that the experience is enjoyable and that one task naturally flows to another.

If you have access to a large whiteboard, you can start out by sketching boxes that represent what a typical user may experience from the very beginning and then connect those with lines to other boxes that represent how they flow through the experience. For this reason, these are called Users Flows or Flowcharts.

If you prefer to work digitally, Google Drawings has built-in flowchart capabilities. Use the toolbar to add different boxes and other shapes, and then add lines. You can easily connect the lines to the sides of the objects, then move the boxes around, and the lines will reconfigure. Type in the purpose for each box in the flowchart.

If what you're building also needs to be designed, you can go further and create what are called "wireframes" for what the users will see. The key to wireframes is to represent only the bare minimum of functionality and the placement of words, images, and buttons in relation to each other. Resist getting too focused on specific fonts, colors, and specific content within each screen. The content should be specific enough to indicate the type of content it represents, but not the exact wording or imagery.

DOI: 10.4324/9781003247012-8

Speaking for myself, I cannot draw. But thankfully, there are a number of prototyping websites that can be used to create compelling wireframes that, in some cases, even mimic the features of a fully functioning experience with the ability to click around and make things happen.

These tools let you choose if you want to prototype an experience for a website, an iPhone or Android phone, or a variety of other devices. You then find and drag typical functionality, such as buttons or drop-down menus, into a wireframe and connect different aspects of the experience together – as if you're making a flowchart that also shows what users will see.

Figma (www.figma.com), Justinmind (http://justinmind.com), and Axure (http://axure.cloud) are three good prototyping systems that have free options. If you have an Adobe Creative Cloud account, which is common among media professionals and students in media-related studies, Adobe XD is also worth checking out.

In some of these tools, you can even create a version that is usable by others through a web link that you send to them. This makes it possible to email a link to people so you can ask them to try something out and provide feedback. But for the purposes of a field test, I don't personally like sending simple prototypes to the final target audience. What you send to your audience should be something real. But in the process of deciding what to build, you can ask friends and advisors to look over your prototype and give you frank feedback on the experience you're designing – long before you send out the real deal.

Building a Minimum Viable Product

Now that you have a good idea of what to build, it's time to get to work. Obviously, the work you do for each project is going to be drastically different depending on the audience and technology. But some common touchpoints apply to building every project.

The first and most important task is to identify the minimum number of features required to get the data you need to make conclusions from your field test. In product development, this is typically referred to as the Minimum Viable Product or MVP.

The concept of an MVP is an outgrowth of the Agile Software Development movement, an iterative process enumerated by 17 software developers in 2001 for how to deliver better software more frequently to customers. Among the 12 principles included in their 2001 manifesto are to deliver working software every few weeks or at most every few months and to keep things simple. It defines simplicity as "the art of maximizing the amount of work *not* done."

The opposite of agile is the waterfall approach, which is very similar to what Eric Raymond referred to as the Cathedral method. The waterfall is a method I know well because I painfully lived through it as a principal product manager at America Online at the turn of the century. It's called waterfall because a team can literally spend an entire year coming up with plans for a digital product before even a single line of code is written. By the time the product requirements are given to the developer – coming down from above, just like a waterfall – the customer dynamics and assumptions have likely completely changed.

With an MVP, you are intentionally creating something simple. As Eric Ries wrote in his 2005 book, *The Lean Startup*, a minimum viable product has just enough features required to "allow a team to collect the maximum amount of validated learning about customers with the least effort," and no more than that.

Let's use our restaurant-ordering chatbot from Chapter 3: Initiating Your Field Test. You can start by simply listing out the bare minimum attributes that *must be present* in order for someone to be able to order food. In product management, these are sometimes referred to as product requirements, and the MVP requirements have a priority of 1 or P1. A product cannot launch if any P1 requirement is missing.

Let's write them out for our restaurant bot:

1.   A chatbot must be created that the user can talk with from any mobile device or computer. – P1
2.   The bot must have a fun personality. – P1
3.   The user must be able to restart the bot from the beginning of the conversation to order more items. – P1
4.   The bot must give users a list of options to choose from that takes them to all of the menu choices. – P1
5.   If the user types a request for something on the menu, the keyword will trigger the bot to ask if they would like to add that item to their order. – P1
6.   When menu choices are made, they must be saved in a Google spreadsheet. – P1
7.   The contact information for the user must be requested and saved. – P1
8.   The restaurant must have a way to see a list of who ordered what.

– P1

To make sure that these are all truly P1 requirements, take each one out and ask yourself: can I still get the data I need to make conclusions if this is missing? I would argue that #2 fit that description. Yes, it would be nice if the bot had a fun and creative personality, but if we run out of time, we could still get information that will tell us if our hypothesis that a chatbot is better than filling out paper forms is correct or not.

Similarly, #5 which allows the user to speak to the bot in plain language would be really cool, but is it necessary? Could we simply have a bot that issues prompts that the user must click or tap on, and emerge with an order? This requirement is highly desirable but also not absolutely necessary to get the data we need.

In your list, you can track the priorities you are assigning by changing anything not required for launch as P2. And as your list grows longer, you can even change some to P3. I think of P3 as the science fiction priority – yeah, it would be really awesome to have, but it's probably not happening any time soon, if at all.

Being ruthlessly honest and methodical about listing requirements and ranking them will save you from losing countless hours or days working on things that you may love but which won't do anything to get you to the testing phase. Also, changing something from a P1 to a P2 doesn't mean you absolutely won't do it. If you find yourself with extra time, you can always throw it in. This gives you an incentive to work efficiently on all those P1s.

Graceful Degradation

While you're working on building your MVP, you will find that some things that you thought would be easiest are the hardest, and things you thought would be hardest are the easiest. Even more, you will inevitably realize that some things you wanted to do are impossible, either objectively impossible for anyone to do or just outside of your skill set.

Just as nobody can predict the future, nobody can accurately predict when they will hit the inevitable road bumps, or even road closures, that occur constantly when dealing with truly emerging media platforms. And they can come for all kinds of reasons. You could be working on a platform, such as a chatbot creation tool, and the tool's features could update right in the middle of you using it. You could discover that something on a no-code platform actually does require coding after all, and you lack the knowledge or skills to do that part in the time you have available. You could even mysteriously lose data and have to start over.

In case you are wondering, all of those scenarios I mentioned earlier have happened to students of mine who were working on field tests. That's when I remind them of the need to create plans A through Z before they start building and to update those plans as they discover new road bumps.

This is where your priority list can help. Even though we said that the MVP couldn't launch unless all P1s are present, are there ways for us to adapt if one P1 has to come off the list? Possibly, if you can identify ways to *gracefully degrade* the specific problematic feature while still getting some of the data you need.

For example, requirement #6 states that the menu choices must be saved in a Google spreadsheet. If the Google connection in the chatbot tool isn't working (maybe even because Google stops supporting that tool, which is another thing that has happened in the past), nothing will be saved there.

How else could you get that data to the restaurant? Could it be emailed? Could it be saved in another service, perhaps Microsoft OneDrive? Could it even be emailed back to the user, and the user is then told to bring that email to the counter?

Remember: our goal for this chatbot was ultimately to reduce line and wait times. If that goal is still achieved because people come in line with their choices already made, line size will still be reduced – just not as much as if their choices were made available directly to the restaurant.

For the perfectionists out there, planning for graceful degradation can be hard because nobody wants to plan on delivering something sub-par. Just remember that by coming up with contingency plans, you aren't choosing to use them. You just have them in your back pocket in case you need them.

Pivots

Perfectionists, there is something even harder for you than graceful degradation, and that's finding that the entire approach you pursued isn't possible. If
you find yourself in this situation, you have a few choices – all of which are
called pivots.

One type of pivot is to use the same technology and general approach but
apply it to a different problem. I know, I know, I said earlier that we should try to
avoid building solutions that are in search of problems to solve. But if you have
already invested a good amount of time in building something and it looks like
it actually isn't a good fit for the audience or problem – or, maybe you discover
that you aren't actually able to reach the types of people for whom you intended
it – it is still worth thinking through how you can build upon the momentum
for what you already built instead of completely abandoning it and starting from
scratch.

As long as you're careful to not actively create the next Horsey Horseless Carriage, fooling yourself into believing your idea is worth saving because of how it
makes you feel about yourself and your own ego, this is a worthy exercise.

Another pivot is to keep the audience and problem focused but change the
technological approach. Let's go back to our restaurant bot.

Imagine that you build the bot and bring it to the restaurant, but they then
tell you that they can't authorize this test because it's saving customer data in an
insecure way that is not allowed by their corporate policy. In this case, if they are
still willing to work with you, you can brainstorm with them about other ways to
get them the data that will help with part of the underlying problem, just not in
the way you thought.

For example, since our goal is to reduce lines, perhaps the chatbot is rebranded
as a different type of customer survey. When people check out, they're offered a
discount for talking with the bot to answer some questions, and the goal of the bot
pivots to finding out what they anticipate they may want to order the next time.
The restaurant would get information to help them plan on what to prepare in
advance so that they can turn around orders more quickly, and thus still reduce
line size and wait time.

The third type of pivot is the least desirable, but it can happen. You can find
an entirely new problem with an entirely different technology. And yes, this does
occasionally happen in my class, and some of the resulting field tests are even better than what the student first proposed. I believe this is the case because sometimes, the best ideas and projects come not from having lots of resources but by
taking resources away. The old phrase, "necessity is the mother of invention," can
be truer than ever when the thing you've lost is time.

But do yourself a favor and don't put yourself in that position. We all know
how to cram for a final exam. But cramming for a product that you launch for
an audience, hoping to get good data to help you make decisions, is a recipe for
disaster.

Ask for Help, Spill Your Guts!

Probably the best advice I ever got when I was running a startup was not just to share my successes but to be open about when I was struggling. I don't mean sharing the struggles with the entire world, but with "friendlies" who may have encountered the same thing.

Telling the right audience when you're stuck is extremely common in open-source communities. In fact, there's an entire website called Stack Overflow (https://stackoverflow.com/) that is dedicated specifically to this. After creating an account and logging in, you can type in practically any technology – a piece of software, an open-source code library, a programming language, and even a brand of drone – along with a problem, and you will find a thread where someone else has shared the same problem. If you're lucky, someone will have already shared a solution.

In the context of a class like Emerging Media Platforms, where everyone is dancing on the edge of various cliffs, the friendlies can be fellow students. Throughout the semester, I have several opportunities where everyone is invited to spill their guts. I even give extra points to students who encounter a sticky problem and post a solution to it for others who are in the class. It's like our own internal Stack Overflow.

Stop and think a little bit about how fundamentally different this mindset is from how things are done in a typical media organization. Is there anything like a Stack Overflow for problems people are having finding sources, achieving a certain kind of video effect, or finding a particular type of public data for a story they're working on? In my experience, this has been extremely rare in media companies, and it is rarely done at scale.

Journalists and content developers of all types tend to hold their processes and sources extremely close, and sometimes there's a good reason for that. The fear of losing your "scoop" and being first can often make you keep absolutely everything close to the chest. But that instinct toward secrecy doesn't have to apply to everything, and it shouldn't. When it comes to building something new, it can even hold you back or cause you to make mistakes that, if you had just been open with some friendly colleagues or connections, you may have been able to avoid.

The person who explained this better than anyone else is Adeo Ressi, an investor and startup coach who started The Founder Institute, a startup boot camp that I went through back in 2008.

When startup founders were encouraged to share their ideas with each other, a few were hesitant. Adeo summed up the danger of that mentality in one sentence: "If your idea is so bad that, by you just telling me about it, I will be able to do it before you can – you need a better idea." He said that execution is what mattered most, not just the idea. In other words, make sure what you're building takes enough serious work that someone else can't come by and scoop you with just a few hours of focus.

So beyond just your idea, don't be afraid to share your progress, including your struggles. Spill your guts! There are lots of fellow innovators out there who are ready to help you climb the mountain and avoid pitfalls and crags, but only if you're willing to be vulnerable and reach out for help.

Finding Testers in Your Target Market

As you get closer to having an MVP that you can test, you should begin looking for a target audience. You can even start building it before you're ready for feedback. These are the rules I set for getting feedback in a Field Test.

First, make sure you have at least 20 people who match the type of user who is likely to relate to the problem you're trying to solve. In most cases, these need to be people you don't know, and definitely should not be your friends or family. As much as you might love your mom or dad, sibling or cousin, do you really think they will be giving frank feedback on what you've built? Their bias toward (or even against) you based on your shared life experiences will inevitably color their input.

Students often struggle to find an audience, but it's easier than you may think. If your audience can be found in a particular area, you can physically go there and reach out to people. You can give them a card with information about what you're trying out and hand it to them. Or, now that everyone on the planet knows how to use QR codes, thanks to COVID restaurant protocols, you can have something with the code on it that will take them to a site that explains what you're doing and invites them to participate.

If you're an introvert and find it hard to reach out to strangers, just remember that what you put out there will be extremely interesting and compelling to most people. Put yourself in their shoes: an innovative student or worker in their community is trying to solve a serious problem, and they want you to check it out and help evaluate it. Who can say no to that? You will find that in most cases, the worst negative reaction will be that someone is too busy, but they will still appreciate being asked.

You can also use social media to your advantage. Posting something on Twitter, Instagram, or Reddit using the right hashtags is worth trying for almost any topic. Finding the right Facebook or LinkedIn group can also deliver good results. And if you're looking for a local audience, check to see if NextDoor has a community for that locality and see if someone in that group can post something for you (if it's not in the community in which you live).

A third way is to find an organization that is focused on your problem – for example, an advocacy group. Talk to them and ask them where they would go to find people, and don't be afraid to ask them if they would be willing to send out a call for testers to people in their community. The worst they can say is no, but they will probably still give you some good leads.

No matter how you find your audience, make sure the final list of testers is specific and describable. Here are some examples from a field test from a student who was using a chatbot to recruit international students:

*   Mother of a 16-year-old daughter and a 14-year-old son, never had a connection to the university.

- Father of 21-year-old triplets (daughters), never had a connection to the university.
- 21-year-old girl, exchange student and freshman.
- 23-year-old girl, exchange student and freshman.
- 19-year-old man, freshman.

Yours will be vastly different depending on your particular field test.

Types of Evaluation Methods

When you query your test audience, you obviously want them to go through the product experience and feel free to share any thoughts – positive or negative – with you. But you want to know more than whether they liked it or not. Here are some other types of data you can collect.

- **Usage Metrics:** If you're using a commercial product, check to see if it has an analytics dashboard and evaluate if the data it collects can tell you anything meaningful to answer your questions. If you do something web-based and you control the content on the pages, you can easily add Google Analytics (http://analytics.google.com) code to the page and use that for some basic analysis.
- **Online Surveys:** There are a number of free sites that make it easy to create surveys that people fill out with a link. Google Forms, SurveyMonkey, and Qualtrics (the latter of which may be available through your university) are just a few. You can set up your survey with multiple choice options, single-word forms, or large text areas that people can fill up with whole novels. Whatever options you surface, just make sure they will give you the data you need to make conclusions about your field test.
- **Interviews:** Sometimes, you want people to be able to talk more freely about their feedback. While it takes more time, don't be afraid to pick up the phone or set up a Zoom or even meet in person over coffee and ask them questions. In order to ensure that you get data that can be used for conclusions, you should make sure you bring up the same questions for everyone – but also allow them to go off script and share other ideas throughout.
- **Compare the Old to the New:** Since field tests typically compare an old, problematic method with a newer, supposedly better or more efficient method, you can almost always divide your testers into two groups. The first uses the old method, and the second uses the new method. Sometimes, this is called an A/B test, though people who do usability testing for a career will tell you that an A/B test is extremely focused on just one product or feature that they are considering launching. Whatever you call it, it's designed to tell you if this new approach really is worth further investigation and investment or not. The old way may, in fact, still be the better way, and your audience will be the one to decide that.

Sensitive Topics

Some topics are just too sensitive to test directly with the intended audience. As just one example, one time, I had a student who wanted to use 360 videos to train young women on how to keep themselves safe from sexual assault. Another wanted to use a chatbot as an alternative to a community support line. Upon investigating the types of calls the support line received, the student learned that there were people calling for suicide support, looking for a homeless shelter, and other truly life-or-death topics.

In cases like these, consider finding people who work with that audience and know them well, and get their feedback. Avoid going straight to their public-facing audience. If you do, only do it while working extremely closely with these experts, and maybe go so far as to only advise them on what's possible versus implementing it yourself. Any field test – or for that matter, research study – needs to start with the desire to help people, and certainly do not harm them. By helping the experts who work with such groups understand what's possible and getting their feedback, you are still getting valuable information that translates into knowledge that will eventually help people indirectly.

You may find yourself unknowingly falling into these scenarios, and when you do, make sure you have a game plan for how to deal with it. As one example, the student I mentioned who created a chatbot directed at international students launched her test right when there was an issue with a potential active shooter on campus.

Parents of students who were studying abroad had heard about this and were suddenly asking the chatbot for information about the safety of their far-away children. You can imagine how stressful this must have been for those parents, and it was also stressful for the student running the field test. We talked about it and agreed that she should keep the bot running, but right at the beginning, direct inquiries about safety to the Department of Public Safety, providing a phone number and email address.

And that frightening scenario leads to what I consider to be one of the best outcomes of Field Tests. I call them French fry moments.

Look for French Fry Moments

One of the many mythologies about French fries (which are probably not even French, by the way) is that a chef accidentally dropped cut potatoes in boiling oil instead of boiling water. Instead of throwing the whole batch out, he tried it, and – voila – the French fry was invented!

So just to be completely open, this silly story is a myth that is based on no facts. But I still like using it as an analogy in field tests because it's what can happen if you look closely at both successes *and* failures. And it's why I say that when you push yourself enough to the edge of innovation, there truly is no such thing as a failure. That failure could be like the invention of the French fry.

Putting field tests aside, one of the most influential French fry moments in recent technology history came from a Podcast company called Odeo in 2006. Odeo had a side feature that allowed users of the platform to send 140-character status update messages to each other.

When Apple's iTunes supported podcasts, Odeo became obsolete, and the investors pushed the startup to change course. Podcasts were thrown out, but the team felt that the little status feature, which they called "twttr" had a future. Out went podcasts, and Twitter became the only focus. Six months later, they renamed the entire product Twitter.

Think of how different the world would be – positive and negative – if that little French fry of Twitter had been thrown out along with Odeo. During the process of your field test, pay attention to things like this that pop up that you would never have anticipated. You may find that this trivial feature, or even what at first looks like a mistake, is the key insight that you would never have been able to make if you hadn't gone on this journey.

Case Study: An Aerial French Fry Moment

Justin's original field test idea was to mount a 360 video camera on a drone in order to get better video of a growing beach-side community development by a Central New York lake. Numerous traditional 2D stories had been done about the development, but he thought 360 video would give people a better idea of the impact the development would have on the surrounding area.

Since he had an FAA Part 107 pilot's license and a drone, he was uniquely set up to run this test. He borrowed a small 360 video camera from the Newhouse School's Innovation Lab and experimented with different mounts that he jury-rigged from fasteners he got from Home Depot. After finally finding a way to securely connect the camera to his drone, he set out to shoot some video.

He shot two videos: one with a traditional 2D camera from a boat and the other from the 360 video camera he had mounted on his drone, which he piloted from the shore. The footage came back, and he realized that he'd overlooked something crucial.

Because the camera was so securely mounted to the drone – which was required so that the drone's vibration wouldn't cause the camera to become disconnected and fall into the lake – that vibration was passed to the footage. The footage itself was unusable and unpublishable. Nothing else he tried would make the vibration go away. His field test hypothesis was a failure. In fact, he couldn't even use the footage to run it past an audience.

But he did find that if he took still pictures, the vibration wasn't a problem. He knew he could do this with the drone's built-in 2D camera, but framing shots created another issue. To frame the shot, he would have to take his eyes off the drone and focus on the image coming through on the controller, and then pinch, drag, and zoom in order to get the right camera angle.

In the United States and most countries, this is illegal because Remote Pilots in Command are required to always keep their eyes on the drone. He was conducting his field test alone, so he couldn't frame the shot.

And then it hits him: with a 360 video camera, the camera captures everything in all directions, and you can use software later to frame 2D shots from those 360 videos. His French fry moment was that having a 360 video camera on a drone would allow a solo pilot to capture still shots, which would be framed in post-production, while still being able to keep the drone in line of sight at all times.

Workbook Exercise 7.1: Start a Field Test Journal

It's time to get serious and run your field test. Exciting! The processes laid out in Chapters 3 and 7 prepare you for what you need to do. But as you go through it, you should keep a journal of your progress.

This is important for two reasons. First, in part of your final field test report, you will be telling the story of your innovation – warts and all. This is what makes you stand out as a true innovator, someone who loves to run toward change even with a few bruises here and there. And second, throughout the process, you should look for French fry moments.

One way to do this is through a daily journal. Feel free to use this template for each entry, or create your own. The most important thing is to be sure you do it every day as you are working on your test.

Daily Field Test Journal

Today's Date:
Days to Launch:
Progress Made Today (2–3 sentences):
Current Status (2–3 sentences):
Problems Encountered (2–3 sentences):
Where Did I Look for Help? Include links:
Pivot Danger (Scale of 1–10, with 1 being low and 10 being high):

Expert Interview: Christina Boomer Vazquez

DP: *I'm really excited to have Christina Boomer Vazquez here with me. Christina was a student of mine a few years ago and has also taught the Emerging Media Platforms class. But on top of all that, she is a working journalist down in the Miami area. Why don't you say a few things about yourself?*

CV: Hello! I'm a field journalist at a broadcast station in Miami. The majority of my 20+ year career has been in broadcast journalism and continues to be.

At one point in my career, I thought I was retiring from journalism, but looking back I now realize it was more like a sabbatical. I left the industry to join the Modern and Contemporary Museum in Miami as part of their executive team. Part of that process was to help the museum think through ways that we could start incorporating digital media into museum spaces to create "pathways to art."

One of those projects was a Knight Foundation-funded augmented reality project. It was really that project that sparked my curiosity about how we can achieve the goals that we have in journalism to tell stories in new ways and to drive new revenue at a time where we have collapsing business models.

How do we engage audiences? How do we cut through the noise of a fractured media landscape to share accurate information so folks can be the informed citizens that democracy demands of all of us? How can technology help solve these problems? It's through that project that I found my way not only back into journalism but also to the Syracuse University's masters program. And it's your class that really anchored me.

We know where journalism has been and that's great, but we also know some of the systemic issues that it's facing. I always loved how your course culminates in a field test on just one technology, and I see it as a way to help fix some of the big issues that journalism and the media industry are facing.

DP: *Thank you for the kind comments, but I reflect them back to you. You're actually experimenting with emerging media platforms in the journalism industry, which is much needed. What kinds of problems do you try to solve in your industry using new technologies and approaches?*

CV: For many broadcast stations across the country, the TV broadcast continues to be the main product. There are some organizations that are beginning to look at both their digital and broadcast footprints, from both content creation and advertising and earned revenue, a little more holistically. But it still remains the case in most broadcast outlets that the broadcast comes first.

This is not only true of resources but also the amount of money that comes in from advertisers. We're just not frankly at a place where we have digital advertising numbers that can fund newsgathering operations.

Within that though, we try to figure out how to start leveraging different technologies and ways of developing products and thinking about earned revenue.

Most of the time, content creators aren't thinking of earned revenue. There's still this bifurcation of "church and state" between sales and news.

There are very good reasons for that which I fundamentally agree to be true, but we're also getting to a point where we're facing a fundamental issue with the business model.

Can that traditional business model survive? If more people are getting their news digitally, then what's the future of sustainability of the journalism we produce that is so crucial to democracy? That whole question will often keep me up at night.

I'm interested in how certain storytelling innovations can also become newly earned revenue streams. You're seeing some organizations do this with video subscription services for niche content or sponsored content that can fund the resources needed to dive deep into a subject area.

DP: *You've picked the Big Kahuna of problems to be solved. But you're right, it's a problem in pretty much all journalism sectors. It's why we have so many news deserts.*

What I hear you saying is that in this day and age, you increasingly need to have a product mentality when you're creating something new. You have to think about how it will be sustained, even if somebody else is doing the selling.

CV: That, and value. For news, this entire concept of product development is very new for journalists, and it still feels very foreign to them. Sometimes when you first hear it, it feels like a friction. We say, "News as a product? No. For an industry that is the backbone of Democracy, I feel that I'm a public service."

For many of us, and definitely for myself, we view ourselves as public advocates. There was a long time where we said, "We make editorial decisions where we decide what the community needs to hear about."

This idea is very noble, and the quest should always be to provide accurate, verified information that underpins the principle of self-governance in our country's Republic. But before social media, there wasn't often a consideration of also asking people, "What would you like to know about today? Is there anything happening in your community, in your neighborhood, at your kid's playground, at your child's school, or anything happening in your ecosystem that you wish we would talk about?"

That's part of product development. You're looking at who is my "buying persona?" Who is the "user?" There are all these different terms depending on what industry you're in, but what they share is this idea of who am I doing all this work for. Let's figure that out first. Let's interview the viewer and talk to them about it so we can build something for them. That concept is often new to some news organizations.

DP: *But it's not antithetical to them. I learned this as a community product manager at AOL after leaving journalism for the first time. At the end of the day, people using community products were doing so because they wanted information, but in this case they wanted it directly from each other. Helping them meet, connect, and share was the problem that we were solving for them.*

In journalism, it's informing people. There's an unmet information need, and you're filling that need by doing the hard work and the journalism.

Whenever you have a true pain killer for a pain like that, there's a business opportunity there. And that can then sustain what then allows future journalists to keep doing their jobs.

CV: When you say it's not antithetical, I couldn't agree with you more. There's a term out there called Solutions Journalism. It's about figuring out what "broke" and why, and what did we learn from that? Did the event highlight an underlying issue or problem? What community stakeholders are involved? What are the possible solutions to prevent it from happening again? It's about investigating some of the solutions to the systemic issues.

DP: *On that note, can you talk about the field test you did, and the process you went through?*

CV: My field test was going to be focused on 3D scanning for news. I wanted to get just one courthouse to allow me to go in and 3D scan evidence from a trial.

I had covered the George Zimmerman trial, and there was one day when we went in and got still pictures and video of Trayvon Martin's hooded sweatshirt. My idea was to add 3D scanning to the mix so people could turn the objects around and experience them more immersively. But to do that, you need to get court approval. Everything has to go through the trial judge. Because I knew that the Zimmerman evidence on our website was one of the most viewed, it was clear that people wanted to see the evidence. But each trial judge is different from the next, and it was clear that this wasn't going to happen easily or swiftly.

DP: *That was too bad, but often things are out of your control in a story when it comes to access. What did you do next?*

CV: I pivoted to looking at the feasibility of using 360 video in our newsroom. At the time I thought it was low-hanging fruit. Compared to other projects that require management approval or oversight or money, 360 cameras are so affordable. I carry a 360 in my back pocket every day, are there good news uses for that?

What I found is yes, and no. Yes, the newsroom was into it, especially because I was doing it myself and bought my own technology. I reached out a lot to the community and did public polls to find out what people wanted to see. Lots of people wanted to see us use 360 for storm coverage. Also, protests. When I was covering the George Floyd protests, I thought that would be an interesting use case for 360 for live event coverage.

DP: *Cool, so you shot some 360 footage and got it online?*

CV: Yes, I shot it, but I couldn't get it out to our audience as intended. The next snafu I ran into was taking those 360 assets and getting them published on the newsroom's CMS. The wheels went off the track because I could get the footage, but in terms of building this into a digital broadcast story, it wasn't possible. I worked with the digital department to see if there was a way that we could hack things a little bit, or talk to the person who created the CMS to figure out if there's a way to easily adapt it.

What I learned is it is difficult to bring innovation to newsgathering when you're the only change-maker in the conversation. The sentiment was that they were supportive, and wished me well in grad school, but there was no time to further develop the concept on their end.

If a TV news station really wants to do something new, they need to have an innovation team or a storytelling lab, even for the low-hanging fruit. I'd first get buy-in with somebody on the digital team and say, "Hey, do you want to just do something fun? We can just do it together." And then if it works, we can figure out how to scale it up. But I didn't even think to do that because I didn't realize until I tried this out that I needed someone on the digital team to figure out the back-end integration with our proprietary platforms.

DP: *Sometimes the human software is harder to change than the digital software. Human software being an organization, and thinking through that.*

CV: This led to my capstone project, which was about trying to solve this macro problem in a newsroom. The organization has to make strategic choices day by day, minute by minute even. And that's when it comes down to organization charts and human resources.

Newsroom managers need to strategically ask, "Do we really need to hire three more beat reporters? Or does it make more sense to hire three more digital journalists?" Then diving deep into the roles and responsibilities of the job and how those would dovetail with a clearly articulated content strategy.

Do the people within our organization have the skills required for digital to respond to where news consumption behaviors will be in five to ten years? If not, that's fine, but do we then need to take existing human capital and shuffle them around and train them on something new? Or does it make more sense as we're looking at budgets to start finding the money to hire the people who have the right skills for the future?

It sounds boring, but it really comes down to that multi-year strategic plan which focuses on human resources, job descriptions, and the line-item budget to pay for them all. If not, it won't happen.

This is all underpinned by a lot of research from a variety of sources. TV news viewers are actually hungry for deeper content and context. When I look at Miami-Dade County's exit polls, what voters say matters to them are issues that are underrepresented in local news coverage. Things like affordable housing and transportation – these are super weighty topics that involve multiple perspectives, nuance, and context, and you have to invest time in them.

DP: *Hopefully your newsroom also learned from that and will focus more on resourcing digital innovation. Can we shift track and talk about interesting field tests that came through your class?*

CV: I have two favorites. My first was a student who built out this beautiful project with AI. Her company had given her permission to build it on her work laptop, which was more powerful than her home computer. We were two weeks into the end of class, and the pandemic started and they had to do layoffs. She lost her job. Along with that, she lost her entire project on her office computer.

DP: *That's terrible! How did she recover from that?*

CV: Based on an assignment she'd done earlier, she decided to create a chatbot for her dad and brother, who run a butcher shop in Pennsylvania. There were all these different dynamics happening with COVID, and people wanted to order meat online instead of going into the shop.

She thought, could a chatbot not only help them with their problem of this new digital requests for orders but also fulfill the orders? She talked to them and they loved it, and they came up with the idea of creating a QR code for the customers in line.

They tried it out and all of these orders were coming in, but they realized that they would need to hire another person to do back-of-house administration. She had all the orders going into a spreadsheet, but someone would need to be seeing all of that and turning the orders around in time. These poor guys literally didn't even have time to go to their computers and see the orders.

DP: *So, the original hypothesis was a failure. Were there any French fry moments?*

CV: Yes! They said that now that they knew what the chatbot does, it would be just as nice to use a bot to show customers what the difference is between different cuts of meat, because some customers often don't know the difference between the cuts. That helped with customer experience as well as reducing wait times in line.

I liked this project because it had a lot of heart, and it was a good example of recovering from the worst-case scenario. We tell the students all the time to get ready for that pivot, which is why they need to start their field tests so early in the course. There might be times when something is failing, but you can still capture insights.

DP: *What was your second favorite student field test?*

I set up a relationship with the Trnio 3D scanning app to allow my class to test out their beta app, which creates higher quality scans. On the first day of class, I told the students that they get to be among the first people to try out this new technology and test it out for Trnio. Not only are you testing it for yourself, but you're testing it for the company to help make it better.

One student took me up on this, and she decided the problem that she wanted to solve was for the digital publication she was already working for. They do videos for a niche community journalism site. She thought a 3D scan with annotations could get people to linger for a little longer than they would from watching a one-minute video.

She tried all these different scans, and the first couple were not so great. I was so proud of her though because she just kept going. Her final scan of a bust was so good that Sketchfab wound up sharing it as one of the top ten "Cultural Heritage and History" scans for that week.

DP: *How did her publication's audience react to the 3D content?*

CV: The feedback she got was awesome. People started writing about so many different scans they wanted to see, and she started developing an idea of becoming a 3D dispatch reporter. It was great. But it was also a lot of hard work.

DP: *These are great stories of innovation. Thank you for all your time!*

Online Resources for Chapter 7

Find more resources for Chapter 7 line at http://emergingmediaplatforms.com/chapter7.

Sources

Cagan, M. (2017). *INSPIRED: How to create tech products customers love*. Wiley.

Demilt, J. (2017, September 12). The origins of Twitter. *Pennington Creative*. https://penningtoncreative.com/the-origins-of-twitter/

Manifesto for Agile Software Development. (n.d.). *Manifesto for Agile Software Development*. http://agilemanifesto.org/

Ries, E. (2011). *The lean startup*. Currency.

Twitter: Complete guide. (2021, January 4). *History-Computer*. https://history-computer.com/twitter-history/

8   360 Photography and Video

One of the easiest and most cost-effective ways to get into immersive media is with cameras that record from all directions at once. The photos and videos produced by these cameras are alternately referred to as 360 video or spherical content. Other terms you may encounter are panoramic, panoptic, or stereoscopic 180. While not all exactly the same, they share the same goal: to break video out of the historic rectangles in which they have been trapped.

Here are some definitions to help you through the sea of terms:

- **Panoramic:** Imagine a long strip of paper that you wrap around yourself and connect at both ends. You are standing in the middle, and pictures appear on the inside. As you look around that strip, you see a scene that is the same as if you were standing somewhere. But there's a catch: you can't see the ceiling or the ground from the scene.
- **360, or spherical:** Imagine a gigantic basketball that is lit from the inside, and you are sitting right in the middle of the sphere. As you look around, you see images that were taken from a scene, and you see it all – the horizon, the sky, and the ground. You may even see the remnants of a tripod that the camera was sitting on. Conversely, if an image is not spherical, it is on a two-dimensional surface or a plane. For lack of a better term, let's refer to that as a rectangle.
- **Monoscopic, or 2D:** This refers to depth. In monoscopic video, what you see is similar to what you see with one eye covered. While you can imagine how close the objects are to you based on the larger context, you don't physically see any distance at all. Everything is painted flat against the inside of a sphere.
- **Stereoscopic, or 3D:** We all know what stereo means in audio: the sound was recorded with two microphones, and because of that you hear depth and even movement of sound based on where the microphone was and what was around it. The same is true for stereoscopic video recording. Your own head sees in stereo because you have two eyes, and that allows you to see depth. In stereoscopic video, there are pairs of cameras for each direction the camera rig is recording, rather than just one.

DOI: 10.4324/9781003247012-9

With an understanding of these terms, you can describe almost any type of video. For example, if you watch Netflix on a traditional TV, you are watching monoscopic rectangular video. If you are one of the few people who invested in a 3D TV, or you pay extra to see a cinematic movie in 3D, you are watching stereoscopic rectangular video.

In VR, most 360 videos you will encounter will be monoscopic 360 videos. They're like a movie that is projected onto the inside of a sphere, and you the experiencer are also sitting inside that sphere. A lot of people will call this "3D video," but that's a misnomer because there is no depth to the image in monoscopic 360 videos.

It is, however, possible for 360 videos to also have depth if the video is shot with stereoscopic, as opposed to monoscopic, cameras. That said, most 360 videos are still not shot in 3D for a simple reason: they cost more to produce. You need twice as many camera sensors in the rig, which raises the price for even consumer cameras. The file sizes are also much larger, and more people – including myself – report feeling nauseous when watching stereoscopic 360 video than monoscopic 360 video.

One of the most interesting, and also underused, formats is stereoscopic 180, which to date has mostly been used for sports and entertainment. When viewed in VR, they can give you the feeling of watching a basketball game from courtside seats, or being at the front row of a favorite concert or play. The experience in VR feels like looking into a diorama at a museum, except everything inside the display case is a real scene – as if you are peering into another world.

How Did We Get Here?

360 video is hardly a new invention, but it has resurged at different technological inflection points in history – most recently, with the launch of the Oculus Rift in 2016. While not the most immersive type of virtual reality experience, 360 video very quickly established itself as the most common type of VR content largely because it could be captured and edited with existing hardware and image-editing software.

The idea of 360 imagery predates even the invention of the camera, with murals painted across multiple walls to make a visitor feel they were somewhere else. The very first panoramic cameras to be marketed came out in the early 1800s, with the first patent going to Austrian Joseph Puchberger for a 150-degree field of view hand-cranked camera. Fast forward to 1898, and we see the first mass-produced Al-Vista panoramic camera, soon to be followed by the Kodak Panoram which proved popular with amateur photographers. The Library of Congress archives have examples of these early panoramas of everywhere from Prague to Davenport, Iowa.

360 video and panoramic photos experienced a brief spike in popularity in 1995 when Apple introduced the QuickTime VR format to its QuickTime video player. But with VR headsets still being far from perfect, and those that were available

being far out of the price range of the average consumer, Apple discontinued supporting the format just a few years later.

The launch of the Oculus Rift, which came out in a developer kit form in 2014 and consumer version in 2016, woke VR out of its 20-year slumber. Media companies around the world started investing in creating immersive 360 video content for what they hoped would be a large new audience of headset-wearing patrons. But the rush to produce 360 video content meant you had to go through quite a bit of pain just to get a single publishable 360 photo or video. There was no affordable camera that shot in all directions (the closest was a camera from Nokia that started at US$60,000), but rather "rigs" of smaller high-resolution cameras that were arranged in a circle or around the focal point of a circular or spherical harness.

I myself created such a rig with colleagues and students which consisted of six GoPro Hero cameras in a 3D-printed case. You would have to synchronize the starts and stops across all cameras, usually by pairing each camera with the same remote. If you were lucky, they would all record at the same time and you could then process the six images into a single 360 video. But often, one or two cameras would lose their connection or fail to stop, or their batteries would die before the others. The result was an *almost-360* that had one or two black spots around the sphere. Hardly publishable!

Finally, if you managed to get six videos of equal length, you had to process them in one of a handful of truly awful (but necessary) software programs and train the software to properly identify "control points" to make sure the different images were properly stitched together. This software was so complex that this step alone discouraged many hobbyists from going too far with 360 video.

All that pain is now in the past, and there are now many all-in-one 360 video cameras available that handle everything more or less automatically. For this reason, I believe that the edge of innovation has moved from simply capturing 360 video – which anyone can now do with a $300 camera – to editing and storytelling.

That's not only good news for you but also bad news because it means you have to work harder to have your content stand out in a large sea of mediocre 360 video. But if you're a professional-trained journalist or videographer, it also means you're better positioned to make a mark with your content because you have those foundational storytelling skills.

My First Experience With 360 Video

Prior to 2014, I had never done anything with 360 video, but that all changed when I found myself working as a summer consultant for the USA TODAY NETWORK. My initial job was to help them create apps for Google Glass, which at that time was considered *the* hot new technology. But a funny thing happened on the way to the forum. Between the time that we'd signed a consulting contract and when I visited for a planning meeting, the original Oculus Rift Development

Kit (known as the DK1) arrived at my lab. I played around with it and was frankly floored, and took it with me to the USA TODAY meeting.

After almost an entire day of discussing what the company could do with Google Glass, I pulled the Rift out and asked Mitch Gelman, the VP I was working with, to look inside. He was equally floored. After about a minute of stunned silence, he turned to me and said in his typically whispery voice: "OK, so don't talk about it, but we're not going to do anything with Google Glass this summer. We're going to produce a major piece of journalism for VR. We're going to be first, and it's going to be big."

In truth, what we created was not the first piece of VR journalism – that was Nonny's *Hunger in Los Angeles*. But it was the first piece of VR journalism by a large commercial news organization at what, at that time, was the largest chain of newspaper and broadcast news outlets in the world.

The piece we ended up producing that summer was *Harvest of Change*, which sadly no longer exists in VR form online apart from a video showing parts of the interactive. Much of the project consisted of a video-game-like recreation of a family farm in Clarinda, Iowa. Users would move through the farm looking for floating icons that would indicate there was another video for them to find, and by the end they experienced the entire history of the place – both through simulation and through immersive video – as if they had been there.

We found and hired a very talented video game producer named Ray Soto to build the simulations, and one of my jobs was to go over what he'd built and compare it to the photos and 2D videos shot 1,000 miles away by journalists at The Des Moines Register. But my bigger job was to figure out how to shoot those 360 videos.

We had tried many of the early 360 videos that were produced for the DK1, but it quickly became clear at that time that the only way to get quality 360 video was to hire a company that had the equipment – and more importantly, that had at least a little experience producing such content. It was that new on the scene, a truly emerging media platform for its time.

After a lot of Google searches and phone calls, I finally located a company out of New York City which had produced 360 video for The Lion King on Broadway, The Smithsonian, and even Michelle Obama. Their crew and ours flew out to Des Moines, and then drove another four hours to Clarinda that reminded me of Dorthy's farm in Kansas. There was nothing but corn fields and rolling hills for as far as the eye could see.

I will be honest that when I saw the "camera" they were using, I was a little disappointed. I was expecting something large, expensive, and impressive, but it was just six GoPro cameras stuck together so they each looked out in a different direction.

Later, when we saw the first rough cuts, they were horrible. You could see clear lines of demarcation between each video (these are called "stitch lines" in the industry). And sometimes you would see someone walking across two cameras and they would slightly disappear, then reappear (this is called "ghosting").

I called over my editor and told him I thought we had a quality problem. He agreed, and we immediately called the 360 video production team we had hired and expressed our concerns. I think we may have even told them that they had to go back and re-shoot everything.

This is when I really dove head-on into the inherent messiness of innovation, and looking back I know that I had the wrong mindset. I was expecting perfection in a nascent technology that very few people had attempted at this scale during the digital age.

The videographer calmly told us that this was a rough cut, and he was still working on "calibrating the stitching." "What does that mean?" I asked in a panic. I truly knew nothing about the process, so he explained that he was calibrating the AutoPano software to identify the common elements between different angles of the video.

"For example, I have to tell the software that this part of this guy's ear seen from this angle on camera 1 is the same as this part from this other angle, from camera 2," he said. He proceeded to go on about noses, baseball caps, tractor wheels, and on and on. "It's a very, very painstaking process! We'll get you a final version in three days."

We hung up the phone and started talking about Plan B if we had to rip all the 360 video out of the project and use only CGI. Would that work? Was there enough time? I don't think anyone slept well that night, and the next three days were nerve-racking.

Three days later, we got the final cuts – and they were amazing. The resolution was higher, and there were no traces of weird stitch lines to be found anywhere. When viewing the videos in the Oculus Rift, we all felt like we were transported back to where we had been in Iowa just a week earlier.

Harvest of Change debuted at the Fall 2014 Online News Association Conference in Chicago with a special setup of PCs and Oculus Rifts. I watched nervously as journalists from all over the world experienced VR journalism, many for the first time. I particularly remember journalists from The New York Times trying it out, and being floored. A year later, the Times launched its own 360 project, The Daily 360.

And icing on the cake was that one year later, *Harvest of Change* – which almost launched with all the 360 videos stripped out because we didn't understand the production process – won a coveted Edward R. Murrow Award in the Innovative Video category.

Your First 360 Video Camera

As I mentioned earlier, you are extremely lucky to not have to go through that kind of pain, and instead you can focus on shooting and editing. The first step is to get a 360 video camera.

There are a number of different all-in-one 360 video cameras on the market that range in price, but most are under $500. They also can produce 2D images that are framed after the fact. For these reasons, I recommend that every journalist or storyteller invest in a good consumer-grade 360 video camera. As long as the output is 4K or better and the stitching is done automatically, you can't go wrong.

As of the publication of this book, my favorite was pretty much any camera by Insta360. My first experience with their cameras was with the 8K Insta360 Pro, which came out in 2017 at a price of about US$3,000. While it's a workhorse, my students and I have since shifted to the 5.7K Insta360 One line which cost around US$430.

You may think: why go with 5.7K instead of 8K? Here are two major reasons. First, pretty much all consumer VR headsets currently can't handle more than a 4K image, and when you upload the video to them or to YouTube, even your 8K will be compressed down to 4K. Second, processing edits from Adobe Premiere in 8K can take all night, as compared to just a few minutes per minute of video for 5.7K.

The other cameras I can recommend are the GoPro Max (5.6K) and Ricoh Theta (4K). But my preference lies with Insta360.

Audio and Spatial Audio

With 360 video, most tend to focus on the visual aspect. But audio is also key. Over time, multiple studies have revealed that audio is an important factor in how present people feel in a virtual scene. Most recently, a 2020 study by Angelika Kern and Wolfgang Ellermeier published in Front Robot AI showed that even ambient environmental sound significantly impacted subjects' reports of how immersed they felt in a virtual scene.

What this means on a practical level is that whenever you are shooting 360 video, you should always be sure to capture high-quality audio as well. Don't assume the audio capabilities from the camera will suffice. Use a separate audio recorder, such as a Tascam or even your smartphone, and use the included audio from the camera only as a reference in your video editing tool to match up audio from your separate recorder.

Even more powerful is the idea of spatial audio, sometimes also called ambisonic audio. This is audio that is recorded in three dimensions, just as we experience sound every day through our ears. The difference between spatial and stereo audio is that the sound also has height and depth. A sound feels as if it's attached to the object from which it emanates in real life.

I first experienced spatial audio in 2016 when I visited a startup in College Park, Maryland, called VisiSonics – an interesting name, as it means literally "seeing sound." They had created a device that they referred to as an Audiovisual Camera. Like a 360 video camera, it had several lenses around it to capture video from all directions. Thanks to each direction being recorded by two cameras, just as our vision comes from two eyes, the video was also three dimensional. But along with each camera was a microphone that zeroed in on sounds coming from different directions.

In their demo, they showed me the head-sized camera, and then put a VR headset over my eyes and special headphones over my ears. What happened next was simply magic, and I felt as if my consciousness had been moved into the camera.

The engineer took out his keys and jingled them while walking around the camera, occasionally also moving a few feet away from it while still walking around. I was amazed at how the sound of the keys exactly matched where I could see the keys.

The engineer then asked me to close my eyes, and as he continued to move the keys around, I was amazed that in my mind's eye I could *see* the sound of the keys moving around my virtual head. This is the magic of spatial audio: it mimics how our brain actually "sees" sound in the real world – even when we aren't looking.

To get a sense of just how powerful this is, either try or watch videos of people playing the game "Don't Let Go." In this game, you hold your hands down on the space bar of a keyboard while seeing virtually created hands on a space bar of a computer in a virtual room. Eventually, a spider comes out of the keyboard and walks up your arm, behind your head, and into your hair. You can hear the movement of the spider behind you, shuffling through your hair as if it's really there. It's at this moment that most people can't take it anymore, and they instinctively move their hands off the space bar to brush the spider off their heads. The audio in this game is simulated via a gaming engine, but an ambisonic recorder could theoretically record those same sounds using a real spider (not that anyone would want to record the sound of a large spider moving through their hair!).

Ambisonic recorders like VisiSonics and a similar one from Sennheiser cost thousands of dollars, and the mixing process has to be done with specialized software that requires significant training. But since then, microphones like the Zoom H3-VR, which costs US$249, have come out that make ambisonics more accessible for the average media producer.

That said, recording is just part of the challenge, and to make spatial audio work in a 360 video you will have to mix it using specific post-production software such as Vordio, Reaper, and Pro Tools. Given how dynamic the spatial audio space is, I will suggest that you Google around for current tutorials if you capture spatial audio with a Zoom recorder.

Workbook Exercise 8.1: Creating 360 Photos From a Standard Phone

You can begin experimenting with 360 photography with your smartphone, even if you don't have a 360 video camera. There are a number of apps available that let you create spherical photos by combining multiple pictures taken from one location into a 360 photo.

The easiest of these is the Google Street View app, which Google created to allow users to contribute their own 360 video content to Google Maps. The app is streamlined to send data to Google – which you can do if you prefer – but you can also just save the output to your phone's camera roll without sending it to Google.

With the Google Street View map open, click the camera button at the lower right and choose "Take Photosphere." The app will guide you to position your camera over dots. Stand in one place, and simply move to each dot. It won't let you proceed until you have found every dot. When you have, the progress circle at the bottom will change to a green check mark.

Tap that check mark, and you'll see a button to "Publish to Google Maps." Just to the right of that is a Share button. Click it and choose "Share Privately," and then Save Image. The 360 photo will then be in your camera roll.

You can find an interesting place near you that you think people may want to virtually visit and take photospheres from different locations. In the next exercise, you can connect these photos together into a tour with buttons that people click to transport between the photos.

Workbook Exercise 8.2: Publish a 360 Photo to the Web Using A-Frame

One straightforward way of taking your audience into a story is with a 360 photo, and you can embed it directly into a story using a little A-Frame code. But if you have a collection of 360 photos, you can go even further and connect them together in a gallery that can be navigated using hotspots.

Figure 8.1 A 360 tour of the Newhouse School as rendered in A-Frame.

(*Source:* Photo/Dan Pacheco)

On the website, you can find an A-Frame template in Glitch for a 360 photo that I prepared for you. It lets you change the text and photos to create your own gallery. I have also provided an example of a finished template that I published on my GitHub Page. Go to this link to find the both: https://emergingmediaplatforms.com/chapter8/.

Workbook Exercise 8.3: Editing 360 Video in Adobe Premiere

Getting Started

Editing 360 video has thankfully always been a light lift for those who already produce video, and Adobe Premiere is what I and almost everyone who works with 360 video recommends. Since this book is aimed at beginners, we'll focus on Premiere, but if you work in special effects you may also want to research what's possible with 360 video in Adobe After Effects. Either way, the editing is actually not really done on a 360 video, but rather on a 2D video that later gets stretched onto a sphere through a 360 projection.

If you already use Adobe Premiere, you can actually edit and produce an entire 360 video without even seeing it in 360 video. It will appear like a distorted picture with a wave moving through it. Anything that you add to that distorted image – such as text, graphics, or effects – will look straight when you first add it but will shift to appear to be painted on the surface of a sphere when you view the video in VR mode.

The first thing you want to do is to add the Toggle VR Video Display button to the toolbar. You can do this by finding the toolbar around mid-right of the screen, click the + button, and find an icon that looks like a circle with a VR headset over it. Drag that into your toolbar and click it, and you will see that you can toggle between the wavy 2D and spherical/VR views.

My recommendation is to always work in the 2D view when you're adding or modifying text, transitions, or effects. After your effects are in place, toggle to the VR mode to get a sense of what it will look like inside a VR headset, then toggle back out to 2D to modify them.

You can work with the timeline to trim and cut just like you would with a standard video. Once you've set up the clips you want and their order, you're ready to do things slightly differently. The next set of workbook exercises cover what you need to do specifically for 360 video.

Adding 2D Video Effects

With the VR view toggled off, create a title by clicking the Type tool to the left of the timeline, then click inside the preview window and start typing.

Your title will look straight on top of the distorted video, but if you turn the VR view on it will look distorted on the 360 video sphere.

You can change the size and fonts for the titles in the Effect Controls window that should appear in a tab to the left of the preview window. Use these controls to determine where and how long the text appears in the timeline (look for a new effect bar at the top of the timeline).

Find the Effects Pane (different from Effect Controls) and navigate to the Immersive Video Effects folder. The 2D text effect is called VR Plane to Sphere. Drag that effect onto your title in the timeline. In standard view, the title will now appear distorted, but when you go into 360 video view it will look flat as if it's floating on top of the 360 video.

Note that if an effect won't render, it's probably because your video quality is too high. You will first need to export at 4K or lower, then reimport and see if that fixes it.

Change the Center Point

Whatever is in the center of your video in Premiere will be where the VR headset will center for the user when the video plays. What happens if the center is looking at a wall or trash can? You need to distort the video so that the action you want people to focus on appears in the center.

For that, use the Offset effect which is under Video Effect > Distort > Offset. Drag this effect to your video, and then in Effect controls change the first number next to "Shift Center To" and you will see the center change.

Adding a Nadir Patch

A nadir patch is an optional, but common, way to hide the tripod in a 360 video. The dictionary definition of "nadir" is the point of a celestial body, such as the earth, that is lowest down from the observer. So, for example, if you were standing at the north pole, the nadir for you would be the south pole. With a classic 360 video nadir, the observers are in the center of a hollow sphere with a scene projected around them, but the nadir is still at the bottom of the sphere.

A 360 video nadir patch is typically circular and often displays a logo and credits for the videographer or production company. But it can also be a photo of the ground on which the tripod stood. If the ground or floor of your video shoot is uniform enough – for example, a field of grass, a uniform pavement, or a single-colored carpet – you can take a photo of that ground after your shoot and after removing the tripod.

Whether you create your patch from scratch or use a photo, it needs to be saved as a PNG (Portable Graphics Format) file, with the background set to be transparent. You or your favorite graphic design buddy can do this fairly easily in Adobe Illustrator.

Create a graphic in Illustrator that has a 1–2 pixel circle, and put anything you want inside the circle (text, the photo of the ground you took, or a logo). Just make sure there is *nothing* outside that circle. Then, choose File > Export As > PNG. On the confirmation page, make sure the background around the circle appears transparent (it should have white and gray checkerboard marks). You can avoid pixelation in the text by setting the resolution to 300 pixels per inch.

Next, import the PNG into Adobe Premiere, and drag it into your scene. It will initially appear right in the middle of the video. You can use the effect controls to change the size of the patch. It's a good rule of thumb to make it as small as it can possibly be to cover the tripod – lest your VR viewers feel like they're sitting on top of a dinner plate!

You should also change the duration of the effect in the timeline so that it appears throughout the entire video. You can do that by simply clicking and dragging the left and right edges of the image in the timeline so that they appear throughout the entire timeline.

Initially, your patch will look distorted in VR mode instead of like a circle. You can fix that by – guess what – applying the same VR Plane to Sphere effect that you use for text. Instead of dragging the effect onto a piece of text, just drag it onto the image in the PNG timeline.

The last step is to move the patch to the bottom of the screen. Find the VR Plane to Sphere Effect control and open the Rotate Projection section. Change Projection Tilt (X-axis) to 90 degrees, and it will move to the bottom.

Now you're ready to export your video. Use the following parameters in the export screen:

- Width and height: 3840 × 1920 (note: this is the definition of 4K).
- Format: H.264.
- Make sure "Video is VR" and "Monoscopic" are selected at the very bottom of the export pane. If you fail to select Video is VR, 360 video services such as YouTube won't be able to display your video as a 360 video.

Your video will export as an MP4. Once you have it, you can upload it to YouTube and the service will automatically display it as a 360 video. If you have an Oculus headset, you can install the YouTube VR app and find your video to view it. Just make sure that you set the video to be public, not unlisted, or you won't be able to find it in the YouTube app's search.

Case Study: Using 360 Tours to Promote an Underused Trail System

Kate took my class in 2018, and she decided she wanted to do something with 360 photography. The problem she decided to focus on was underutilized trails in her Connecticut town. Knowing that Facebook had native support for 360 video, she wondered: could 360 videos of the trails on Facebook help build awareness of this great natural resource, and actually drive people to get out and hike them? The park system already published 2D photos of the trails, but they had never done anything with 360 video.

She checked with a local trail steward and a town planner, and they confirmed that they were having a hard time getting people interested in using the trails. One said that many weren't even aware that there were trails within a short walking distance of their homes.

She purchased a $145 Insta360 Nano camera S, which she chose because it would automatically process images and it integrated with her model of iPhone. Then she headed out to a trail that goes by an old cranberry bog. At each point, she captured 360 video and 2D video.

She published the videos on her Facebook page and began asking local people to try them both out, ultimately getting feedback from an impressive 79 respondents. She asked two questions:

1. "After watching the 360 video, did you feel immersed in nature?"
2. "After watching the 360 video, are you more likely to visit one of Tolland's 13 public conservation areas?"

Eighty-seven percent of the people who watched the 360 video said yes, while 67% of those who watched the 2D video said yes.

In addition, 73% of those who watched the 360 video reported that it made them feel more immersed in nature.

She was especially excited to see the qualitative feedback from people, which included some emphatically stating how they felt like they were actually there in the trails, or "being wrapped in nature." But at the same time, a minority reported feeling sick, or that they didn't feel immersed at all.

Finally, she shared the results with the Conservation Commission. "I'm very pleased that so many people responded. . . . Anytime we can have more people learning about the trails and be more user-friendly, that's a good thing," he reported.

Read more about Kate's field test at https://emergingmediaplatforms. com/chapter8

Expert Interview: Thomas Seymat

Thomas Seymat is currently a Projects Editor and Development Manager for Euronews, a European-based visual news network that publishes in 12 languages. In June 2016, Seymat conceptualized, launched, and managed a 360 video portal for Euronews that ultimately resulted in over 200 pieces of immersive content. I asked him to talk about that experience, how he landed that role, and his thoughts on innovation and intrapreneurship.

DP: *How did you find yourself running something as large as Euronews' 360 video program?*

TS: I was just a regular digital journalist, and my boss sent me to cover a trade show at the Cannes Film Festival in 2015. There were a bunch of people in suits looking at deals, Netflix was just coming up, and all those sorts of industry events.

There was a panel discussion on 360 video, and I was like, "Oh, that's amazing!" It was this whole new media innovation, a new iteration of video with the VR headset, and with the phone. YouTube was also getting into the space as well with Google Cardboard. So there were lots of things going on. I immediately thought it was all very interesting.

It took about six months of badgering my boss for him to let me actually apply for funding from Google through their Innovation Fund. We asked for almost 1 million Euro, and we got half of that. Then all of a sudden, we had to deliver a three-year-long project, and I became the project manager.

I had no idea what to do. That's how we got into producing a lot of content rather fast, because we had milestones to meet in the industry innovation project.

DP: *So you had asked for the money, they gave it to you, lit it on fire, and you had to produce something quickly?*

TS: Exactly. At the same time, we also had a deal with Samsung with their 360 camera and the Samsung Galaxy S8. Through a deal that included some of my colleagues from the sales team, I went to South Korea and eventually we got some more funding. We had very strict content objectives and we had to co-brand videos, but it was basically the same type of deal [as with Google].

DP: *So your company wasn't looking into 360, but you discovered it and then sold them on trying something with 360?*

TS: Yeah, exactly.

DP: *So what did you remember about what happened between you pitching your boss on this, and being able to apply for funding – if you can go back that far? . . . I'm sure you didn't just walk into your boss's office and say, "Hey, can I have a million euros?"*

TS: So first of all, outside of work, I was already really into [360] as an emerging technology.

I read a report from the Tow Center, where they looked at ten projects that had been published so far at that time using 360. I realized that with Euronews' focus on multilingualism, we could have an early mover advantage in using 360 across several languages including Greek, Hungarian, Arabic, Farsi, Portuguese, and Spanish. So, you know, there was a space for us.

There's also the fact that internally, I had earlier managed a couple of innovative projects, including the rollout and implementation of a live blog solution. Being known as a little bit of a digital Sherpa, being able to bring some new tools into the newsroom, helped. My boss already had identified me as such.

My boss decided that we should submit some fundraising proposals. He had some ideas, and I came up with a whole package.

I had done a bit of benchmarking and I noticed that these types of projects always had six-figure production budgets, long turnovers, were always in just one language, and incorporated CGI. We thought, let's go the other way completely: short turnaround using the platforms we already have with audiences that are ready to maximize ROI (Return on Investment).

The language angle was, of course, a big selling point. And at the same time, there was a strategic interest because we had just gotten a new shareholder and the company had renewed digital ambitions. . . . The new company tagline was "All Views." So pitching this as a medium where you can have a multitude of perspectives on a single event based on where you look when you are in a 360 scene kind of helped to sell it as giving the audience more of the story.

The last convincing I did was to get a VR headset to my boss's boss, and he put it on. He was kind of like a kid with it, and he played with it for ten minutes. It wasn't the defining factor or the decisive moment, but it helped.

DP: *It always helps to let the boss try something new. Let's go back a little bit, because it sounds from what you are saying that 360 didn't come out of a vacuum. You had already built a reputation internally.*

What were you originally hired to do? Were you somebody who focused on new, innovative, and emerging things? Or did you kind of create that space for yourself? What did you do before you started moving into those emerging areas, and how did you navigate that?

TS: When I started at Euronews back in March 2012, I was one of their first six or seven fully digital journalists. The rest of the company was doing TV and reshuffling their TV scripts to go on the website.

I pitched myself as someone who could help them with social media, when Twitter was a big thing. I was also on Tumblr back then. And I had also done an international Masters in journalism, so my English was quite good.

Once I started, I stayed on the digital side. Initially, I was just producing content and helping others publish their articles, and helping them with social media a little bit. I was also the reference point for user-generated content verification.

We had a new boss come in 2015 and around that time, our CMS wasn't flexible at all. It took 15 minutes from the time something was updated in the CMS to when it showed up on the website. For this reason, Euronews had bought a live blogging solution. All of a sudden, they needed someone to implement it and train people.

I must say, I came to it with a bit of preconception about my TV colleagues. But actually, they were used to being live on TV for hours on end, commenting sometimes without a lot of info.

I told them: you don't have to speak all the time. You can take ten minutes to find some pictures and wire stories and update that on the live blog.

They got it really fast, and I think I learned as much from them as they learned from me. I was then identified as someone who was keen on those new technologies. Not just the technology and CMS, but how to use it to cover events.

DP: *It sounds like you really found a way to kind of translate that into the familiar patterns of the people who are working there. Which is always a big part of it, right? It's not just about technology, it's about someone's job and how to use the software that exists as gray matter in their heads.*

TS: Whatever extra value I brought in, I had to make sure that it would also fit other peoples' existing workflow or mental space, so to speak. They were used to doing live coverage for special events, so just adding a digital element to it with this new tool made it a lot more active.

I remember doing a 48-hour plus live coverage of the independence referendum in Scotland in six languages, for instance. All my colleagues would come in and live blog about it for two to three days.

DP: *One of the themes in this book is that not everything works the way you think it will. Sometimes things spectacularly fail, and you learn from those experiences. Do you remember a case where you thought you should go in this or that direction, and it resulted in everything going splat on the wall?*

TS: There's a lot of inertia [at Euronews] that sometimes stifles speed, because you can't do something for just one audience. Often, it had to be across 12 languages.

If we were covering the French election for instance, French speakers were not necessarily going to Euronews. Many were going to go to their own preferred media in France. And then, the colleagues working on those live blogs were seeing real-time numbers on who was watching the live blog. They weren't used to that because they're TV journalists, and that was sometimes de-motivating.

DP: *Hasn't that been true for a lot of early things on the Internet? I remember that happening in the newspaper world when we first started putting things online. It was the first time that print journalists could really see how many (or few) people were reading their individual stories, and it resulted in that same deflated ego issue you're talking about.*

TS: Back then, our reporting system's metrics were not where they are today. But with the live blogging solution, suddenly you could see how few people were there [on certain stories].

There was this small number, but then I started looking a little bit deeper into the metrics and looking at time spent. I'd take average time spent and total time spent divided by minutes and divided by 24, and then you real-ized that this modest number of people would spend days and even weeks in the live blogs. So that was a way for my colleagues to understand that yes, it worked in some ways.

The numbers were higher with coverage of tragic circumstances, such as the November 13, 2015, attack in Paris. At this point, the figures start to matter a little bit less, but it's nice to see that you're actually doing it for something.

DP: *The metrics that work in one medium aren't the ones that work in a new medium, right? You really have to take a look at what's unique about them. Speaking of metrics, a lot of early 360 projects have gone on hold in newsrooms. What are your thoughts on that? Where do you see 360 in the Hype Cycle?*

TS: The hype for 360 is no longer there. But I feel like at the same point where people were starting to get drawn out of it, we had reached maturity regarding something that is technically sound, journalistically correct, and engaging.

Maybe it was due to the fact that when we started, people said 360 is new and you can do whatever you want. But the audience wasn't necessarily as open.

360 is also a demanding medium. You can't just scroll through a 360 video like you do on Twitter, TikTok, or Instagram. All those user interfaces have been tailored to increase engagement through a very easy swipe movement. Even on your phone, just turning your phone around to view a 360 is already more demanding than swiping.

DP: *It seems like the rumor exists every year, but lately a lot of people with con-nections are saying next year Apple will finally release a VR headset. Do you see that changing things?*

TS: Maybe, if they have a cool product with the cool factor, and it's not too expen-sive. The content is going to be key, of course, but I'm not holding my breath. And I don't think it's going to be focused on 360 video.

DP: *What about the ethics of 360? Is it OK to just put someone in the middle of a war zone?*

TS: We have an ethics guide for TV, and we adapted it for 360. Showing someone severely wounded or showing a dead body was a no-go for us. With 360 video we weren't as daring to send someone to the front line. . . . Back in 2016, we sent someone near the front line of Eastern Ukraine in the no-man's land, and you can see villages completely bombed out and destroyed, but there are no bodies.

We also focused on privacy, which is obviously linked to ethics. When filming in public in France, you can't film kids without their parents' consent, even in a news environment. Fortunately, the quality of the cameras we were using was not that great, so people were not very identifiable.

If we go into someone's house with a 360 camera, we have to tell them that if you have a basket of dirty laundry in the corner, it's going to capture that.

DP: **What advice do you have for a student or media producer who is just starting out, and wants to move into working with emerging technologies?**

TS: I would say that you need to be at the right place at the right time. There's some luck involved in a resource-constrained environment to be given the resources to experiment with something new. It's not an opportunity that's granted to everyone.

Preparation is also important. Luck favors the bold but if you're prepared, it's easier for you to seize the opportunity.

You need to be OK with leaving your comfort zone as well, and maybe you're going to have to nerd out a little bit.

DP: **What's one thing in the technology space that really scares you, and what's something that gives you a lot of hope?**

TS: Well, we haven't mentioned the M word, the company Meta and the Metaverse. The scale of what Meta has promised, and building these permanent worlds that are interconnected with real life, with the involvement of a for-profit company that is already very good at monetizing activities online, I don't think is ideal. But who else has the capital to make a $10 billion bet on people having Zoom meetings in the Metaverse?

But what I think is something that gives me hope is companies giving people the tools to build those Metaverse worlds. No-code tools, or something you can build with limited technical knowledge.

A lot of my generation's first experiments with HTML was customizing MySpace pages. There are several companies working on building tools to make things in the Metaverse. This would unleash creativity and allow people to experiment – the same way DSLR cameras allowed so many people to get into photography. I'm hoping we're going to see this with immersive as a whole.

Online Resources for Chapter 8

Find more resources for Chapter 8 line at http://emergingmediaplatforms.com/chapter8.

Sources

360° video: Experience life on Ukraine's front line in Stanytsia Luhanska. (2016, August 5). www.youtube.com/watch?v=F157KztePwM&feature=youtu.be

A brief history of panoramic photography. (n.d.). Retrieved August 28, 2022, from www.loc.gov/collections/panoramic-photographs/articles-and-essays/a-brief-history-of-panoramic-photography/

Baker, B. (2022, May 3). *Spatial audio*. Retrieved October 24, 2022, from https://transom.org/2022/spatial-audio/

Chen, E. S. (1995, September). QuickTime VR: An image-based approach to virtual environment navigation. In *SIGGRAPH'95: Proceedings of the 22nd annual conference on computer graphics and interactive techniques*. https://doi.org/10.1145/218380.218395

Don't let go!. (2016, May 26). Retrieved October 24, 2022, from https://store.steampowered.com/app/519030/Dont_Let_Go/

Hannavy, J. (2008). *Encyclopedia of nineteenth-century photography*. Taylor & Francis Group.

Hendrix, C., & Barfield, W. (1996). The sense of presence within auditory virtual environments. *Presence: Teleoperators and Virtual Environments, 5*, 290–301. https://doi.org/10.1162/pres.1996.5.3.290

Immersive case study: Euronews 360 video. (2020, July 15). https://journalists.org/resources/immersive-case-study-euronews-360-video/

Kern, A. C., & Ellermeier, W. (2020, February 21). Audio in VR: Effects of a soundscape and movement-triggered step sounds on presence. *Frontiers in Robotics and AI, 7*. https://doi.org/10.3389/frobt.2020.00020

Presenting "harvest of change." (2014, February 21). www.usatoday.com/videos/news/nation/2014/09/21/15894879/

Snow, M. P., & Williges, R. C. (1998). Empirical models based on free-modulus magnitude estimation of perceived presence in virtual environments. *Human Factors: The Journal of the Human Factors and Ergonomics Society, 40*, 386–402. https://doi.org/10.1518/001872098779591395

9 Photogrammetry

Every once in a while, a truly paradigm-shifting technology comes along that has the potential to completely change the way we think about media. You never forget where you were when you encountered it, either by a friend showing it to you, reading about it in an article, or if you're lucky, meeting someone who created it.

I had such an experience in 2013, one year after starting my career as a journalism professor. A colleague of mine named Sean Branagan, who is one of the best curators of entrepreneurs and innovators that I know, invited me to a demo from a Cornell professor named Noah Snavely. In that demo, Snavely showed us all this software technique he had developed that would analyze hundreds of photos taken by different people of a city and generate "point cloud" models of them.

The example he showed, which you can still view online in a 2011 conference presentation he gave at MIT, took several hundred pictures of the old city of Dubrovnik to create a ghostly fly-through of the city. I say ghostly, because many of the buildings in the fly-through were destroyed in the 1990s during the Croatian War of Independence.

My jaw dropped during his presentation, and afterward I approached him with questions. "Noah, are you saying that if you have enough pictures taken by anyone of places that may not exist anymore, we can bring them back to life digitally?" He replied, "Yes, as long as they were taken from the right angles." I think I told him that he had invented a digital time machine, and he laughed.

He went on to explain how he didn't invent this method, but that he was using it in a way that was important to him because of his interest in his own family history in that part of the world. And he also told me the name of this approach: photogrammetry.

A Short History of Photogrammetry

Photogrammetry is the art of using multiple two-dimensional images to interpolate an object's three-dimensional data. While it has become more popular in recent years as a way to create 3D models for XR environments, it is hardly new. Its origins can be traced back to artists applying the rules of geometry to paintings to create an accurate perspective.

DOI: 10.4324/9781003247012-10

After the invention of photography in the 1800s, architects and map-makers realized they could interpolate angles and distances by analyzing the geometry of photographs taken of the same places from different angles. Over time, others realized they could use the same method to create topographical relief maps from aerial photos shot from balloons and airplanes.

Over the next hundred years or so, various mathematicians, architects, surveyors, and scientists perfected the algorithms used to interpolate perspective. After the invention of the computer, the math used for photogrammetry moved into software. At the same time, the defense and space industries figured out how to use lasers to measure depth for practical use cases, such as accurately docking a space transporter to a space station. LiDAR, a version of this type of laser scanning, is now starting to show up on iPhones.

The magic of photogrammetry remained largely out of the public's eye until the 2003 Invasion of Iraq when a startup named Keyhole created 3D virtual flyovers of Baghdad that were broadcast on CNN, ABC, and CBS to illustrate the progress of the war using photogrammetrically created 3D buildings. In 2004, Google purchased Keyhole and rebranded it as Google Earth, later followed by Microsoft and Apple both adding 3D buildings to their mapping services.

Even by this point, the idea of being able to create your own 3D models was considered to be out of the range of regular people. But in the 2010s, the introduction of creator-friendly software from companies like Autodesk and later Reality Capture made photogrammetry accessible to creatives working in architecture, mining, and media. And in the 2020s, there are now multiple mobile phone-based apps that are either inexpensive or free that anyone can use to capture 3D models as easily as taking a photo.

Photogrammetry in Education and Media

One of the early industries to experiment with photogrammetry for the general public is museums, which have been investing heavily over the last couple of decades into 3D scanning their collections. As part of museums' larger digitization efforts, photogrammetry and laser scanning serves multiple purposes. Scanning preserves cultural heritage long after artifacts break down, but it also makes more items from their collections available than could ever be possible in physical gallery spaces.

The Smithsonian Institution is at the forefront of this movement with a whole website called Smithsonian 3D (https://3d.si.edu/) dedicated to making its collections available online. The institution has 155 million artifacts in its collection, and is only able to exhibit 1% of them in gallery spaces at any one time. Its wildly ambitious goal is to ultimately scan everything in its collection. This is no small feat, as the 3D team says that it would take 300 years to scan every object even if they were able to scan one item per minute.

So far, the museum provides 2,613 high-quality models on its website along with annotations, articles, and other information. In essence, it serves as a digital expression of their museums, in some cases giving access to objects and spaces that aren't available to the general public in person.

For example, when you open the 3D scanned Apollo 11 Command Module, you can zoom in to go inside it. Since the Smithsonian allows the public to download these models, with a little coding you can even create your own virtual reality experience where you go inside the module, just as if you were astronaut Neil Armstrong.

Hundreds of other museums around the world are doing the same thing, so much so that in 2015 the 3D model hosting service Sketchfab created a program specifically for museums. Over 20,000 such cultural models are available for re-use under Creative Commons licenses.

Media companies began to follow museums around 2017, using photogrammetry to 3D image all kinds of newsworthy objects and incorporate them into multimedia stories. FRONTLINE, NOVA, and Emblematic Group launched Greenland Melting about the science of climate change, using photogrammetry to put viewers inside a NASA research plane and ship in virtual reality. USA TODAY launched multiple experiments, including an immersive augmented reality feature about iconic Hollywood costumes. And The New York Times created a piece about China Town, 3D scanning an entire street and overlaying it with historical photos from the early 1900s.

While the storytelling techniques for 3D models are very diverse, what they all share in common is that the object or space itself serves as the centerpiece of the story. In this way, the story is revealed much in the same way that information is conveyed in a museum: through interaction.

Users are invited to interact with objects, and information in the form of annotations, articles, audio, or even animations of the scanned objects themselves are triggered by those interactions. This is a fundamentally different method of storytelling, and something that I prefer to call story-experiencing. Just like in a video game, the exploration itself is what allows the viewer to discover information. If crafted well, the story reveals itself through the experiencer's agency.

The Architecture of 3D Models

3D models come in all different types of formats, many of which were created for different industries – architecture, media, gaming, you name it. For this reason, working with 3D models can sometimes be a complicated and occasionally infuriating process. Just ask any of the students I've had who have delved into 3D and they'll tell you the same thing. But they'll also probably tell you that it's worth it when you get something to work.

3D models generally consist of two components. The *mesh* is like a work of origami that is folded into many thousands of triangles in order to create the three-dimensional shape of something; and the *texture map* is like a picture of the outside of an object, but with everything splayed out like a Pablo Picasso cubist painting.

It is common for software and services to lose the texture map, so whenever you obtain a 3D model make sure you see a JPG or PNG somewhere that contains what looks like a texture. In some formats, the texture is baked into the 3D model file itself, but it's usually included as a separate image which you need to later "wrap" around the model in whatever program you're using. As long as the texture was created at the same time as the model, it will usually automatically wrap around the object in a uniform way.

A few 3D model formats have slowly emerged as preferred for media:

- **OBJ**: This format is like the lingua franca for *working with* 3D models. If you create, capture, or discover a 3D model and want to use it for anything, always grab the OBJ file. Almost every 3D program and website you use will be able to read it.
- **FBX**: An FBX is similar to an OBJ, but optimized for Autodesk which is a popular 3D model creator from the gaming industry. Like OBJ, for the purposes of storytelling it typically serves only as a source file that you turn into something else, with one exception. The Unity gaming engine has native support for FBX.
- **PLY:** Like OBJ and FBX, this is another source file. Some mobile photogrammetry apps use PLY as a default.
- **GLB** or **GLTF**: These files, known as Graphics Language Transmission Format, are native to the web. Created by the Khronos Group 3D Formats Working Group, a nonprofit consortium dedicated to interoperability of 3D formats, it is widely supported by anything that uses a web browser. That browser can be on a computer, or on a phone, or even on other types of devices such as smartwatches. As long as the device has a standard web browser, JavaScript code libraries can be used to surface the file in the browser.
- **USDZ**: This relative newcomer of a format, which stands for Universal Scene Description, is based on a format open sourced by Pixar in 2016. Apple officially launched USDZ in 2018 with iOS12 for use with augmented reality on Apple devices.

In the sea of formats, the important thing to remember is that there's typically always a way to convert from one format to another. But currently, doing so often means using several different programs in tandem – opening the file in one, saving in a different format, and sometimes opening that latest format in yet another program, making some modifications, and saving it again.

Using Photogrammetry to Capture Objects

Regardless of the method you use for photogrammetry – desktop software or mobile apps – there are some hard and fast rules for getting good outputs. Keep in mind that photogrammetry software is constantly evolving, and many of the "don'ts" on this list will likely be fixed with software over time.

   Multiple Photos: The general approach, whether you're taking photos directly or using an app that handles the capture for you, is to get photos around the object from multiple angles – ideally with about 30% overlap between each photo. If you can imagine an invisible sphere or cube around the object, you can "paint the sphere" with overlapping photos. Some photogrammetry apps automatically display a sphere for you, and you move your phone around the virtual sphere until you've covered every spot. In my experience, you need at least 100 photos – but possibly as much as 300 – to get a good model, so be ready to take your time.

Uniform Lighting: Lighting must be both adequate and uniform. You don't need extremely bright light, but if you're shooting indoors, make sure that there are enough lights above and around your object. If you're outdoors, any light will work but you will have the best results on a slightly overcast day.

Uniform Focus: Similar to lighting, the focus of the camera for each picture must not change. This can be tricky if you're using your smartphone or an automatic digital camera to take photos, because their cameras constantly adjust focus. This is where mobile photogrammetry apps can be helpful, as they control the focus (or try to) as you're getting the required angles that you need.

Minimize Glass and Reflection: This is probably the trickiest limitation of photogrammetry to manage. Glass and shiny surfaces such as metal will most likely confuse the algorithms, and the resulting model will look slightly melted. Some metal is OK, as long as it's brushed or has some kind of texture. A chrome toaster is simply not going to work, but a brushed mattefinish metal toaster may. If you can't avoid glass, one method that sometimes works is to use gaffer tape to put a few small X patterns on the glass.

Hair and Fur: If you're scanning a person (and yes, you can do that with photogrammetry!), or something with animal fur or carpet, you will have varying degrees of success. The fur of stuffed animals tends to come out extremely well, but some types of hair or hairstyles can look almost like plastic or silly putty. If your subject has a very "busy" hairstyle, you can bet that it's going to come out funny, but someone with a recent tightly cropped haircut will look normal.

Avoid Plants: Leaves on plants tend to always come out funny – especially lots of small leaves. If you can avoid or remove plants, you will have better results. The exception is plants with a few, larger appendages such as succulents.

Using Photogrammetry to Capture Spaces

For capturing a space, such as a room, many of the earlier rules apply. The exception is how you take the photos.

You may assume that you should point the camera at the walls or stand in the center of the room with the camera pointing out – just as if you were shooting a 360 video. But I have found that it's better to stand with your back against each wall and take photos with the camera pointing at the center of the room.

Go around the room two or three times. The first time, have your camera pointed straight ahead. The second time, have it slightly angled toward the ceiling. And the third time, have it slightly angled toward the floor.

3D Model Editing and Formatting

While the photogrammetry space is rapidly evolving, at the time of this writing it was still important to do some light editing of the 3D models that come out of photogrammetry software and apps. And by editing, brace yourself because editing a 3D model is definitely a brain stretch for someone who has never spent much time with 3D.

One of the things I have learned over the years is that students in my classes who have spent a lot of time in 3D games with builder capabilities, such as The Sims or Minecraft, have an easier time editing 3D models.

If you have done neither, I have a suggestion. Carve out a couple of hours of your day and spend some time building 3D models at Tinkercad.com. Tinkercad is a tool that's created for 3D printing, but the interface is so simple that almost anyone – especially a child – can figure it out.

In Tinkercad, you start with primitive objects, such as spheres, cubes, and cylinders, and put them on a surface. Each object can either be a "solid," which means it's visible, or a "hole," which carves its shape out of whatever shape it intersects with. So, for example, if you want to make the shape of a bead, you add a sphere and a cylinder that intersects with the sphere. Set the cylinder to be a hole, and you now have a round bead with a hole through it.

After spending some time with Tinkercad, you can graduate to Blender, a free open-source program that lets you do almost anything imaginable with 3D models. The interface in Blender is a beast, and it will make you angry at times. On the website for this book, I have some tutorials and videos that show you very focused "tunnels" to optimize the polygon count and size of models, and save them in the formats you need for XR storytelling. You can also find many tutorials for optimizing 3D models on YouTube.

Workbook Exercise 9.1: Photogrammetry From Your Phone

You can experiment with photogrammetry using a number of mobile apps. Some are free, while others charge a few dollars for the app or per export, or a small monthly subscription.

As of the writing of this book, I can recommend three apps, all of which let you capture impressive 3D models that you can use in stories:

- **Trnio** (www.trnio.com/): iOS Only. Trnio also has a very good pro app called Trnio Plus. As of the publication of this book, Trnio basic was available for a one-time US$4.99 fee, and Trnio Plus cost US$9.99 per month or US$71.99/year. Trnio basic is best for objects, but the Plus version can also be used to capture environments such as a room or an intricate doorway.
- **Qlone** (www.qlone.pro/): iOS and Android. Qlone works only with objects, and they must be small enough to fit on a matte that you print

on a standard-sized piece of paper. You can now scan without a matte, but the object size is similarly limited.

- **Polycam** (https://poly.cam/): iOS, Android, and Web. Polycam works great for both objects and spaces, and as of publication offered the highest quality models of these three apps. But after the first few three models, you are required to pay a subscription fee that costs a few dollars per month or about US$60 per year.

In all three apps, the best quality model will be created on cloud servers rather than right on the phone. You must tell the app to process the model from photos and/or LiDAR data the app collected, then wait for the model to process in the company's servers and then download it to your phone. This typically takes from between a few hours to, sometimes, a day or more.

If you have a phone with a LiDAR sensor, you will have the ability to create the scan from photos or using LiDAR. Generally speaking, using photos works better for objects, and LiDAR works better for environments such as an entire room. But as they say in the car industry, your mileage may vary. For every new photogrammetry project you start, it's good to do a few tests using both methods just to see what works best for the particular object or environment you're attempting to image.

When you see your completed model in your chosen app, you'll want to inspect it from different angles to make sure all surfaces were rendered equally.

Figure 9.1 What the Trnio Plus app sees for a typical indoor scene on an iPhone 13 Pro. From left to right: the visual picture from the phone's camera; the augmented reality capture using AR Capture; and the structural data from the phone's LiDAR sensors.

Workbook Exercise 9.2: Upload and Embed a 3D Model

Once you have a 3D model, it's not much more work to embed it into a web page. You can use one of the models you captured in the 7.1 exercise, but you can also use a royalty-free model from Sketchfab's Cultural Heritage and History archive.

To bring up a list of freely available models, click Explore on Sketchfab and choose Cultural Heritage and History, and then check the "Download-able" filter. To protect yourself from unintentional copyright violation, it's also a good idea to check the "CC-BY" and "CC-SA" licenses, which allow commercial use with attribution to the author.

Once you find a model that works for your story, click the link to download it and then select "GLB" or "Autoconverted GLTF" as the format. Note that you will very likely need to optimize the model to reduce its number of polygons, as well as the size of the image that makes up its texture map. Go here to find a Glitch that you can remix to edit: https://emergingmediaplatforms.com/chapter9.

If you already followed the steps from a previous chapter to set up a GitHub repository, you can upload your GLB file there and create a URL to it. Just make sure the file is under 20 MB. Replace the file name of the default GLB in the index.html file with the URL to the new file you added. You should then be able to move around the model using your mouse and arrow keys, right in the browser.

After your model is live online, you can use HTML embed tags to include it in a story on whatever platform you use – WordPress, Weebly, your newsroom's CMS, or even HTML code that you write.

I've taught this for a while, so I can already see some of you asking: "Ugh, is there a no-code way to do all this?" And the answer is a little bit of yes, and no.

I talked about Sketchfab earlier. If you have a scanned model in any of the apps listed earlier, there should be an Upload to Sketchfab button in it. You will need to enter an API key for your Sketchfab account, which you can get from your account page on their site. After that, models upload directly from the app into Sketchfab, and you get a link that you can share with anyone. Sounds easy, right?

The downside of this approach is that Sketchfab only allows so many free model uploads per month before they charge a monthly subscription fee. Costs are not exorbitant (US$15/month at publication of this book) but still higher than most streaming services you may pay for. For just experimenting, using a free account to upload will cost you nothing. You can then embed the code for the 3D model into practically any web-based content management system such as WordPress just like you would a YouTube video.

Workbook Exercise 9.3: Put a 3D Model in a Mozilla Hub

In Chapter 4, we went over how to create Mozilla Hubs. In Exercise 4.2, you learned how to browse a collection of models in Sketchfab and add them to your VR scene. How do you add your own 3D models?

Thankfully, if you were successful in getting your model into the GLB format and it's under 20 MB, you're nearly finished. Enter Spoke and edit the hub you created. Select Model in the Elements pane and place the default model (which will be a rubber duck) where you want your model to appear. In the info pane to the right, change the Model URL to what you uploaded – either to GitHub or to Sketchfab.

For example, at this link you can find a scan I created of a Little Free Library in my neighborhood park. Open the link you find there in a new tab, and then add it to your Mozilla Hubs scene: www.emergingmediaplatforms. com/chapter9.

If you're afraid of GitHub and you uploaded your model to Sketchfab, you can make it appear in a hub using the main URL for viewing the model. But you first need to make it publicly downloadable. To do this, choose Edit Properties in Sketchfab, and then toggle the Download option to Free. After a few minutes, a Download button will appear on the model's page. That's your sign that you can add the model's URL to Hubs.

Expert Interview: Ken Harper and Sonny Cirasuolo

DAN PACHECO (DP): **Alright, I'm joined here by Professor Ken Harper who I've worked with for almost a decade now. And Sonny Cirasuolo, who is an alum of the Newhouse School, was a student of mine, and has been doing some really cool stuff with photogrammetry, among other things.**

Please introduce yourselves and tell us what you've done in your career and how you got here.

KEN HARPER (KH): Sure. My name is Ken Harper. I'm an Associate Professor of Visual Communications at Syracuse University, as well as the Director of the Newhouse Center for Global Engagement. And I've been teaching at Newhouse for about 15 years now.

DP: **And what did you do before Academia?**

KH: My background is in photojournalism, and it greatly informs what excites me today. I got my undergraduate degree in photojournalism from Western Kentucky University. As I moved along in my career, my first job opportunity was in design. I'd had one design class, but I said, "Well, cool, alright, I need a job."

I didn't have anywhere to live, just having come back from studying abroad, and I ended up learning graphic design and page layout in Chicago for Copley Press.

At that time, a new product had just been released called Future Splash and it ended up becoming Macromedia Flash. That got me interested in interactive design and movements and new technology, and how visual communications can really be dynamic and exciting.

I've worked at newspapers all around the country; I worked at MSNBC for a while; I've worked on projects for the United Nations and NGOs, and worked extensively in various countries throughout Africa. Eventually, it led me to actually working in the commercial sector for a company called Answer Think, where I was an interactive designer doing commercial work for companies like Bausch and Lomb and New York Life.

After being laid off several times from newspapers, I got a job offer at the Newhouse School, teaching interactive design. Since that time I've been able to do really interesting, exciting work, especially internationally. And I think the power of visual communications is what really drives me.

With all the diversity of thought and the way we walk around the world, I've found that visual communications is a bridge that helps cross those divides no matter where you're coming at it from.

DP: *Sonny, why don't you say a little bit about yourself?*

SONNY CIRASUOLO (SC): My name is Sunny Cirasuolo. I'm a pretty recent graduate of Syracuse University in the Newhouse School. I graduated in 2021, and directly after graduation, I started working for Yahoo Sports as an augmented reality and video producer. And now I currently work as a creative technologist and XR engineer for a startup called Nowhere. Prior to all that, I was a research assistant for you during my senior year. I got to research WebXR, AR, and VR, and that was what really showed me that I could do this as a career.

XR and AR in general are things that I've always been interested in ever since the first VR headset started coming out, and Oculus first announced their headset. I was always inspired by photogrammetry as well. Back in ninth grade, me and my buddies tried to make 3D models of each others' faces using photogrammetry apps. They were horrible, but we thought it was the coolest thing ever. We even tried to 3D-print little action figures of ourselves.

I went to Syracuse starting off as a mechanical engineer, so I always had a 3D-modeling aspect to my education starting from my first year of high school. But even back then, we always asked, "How can we make this more artistic?" rather than just using it for engineering. There wasn't a way to do that just yet, but eventually that came.

DP: *I didn't know that you had experimented with photogrammetry earlier when you were in high school. When you first started to play with the technology it was really bad, but you kept with it over time. You saw some future possibility in it, and you stuck with it?*

SC: Yeah. The ability to take something that physically exists in our real world and bring that into a digital space in a photorealistic way is very powerful. You can show people something you couldn't show them otherwise, and give them an experience that they couldn't experience otherwise.

Going back to high school, we could barely get any models to work. I think we were using Autodesk Inventor, and we were trying to import it as an FBX and print it out as a 3D-printed file to make a little action figure of our teacher. We just had a great time doing it, even though it didn't work. But we sort of all saw the potential for it.

DP: *Then in college, I know that you and Professor Harper did some photogrammetry experimentation together. Ken, how did you get into photogrammetry?*

KH: What really makes me excited about new technology is just being around cool humans who aren't afraid of failing and are just excited about creating new stuff. It brings people that have energy together.

I was lucky enough when you came on board to reignite my excitement about doing innovative technology and be a part of that. Dan, you, and I were doing all those things with 360 and 3D-printing rigs to combine GoPro cameras together. That was all very frustrating, exciting, fun, and interesting.

In 2016, photogrammetry just started becoming more accessible with the release of the professional-grade app, RealityCapture. I just needed a project to try it out on. In 2018, I took a number of high school and graduate students from Syracuse to Makhanda (formerly Grahamstown) South Africa, to do collaborative storytelling with community members.

One of those community member organizations was in the Joza Township, called the Egazini Outreach Project. They are housed in a former police interrogation building where they used to actually hold and torture residents during the apartheid regime. Subsequently, artists took over this space and converted it into art studios. I was so blown away by that transformation, and I'm like, "How can I take this with me?"

We had some really great students with us and were able to basically get a whole bunch of people to work on capturing a whole lot of photographs of this space. It was one of the dumbest ways to possibly do it. We didn't know what we were doing, but that didn't stop us. We ended up with two terabytes of still photographs, way more than is needed to get a good model.

We brought it back, and a student named Aubrey Moore was able to go in and make this really cool 3D model that made us go, "Wow, this is interesting." It was a little janky, but we learned a ton and it just opened up our eyes.

Fast forward about a year and a half, and Sonny came on the scene. He was clearly a leader in this space. I was working with a local artist, illustrator, and sculptor named Jaleel Campbell here in Syracuse who does all kinds of interesting work in the Black community. Jaleel has worked with us on addressing issues around art and culture, race, and justice. As we've been working with artists alongside in South Africa, we were like, "Well, how can we bring these two communities together?"

So I said, "Hey, Sonny, you've done so much photogrammetry. Can we transport people into Jaleel's gallery space?" And so we went there and spent many nights photographing every nook and cranny of his space. Sonny, I remember you being really sweaty.

SC: Oh yeah. No, that was fun.

KH: Running out of batteries and using our phones . . .

SC: I remember being very hungry at certain times. I'm like, "I've been here for like seven hours."

DP: **Wow. That's dedication.**

KH: Yeah, exactly. Jaleel is super cool and was so excited to be able to do something unique. This was a technology that could be used as a bridge to bring people together, to do something unique. The results were actually decent enough certainly to make us go, "Wow, there's so much here."

Coming from photojournalism, with photography being my first love, it was all about meeting people. It wasn't really about the photography. I mean, the photo was this great artifact that came out of a moment that you got to share with other people.

I think the specific cross-section between photography, technology, and experiencing things together, makes photogrammetry exciting. It's really the future, and that makes me pumped. But really, I just like working with cool folks like yourselves.

SC: It was a really good time. We both learned a lot doing that, especially about doing interior photogrammetry. It was difficult, but it was totally worth it. I think we got a pretty good outcome.

KH: One of the things I found awesome about this, being a tenured assistant professor, is that titles don't mean crap. I just want to learn stuff. Sonny knows more than I do in many areas. I know more than Sonny does in other areas, and that's cool. That doesn't intimidate me or make me upset. It makes me excited.

Sonny shows me things that he's learned going deep into these neat, niche areas. I can then take that back to the classroom and share that with new students. That to me is awesome.

DP: **When I saw what you were doing with Egazini and Jaleel's studio, I thought this approach could be a good focus for a school project called Deconstructing the Divide, and I pulled Sonny in to focus on that. The section that you, Amanda Paule, and I worked on, Sonny, was called Visualizing 81 and you 3D-scanned the inside and outside of the People's AME Church of Zion. Can you talk about that a little?**

SC: Of course. I think we started with the outside of that building actually, and that went through a couple of renditions. The first thing we did was on our phones to see how it's gonna turn out, and then went back and shot with a DSLR. We had to do a little bit of cleanup on the roof, which was challenging because we couldn't fly a drone due to FAA regulations in that area.

I tried to climb the parking garage next to it and get on top of the roof and some of the other buildings, but they wouldn't let me. So we decided to stay on the ground and get decently far away from the buildings to get some of the roofs in there. We got a decent model that turned out pretty well. But the much more challenging part was inside because it was pitch black and there was no electricity.

Figure 9.2 Sonny Cirasuolo and Amanda Paule using a 60-megapixel camera with ring flash to 3D capture the inside of the People's AME Church of Zion in Syracuse, New York.

(*Source:* Photo/Dan Pacheco)

DP: **And I remember that there were years of bird feathers and rat excrement all over the place.**

SC: Oh yeah. When you think of a dilapidated, disgusting, creepy, terrifying old building, that's exactly what it was. With photogrammetry, lighting and the crispness of the photo is very important. In a dark environment, it would be very difficult to take a lot of photos with just a minute or two minutes of exposure time, which you'd need to do without special equipment, and get the 1,000 photos that you need to get a good model.

We had to buy a special thing called a ring flash, along with a few other pieces of equipment, and polarized filters for both the ring flash and the camera. That way we wouldn't have any glare.

We used ten-second exposures. The raw photogrammetry model from Reality Capture ended up being amazing. At the same time, Amanda ended up getting some great photos that we used in the story as well.

It was challenging, but again, we learned a lot. I learned a lot about using specified equipment to achieve certain tasks; especially in low-light environments, those ring flashes are really helpful.

DP: *We talked about how there were these early mobile photogrammetry apps weren't that great. And then along came Reality Capture, which runs on a high-end Windows PC and uses DSLR photos. But now things are coming full circle back to mobile.*

   Ken, you, and I have done a lot of tinkering with mobile photogrammetry lately. Do you want to talk about what you can do on your phone now, especially with LiDAR?

KH: Oh, it's crazy!

   I use an app called Polycam that lets me get a scan in a few minutes that just a couple of years ago would have taken hours; That with Apple coming up with their mixed reality headset, and Object Capture on the server side to process photogrammetry models, there's a lot of potential for mobile photogrammetry.

   The person who's been a leader in the community who got me interested in the mobile side of it is Azad Balabanian. He just bangs away at things and does YouTube tutorials on how to do it all after he figures it out. When I saw that, I went, "Wait, you can use your phone? That's amazing."

   Now he's working with Realities.io, a German photogrammetry studio, and he's the brain behind Puzzling Places which takes detailed photogrammetry models and turns them into interactive puzzles for VR. The community of people working in this space is really amazing.

DP: *There's also Trnio Plus, which is pretty good too. I use it because they gave us access to the Beta.*

KH: I've grown to appreciate Polycam because they have a really active Discord community with hundreds of people answering questions, critiquing scans, and coming up with new feature ideas. That modern sense of community behind a startup is really there.

   There's this guy, Brent Underwood, who's revitalizing a ghost town called Cerro Gordo in California. He's, like, rebuilding it. Polycam partnered with him to go into the old, decommissioned mines and these old buildings, and do 3D scans. And they did a whole YouTube episode about that.

DP: *As a professionally trained photographer, do you feel like this is the next evolution of photography?*

KH: 100%. Still photography is poetry, and no one's ever going to take that away. Photogrammetry has its own unique form of beauty. Recently, I found myself in Iceland with my son, Rio, for his birthday. We went hiking, and I found myself doing photogrammetry captures of things in the landscape instead of taking still pictures. It's like my new scrapbook.

   I think it's great because I can project it in AR, right through my phone into different spaces, and go back and relive being in those places. I can mix it together with video footage. It reinvigorates this really wonderful classic tradition of photography in a way that makes me want to stay up really late and learn new things.

DP: *It makes me wonder if 20 years from now we'll be looking through our photo archives, and what we will call them. We'll have all these 3D captures. Will we even call our current 2D photos "photos," or will we call them something else, like "flatties"?*

It's like how early movies had no audio, and then when audio came to movies they called them "talkies," and then the old ones were renamed "silent movies."

KH: Yeah, I could see that happening. I think there will always be a place for still photography. It's an art. But this is a different kind of art. I think the complexity will increase, with Apple developing their mixed reality headset and others coming out with all this new technology that's gonna be more accessible over time.

DP: *So . . . can we talk a little bit about the potential dark sides of this technology?*

SC: I had a potential segue there, to be quite honest. With all this photogrammetry becoming very easily accessible on phones, the implications or potential possibilities for using DALL·E (an AI image generator) to supplement photogrammetry is awesome, but it's also pretty scary.

You can use DALL·E to fill in textures that you're missing because you couldn't get to that part of the room. The fact that you can clean up your photogrammetry work using AI is pretty cool.

KH: If you think about fake news and deception, AI generation certainly opens up a whole other can of worms as to the possibilities. There's a modern Twilight Zone-like warning in all this about the kind of reality that we may be leaning into a little more than we want to. And that's why I think it's important that good people who are excited about technology are also the stewards of this space. . . . There are great people who are using this technology for good, and they need to be the guardians of using it for something that is helpful, not harmful.

DP: *Do you ever worry about fake news evolving into fake experiences, especially with all this focus on the Metaverse?*

KH: It's going to happen.

DP: *With cameras everywhere, even on peoples' doorbells, what's to stop any of these companies that collect that data from using it to create 3D models of people? Could there already be digital twins of all of us and everything being created right now, and we don't even know it?*

The ethics around this, such as what you think should and hopefully can be done to prevent those kinds of misuses of this most personal data, is important. Other than our minds and souls, our bodies are our most personal, private data.

SC: Yes and no though, right? We put our bodies out on social media for everybody in 2D form all the time. I get what you're saying, but at the same time, people seem so eager to share their 2D bodies digitally. Maybe they'll be just as eager to share their 3D bodies.

DP: *Maybe, maybe not.*

SC: Maybe not.

DP: *But I think it's worth educating people about what's possible and how it can be used – for good or for bad.*

SC: There are already companies that let you take a capture of yourself, and you get a perfect 8K resolution scan of yourself back. Now imagine in the future that you can sell yourself to be used in movies, or sell yourself to be used in video games.

Rather than having to cast extras in the background of movies, a director could be like, "I want this specific type of person" and go through a catalog of ten thousand of them. If you get chosen, now you get a royalty check for being in that movie. If somebody in a video game wants to use you as a character, they can pay you for it.

DP: *The digital human marketplace.*

SC: There very well will be a digital human marketplace for selling the use of your own persona in video games and media across the Metaverse. And if you don't want to, you probably will be able to lock that down.

DALL·E currently blocks out the ability to create faces. But if they wanted to, they could stop blocking that and probably generate 3D meshes of all of us. Which is scary. It doesn't scare me that much, but I can see how it could scare a lot of people.

In the future, I think we're going to all want to go out and get better, higher-resolution models made of ourselves so they can be used in 3D.

DP: *Or how about if they could just be used as our own avatars that we control in the Metaverse? It's already happening to some degree in Spatial.io. To even use the tool, you have to create a simple 3D scan of your face and they put that onto your avatar.*

It seems logical that this will eventually move to your full body. In the current versions of the Metaverse, in the year 2022, our avatars don't have legs, and everybody comments on how weird that feels. People want to see full bodies in Metaverse worlds.

Sonny, I know that you've also been looking into NFTs. I've had some students who have thought about this idea of bringing 3D capture together with NFTs. How do you see photogrammetry living as NFTs in whatever the Metaverse becomes in the future?

SC: I think you really hit the nail on the head right there with NFTs and photogrammetry, especially 3D assets and NFTs. . . . The ability to buy and sell digital goods in a way where there are only a certain number of copies is pretty unique. But I think there's a lot of potential for 3D sports collectibles as NFTs.

When somebody hits a home run, the player wants to keep the home run ball for themselves. But if you scan it, now you have a one-to-one digital copy of it. You can sell it as an NFT.

Same thing for every single piece of sports memorabilia in the Hall of Fame, or in the back rooms that nobody ever gets to see. Imagine them doing a digital exhibit of everything in the back catalogs that nobody ever gets to see because it's never on the shelves, and they don't have room. In the future, maybe you'll be able to buy it and display it in your own Metaverse.

DP: *Museums are doing that already with their collections. With cultural heritage, Sketchfab has a whole category around that in a program. But in this case, it's the potential commercialization of that kind of material beyond museums.*

KH: There are limitless possibilities in the commercial world. I see this as an opportunity to even lessen the need for traveling. These types of virtual experiences could lessen the carbon in the atmosphere. For people who want to experience something, this gives you a whole other opportunity to create those visceral photorealistic 3D experiences without having to leave your home.

CyArk (www.cyark.org/) has instances where ISIS had blown up world heritage sites, or they'd been destroyed by earthquakes. But they have an actual 3D record of those things that can be reproduced. I think that's really, really exciting.

I give a lot of credit to early thinkers about this in entertainment, like David Lynch, with his series Wild Palms. It's basically a soap opera that uses technology to project holographic 3D images into your room. People fell in love with interacting with the stories' characters, and mayhem ensued.

I think that's exactly where things are going, and that's great and terrifying, like most things. I think there's just an interesting gradient of opportunities here, from entertainment to fashion to journalism. As this becomes more readily available, how fast can you do something that actually looks pretty good? That seems to be evolving very quickly from where it was not that long ago.

DP: *Definitely. Last question: what's something on the horizon that excites you?*

SC: The accessibility of it all excites me. Everybody is going to be able to create photogrammetry a lot more easily in the next five years, and everybody's going to be able to view it as AR content.

The number one thing that excites me is AR glasses. They're coming soon, and with that comes realistic accessibility to everyone for this type of content. I've been creating so much AR for two years, and currently only a certain portion of the population actually sees it because only certain people have the technology in their hands to make it look realistic in AR. When that increases to a number where a large percentage of our population is seeing this stuff, it's going to be pretty cool.

DP: *Alright. What about you, Ken?*

KH: I'd echo that, and expand it to accessibility throughout different parts of the world – especially to different socio-economic groups, such as in the Global South.

Things like mobile banking were famously invented on the continent of Africa. For instance, this technology will be getting into the hands of folks in developing countries like Nigeria. My friend who is a photojournalist there discovered photogrammetry just a few weeks ago and is already cranking out models like nobody's business.

I think people are going to come at it from whole different angles in the Global South. I can see people getting together there, banging on new ideas and new technology, and helping make the world a richer place.

Online Resources for Chapter 9

Find more resources for Chapter 9 line at http://emergingmediaplatforms.com/chapter9.

Sources

Chinatown: Time travel through a New York gem. (2020, December 2). www.nytimes.com/interactive/2020/12/02/arts/design/chinatown-virtual-walk-tour.html

Cultural heritage & history 3D models. (n.d.). *Categories*. Retrieved August 28, 2022, from https://sketchfab.com/3d-models/categories/cultural-heritage-history

Google acquires keyhole. (2004, October 27). *Wall Street Journal*. https://www.wsj.com/articles/SB109888284313557107

Meet 2011 TR35 winner Noah Snavely. (2011, December 2). www.youtube.com/watch?v=r8PlpABP6Mk

Photogrammetry. (n.d.). *Close range surveys and mapping*. Retrieved August 25, 2022, from www.close-range.com/docs/History_of_Photogrammetry–Dermanis.pdf

Realities.io. (n.d.). Puzzling places. www.realities.io/puzzling-places

Roose, K. (2022, August 24). We need to talk about how good A.I. is getting. *The New York Times*. www.nytimes.com/2022/08/24/technology/ai-technology-progress.html

Spring, A. P. (2020). A history of laser scanning, part 1: Space and defense applications. *Photogrammetric Engineering & Remote Sensing, 86*(7), 419–429.

Storytelling in new dimensions. (2022, August 16). *Syracuse.Edu*. www.syracuse.edu/stories/sonny-cirasuolo-newhouse-virtual-reality/

10 Data, AI, Automation, and Bots

One of the most rapidly developing categories of technology is the automation of content based on data analysis, machine learning, and artificial intelligence. And it's been happening for a while now, at least ten years in journalism and even longer in business analytics and data science.

As just one example, in 2018, Google's Digital News Innovation Fund supported an organization called RADAR, which stands for "Reporters and Data and Robots." In its first 18 months, RADAR filed 250,000 articles that were published in digital, print, and broadcast media in the United Kingdom and Ireland.

When people who make their living by writing, reporting, and publishing hear stats like this, a chill goes through the room. You can sense the palpable fear of an Asimovian robot rebellion that takes over journalists' jobs and eventually turns them into batteries, like in The Matrix.

But what's happening is actually quite different from that. In my opinion, the term "AI" itself is part of the problem because at least at this point, there is nothing even remotely "intelligent" about what these programs are doing.

If anything, they're just the latest iteration of Computer Assisted Reporting, in the same category of what has been happening since the 1980s when journalists began using spreadsheets and databases instead of file folders full of printed documents. Today, automation has evolved to also help journalists with boring, repetitive types of stories like quarterly reports, SEC filings, high school sports stats, political race results, and government statistics. If data are published anywhere in a predictable and standardized way, they can be reformatted to read more like something a human wrote.

The real innovation that's happening in AI has to do with data, some of which is structured and some of which has structure added to it by algorithms, that flows into standardized story templates.

You can think of AI like a more sophisticated version of the Mad Libs you may have played with as a kid. But instead of writing silly stories about your friends, it's spitting out a weather story that looks almost exactly the same that it was reported a month or a year ago – just with different temperatures and specific weather events.

The larger category of this technology is what's known as Natural Language Generation (NLG) which was originally developed to help business analytics firms

DOI: 10.4324/9781003247012-11

to deliver business intelligence to clients in a form that was more enjoyable to read than loads of spreadsheets.

NLG began to appear in the news industry in the early 2010s. The Associated Press was one of the early adopters, partnering with a company called Automated Insights to produce stories on corporate earnings reports. In 2014, the AP began experimenting with automating earnings reports so that its human business reporters would have more time to analyze larger trends.

But even now, over eight years later, AI program managers tend to preface any news about their innovations with a plea for calm. For example, in a story published on Poynter in October 2021, the AP's AI lead Aimee Rinehart was quoted as saying, "We are not building tools to replace people. We are building tools to automate tasks and hopefully broker opportunities for journalists to do deeper, richer reporting." And only after that did she address what the AP was actually doing with AI.

Moving Past the Fear and Into the Practical

Regardless of how you feel about AI, try for a moment to believe that it's not going to replace your job. Instead, imagine that it's going to help make your job even easier to perform, freeing you from rote repetition and left-brain tasks, and allowing you to be more efficient and creative.

And it can go beyond the reporting aspects. Maybe it can also handle some audience outreach, taking the information you feed into it and sharing it in well-written tweets – in fact, using language that you wrote yourself, as if you were writing a news-based Mad Lib template.

AI means that your job as the journalist just got a lot easier. Instead of becoming an even bigger slave to feeding the social media beast, you can dig even deeper into stories and data, identify trends and patterns, and then connect those data points to templates, WordPress blogs, social media feeds, and more.

Want to modify the style of the thousands of stories that go out? Instead of rewriting thousands of stories, you update a few templates.

Does your publication publish in multiple languages, and in multiple countries? No problem, just create a template in the language for each audience.

Do you want a version for kids that uses more kid-friendly language? That's another template.

Want to quickly get out stories about every high school football game in a large city? Odds are that you can make just a few templates, and have them updated based on nothing but box scores.

This is exactly how "AI" or "Automated Journalism" works in the field. The tools that make it easy often have a high subscription price that's focused on the enterprise news market (like the AP or BBC), but there are some free tools that you can use to play around with this idea of data–template–audience workflow described earlier.

Finding and Analyzing Data

Before you can feed data into templates, well, you need to find some data. There are entire books about data and data journalism, and in fact I teach a whole separate class about this called Foundations of Data and Digital Journalism. The following is a very high-level summary of how to find and analyze data.

The first fundamental skill you need to spend some time developing is working with spreadsheets like Microsoft's Excel. In recent years, many journalists have been shifting from Excel to Google Sheets. It not only works very similarly to Excel but also uses APIs to integrate with a large number of services. Once you have a spreadsheet in Google Sheets in the right format, and the data are clean, you can connect it to those services and the data flow right in or out.

You can see a very basic example of this through the Knight Lab's Timeline tool, which automates the layout of an interactive timeline by using data that are in a Google Sheet. You can find it here: https://timeline.knightlab.com/.

The timeline tool walks you through how to set things up and even gives you a link to a Google Sheet template. Update the template, share the link and paste it into the Timeline interface – and voila, you have an interactive timeline. See? What you may have thought was a scary robot bent on taking over your job is just a cool visual tool that automates layout from data.

A lot of data in journalism comes from public sources, just as governments or nonprofits. Many governments around the world now provide public data in "machine-readable formats," which is shorthand for what programs like spreadsheets can read. The key to something being machine readable is that each distinct type of information is separated into its own "field" through a "delimiter."

Let's say that we want to automate stories about the number and types of crimes committed in a particular city. If the local police department simply uploads PDFs of crime reports for that week, a piece of software can't easily read it. You need to have those data in a format like this:

```
Date, 1/1/2022, 1/2/2022, 1/3/2022
Murders, 0, 1, 2
Stabbings, 4, 1, 3
Shootings, 0, 5, 3
```

For each line, which is called a "record," you have a label (date, murders, etc.) and numbers (dates, number of stabbings, number of shootings).

The individual pieces of data are separated by using a comma as the delimiter.

This is a very common type of machine-readable data known as a Comma-Separated Values file, or. csv. You could type this out in a text editor like Sublime Text, save it as "crimes.csv," and then you have a CSV file. Another less common format is TSV, which uses tabs as delimiters. And very occasionally a pipe (|) is used.

If you were to upload the CSV into a spreadsheet, each of the data points would flow neatly into columns and rows, like it does here in Google Sheets:

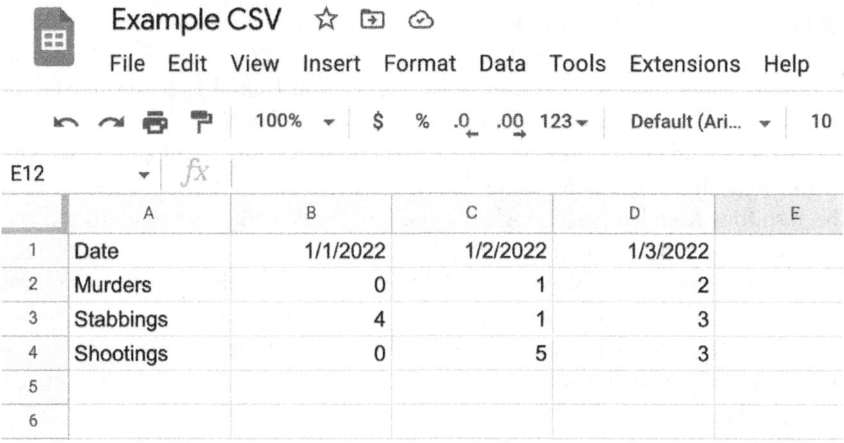

Figure 10.1 How data appear inside a spreadsheet program. This is from Google Sheets, but you could just as easily use Excel.

(*Source:* Screen capture/Google Sheets. Used with permission.)

In this example, the Date, Murders, Stabbings, and Shootings are in a row, but most tools will want them to be column headers. To rotate it so that headers are at the top, select all the data and copy it, and then go to blank cells. Right-click and choose Edit > Paste Special > Transform. Remove the other columns and rows so that only the data you want to use appears, all starting at cell A1.

If the data you find are only available in a PDF, or worse, in printouts that you have to scan into PDFs, there are tools out there that will try to extract individual data fields (a process known as parsing). But most are still rather expensive, and they require a lot of manual cleanup. In these cases, you may find yourself manually typing data into a spreadsheet.

The best way to practice using public data is to find a government website that specializes in data. In the United States, all federal agencies are required to make their data machine readable. You can find those datasets by going to http://data. gov and finding the agency that collects the data.

Many cities and counties also have their own public data sites, and you can find them by going to the municipal websites and looking for a "Data" item in the menu. Or, go to a search engine and search for the city name along with "open data."

Once you find an open data portal for the agency or location you're researching, look for a tab at the top labeled "Data," or some way to search or browse through what they have. What you want to look for is a preview that shows the fielded data in a spreadsheet view, right in the browser. If the data work for the story you want to tell, look for a Download button and choose CSV as the format. If you don't see CSV, Excel may work – but an Excel file may have more visual formatting that you will have to remove. Both CSV and Excel can be uploaded into Google Sheets.

A good rule of thumb is to make sure the grid of columns and rows is even. If you see one column or row span across two spots, you will need to remove that from the spreadsheet which is not always straightforward. This is the main reason that I advocate for seeking a CSV file, as a CSV doesn't support that kind of formatting.

Creating Charts With Datawrapper and Flourish Charts

Data visualization has become more popular in recent years, largely driven by software and services that make it easy. Datawrapper (http://datawrapper.de), a company based out of Germany, offers a number of attractive-looking charts and graphs, as well as some animated visualizations, and is used by a number of news sites large and small. Flourish Studio (http://flourish.studio) is another with a more magazine style.

Commercial news sites usually pay for subscriptions that remove the Datawrapper or Flourish branding, but you as a student or hobbyist can create the same types of charts for free.

Datawrapper is particularly easy to use. The first step is to copy and paste a data table. If you copy only the column headers and rows that contain the data you want to visualize, you can paste it into the site and it will import your data into fields. Next, you choose a chart type. If it looks a little off at first, scroll down and click a small link labeled "transpose the data," and you will see it rotate to the right.

The AI behind Datawrapper does a lot of guessing to figure out which chart and configuration are best for the data you gave it. Most of the time, it gets it right, but sometimes it makes the wrong choice. You can usually override its choices in secondary tabs on the chart step.

Finally, you go to the Publish and Embed step. Click Publish Now, and then scroll down to find the Embed code. You can put this Embed code right into HTML for a story that you can then publish to your GitHub Page.

You can also typically embed the code into a company Content Management System or WordPress, though sometimes these CMSs will prevent you from doing that for JavaScript security reasons.

Flourish works in a very similar way, with data import, visualize, and publish steps. I mention it because it has some more fun, dynamic types of visualizations. A few examples are as follows:

- **Bar Chart Race:** Shows the changes in different categories of a story over time, and how they evolve.
- **Chord Diagram:** Shows the relationship of items to each other around a circle. This has been used to visualize relational data, such as how many times different Supreme Court justices agree with each other or not.
- **Sports:** Visualizes a player's position on a field or court.
- **Survey:** Represents survey results on a petri dish which reorganizes itself when you select different categories. For example, you can re-sort it by gender, age groups, and so forth.

In all of these cases, don't assume there's only one type of chart you can or should use for each type of story. Have fun and try different things. This could even be a field test, where you compare different types of charts for the same story and see how chart choice impacts understanding.

Application Programming Interfaces

One of the most common types of automation is for data that's published or updated in one service to magically flow over to another. Serious software coders usually accomplish this by using an Application Programming Interface (API). An API is a set of instructions to coders to pull data from a service or to push it to them.

Fully taking advantage of an API typically requires a base knowledge of a true programming language such as Python. But sometimes you just need to create what's known as an API Key which you give to another application that pushes and pulls data for you.

You can learn about what a service's API will let you do by finding its API documentation. Sometimes you'll find a link to the documentation in the navigation of the site itself, but often it's on another domain with "developer" in the title. For example, here are the developer documentation links for Facebook, Twitter, and Sketchfab:

- **Facebook/Meta:** https://developers.facebook.com/docs/
- **Twitter:** https://developer.twitter.com/en/docs/twitter-api
- **Sketchfab:** https://sketchfab.com/developers

Even if you don't have any programming skills, simply knowing that a service has an API is useful because you can dream up ways to use data you get from a service to create another type of information service.

One extremely common utility for APIs is aggregation – pulling headlines, paragraphs, and photos that are shared about a topic in disparate places and aggregating them in a single place. Another is to log in to a service using the account of another – such as the "Log in with Google" or "Log in with Facebook" buttons you're probably familiar with.

IFTTT and Zapier

Since most creative media people don't know programming languages, a new type of middleware has emerged that provides an interface for non-coders and allows them to create automated workflows that move information from one place to another. They tap into the APIs of multiple services and program the hooks between them for you, so all you have to do is click a few buttons and modify a template.

The two most common API middleware services are IFTTT (http://ifttt.com) and Zapier (http://zapier.com). Started just one year apart, in 2010 and 2011, respectively, they have emerged as a kind of lingua franca for moving data around the Internet.

IFTTT stands for "If This, Then That," and its automations are called Applets. When you click Create, you see large "This" and "That" links. Click on the "This," and you see a list of products and services that give IFTTT access to their APIs.

For example, if you want something to happen when someone posts something on Twitter, you select Twitter. You then see a variety of actions that can trigger a "That" to your "This." A few examples are as follows:

- New tweet by you.
- A new tweet by a specific user.
- A new tweet by anyone in an area.

After you make your choice and enter other information about what you want it to look for, you click on the "That" button.

Let's say you want to automatically save every new tweet – including the deleted ones – from a local politician. For the "That," you could choose Google Sheets, and then Add Row to a Spreadsheet.

At this point, you will see a template – just like what we talked about at the beginning of this chapter. For the spreadsheet name, you'll see a formula like this:

Tweets by @{{UserName}}
{{UserName}} will be replaced by the politician's Twitter handle that you
    entered in the This step.

Under that is a Formatted Row section, and it lets you add what IFTTT calls Ingredients to it. For the Google Sheets app, the available ingredients are

{{CreatedAt}} ||| @{{UserName}} ||| {{Text}} ||| {{LinkToTweet}}

In the template, you enter three pipes (|||) to indicate where the next set of data should go into another column. And below that you will see other information you can have pulled from Twitter, such as the embed code for the tweet.

When you're done, click Create Action. It will run within an hour and will be saved as an Applet in your account. It will continue to run on a periodic basis for as long as you have it turned on.

In 2016, when United States President Trump was elected, I set up such an IFTTT recipe that was focused on the @RealDonaldTrump account. For the next four years, it saved every tweet – as well as deleted and re-posted tweets – Trump ever posted. This became useful when he would delete something he was criticized for and re-post it with an edit. I still have a copy of that spreadsheet. It generated at least 4 worksheets of around 1,000 rows each over the next few years before I turned it off.

Another nice feature of IFTTT is the Explore tab, which lets you find and use Applets others made. Anyone – including you – who wants their Applets to appear in this list just has to toggle a Publish button when setting up the Applet.

One interesting thing to consider is that you can string Applets together, with the action from one Applet triggering something to happen with another. For example, if you wanted to publish such tweets into WordPress but don't see that option in a service's "That" list, you can make two Applets: One that pushes the Tweet to Google Sheets, and another that pushes updates to that Google Sheet to WordPress. You could even create a third Applet that posts a link to that Word-Press post back to Twitter!

Zapier works almost the same way, but its apps are called Zaps or Workflows. The trigger (If in IFTTT) is called an Event, and what happens after that trigger is called an Action. Zapier also has an Explore tab to find other Zaps and get inspired.

Airtable

Let's be honest: most people really hate spreadsheets. OK, maybe not everyone, but they don't tend to get people excited. There's a reason data visualization has grown in popularity: people prefer pictures over words, and definitely both over pages and pages of tightly packed numbers.

Airtable is like the spreadsheet tool for spreadsheet haters. Started in 2012, it combines typical spreadsheet functions with a friendlier interface and a powerful database behind it. Airtable doesn't even use the term "spreadsheet." It refers to a dataset as a Base.

Another nice feature of Airtable is that each cell can contain more than just numbers or text. An Airtable cell, which it refers to as a Field, can be a checkbox, phone number, email address, drop-down list, or even a full file such as a Word or PDF document or image.

Airtable works with Zapier and can send and receive data to and from other services using it. But it also has a more sophisticated type of integration that it calls an Extension. Extensions are like little programs companies offer to Airtable that create something or perform some task. Beyond what Zapier alone can do, an Extension can potentially create an entire new information product.

As just one example, the SendGrid extension is worth a look. SendGrid is an email delivery service that both increases the chances that mass emails won't be seen as spam and allows customization and personalization of the emails using – you guessed it – templates.

Here's a real-world example of how you could use Airtable and the SendGrid extension on election night. Let's say you set up a Base that has fields for every election precinct in your town, with other fields for every candidate running in those precincts. You could set up an automated email as a SendGrid template that goes out to all of the members of your audience sharing the latest results.

The SendGrid template would look something like this:

Hi, {First Name}!

It's {TimeStamp} on {Date}. Here are the latest results for {Precinct}:

{Candidate1}: {Votes}
{Candidate2}: {Votes}
{Candidate3}: {Votes}

You can get the latest updates from our site here: {Sitelink}

In other words, it's an election-night Mad Lib!

Airtable also lets you create public views of some of the data in your Base, and share that link with your audience. You can also choose which columns to display in a public view, and which not to. This can be particularly useful if you have a lot of broad-based data in a base but want to share only certain information with specific audiences.

The visual look and field of views are somewhat customizable. But if you want to go old school, AirTable also offers a Page Designer extension that automates the creation of PDFs with a layout you design and populates each page with data that comes from a different row of the Base.

One last feature I want to highlight in Airtable is its forms, which can be very useful for crowdsourcing information from practically anyone. You can add a form for any Base and choose which fields you want to surface in the form. In the magazine world, this is used a lot to manage freelancers and their submissions.

As with IFTTT and Zapier, AirTable lets people publicly share Bases they have set up as templates that others can use, and they're categorized by industry. You can browse many of the Bases people have created for journalism and publishing here:

*   www.airtable.com/universe/category/journalism-and-publishing

Case Study: The Bloomfield Information Project

In the 15 years leading up to 2020, more than 25% of the newspapers in the United States disappeared, according to the News Deserts report from the University of North Carolina's Hussman School of Journalism and Media. This allowed even more misinformation to spread, as peoples' appetite for information didn't diminish and was replaced by fake news and rumors.

This was the case in Bloomfield, New Jersey. At the start of the COVID-19 pandemic, Simon Galperin, who runs the nonprofit Community Info Coop (www.infodistricts.org/), saw that his community was particularly suffering from lack of local information. In a listening session, residents said the information they received was coming from a variety of sources, but there was no single reliable source.

The Coop used a combination of Crowdtangle, a service by Meta that helps analyze and report what's posted across social media sites, Google Sheets and Zapier to generate newsletters that contain stories aggregated from multiple sources. Some of those come from county and municipal press releases, which are automatically parsed into fielded data using a service called Mailparser.io.

As reported in Zapier's blog, the site wouldn't be possible for the nonprofit to create due to all the manual work that would be required to aggregate and publish everything by hand. They use Zaps and connected services to automate much of the work. Human beings can identify and tag articles, but the actual publishing is largely handled with AI.

You can view and use the Bloomfield Information Project's Zaps on the Zapier blog:

- https://zapier.com/blog/how-a-journalist-uses-automation/

Workbook Exercise 10.1: Envision an Automated Workflow

Think of a news desert near you (maybe even your hometown), or choose one from one of the maps on USNewsdeserts.com: www.usnewsdeserts.com/. Remember that a news desert doesn't mean there's no news at all. It can also be an area with only one source of news, or a source that is under-resourced.

Next, spend some time on Google, Twitter, and Facebook and identify at least three reputable sources of information in that community. They can be any of the following:

- City and county websites
- News providers
- Nonprofits
- Social media influencers
- Schools

Write up the steps you would have to manually go through in order to aggregate and publish information gathered from these places. The more detailed you can get, the better. For example, if you find county press releases on budget meetings, examine the style of the releases and look for standard and repeatable patterns in them. Do they have a regular headline? Date? Several paragraphs with the most important information at the top? If you see a clear pattern, note that as a candidate for automation.

Now, write up a workflow for who the content needs to go to, and where, all the way until it reaches your intended audience. Be sure to address the following:

- What triggers content to be identified as a candidate for republication?
- Who chooses what is republished?
- Where do they review candidate content – in a Google Sheet, Airtable, or somewhere else?
- Where does editing happen, if at all?
- What is the final publication form – a website, an email newsletter, a social media post?
- What simply cannot be automated and requires human involvement?

Finally, look through Zapier and IFTTT and identify which services can be used to move information through your workflow for the tasks you listed.

Conversational Interfaces

Now that you have an understanding of how data and templates can work together, and how APIs and middleware API services like Zapier can move data around, you're ready to learn about how to explore another new frontier: conversational interfaces.

Conversational interfaces cover all the ways in which templates, combined with more software such as Natural Language Processing, are used to make data appear to talk to us. The idea has been around for a while. For example, back in the days when I worked at AOL in 2000, a service called SmarterChild began communicating with users on the AOL Instant Messenger platform.

During that same period, we all began to be more acquainted with the universally loathed practice of automated customer service telephone agents. Fast forward to today, and it's almost impossible to get to a real human customer service agent without first tricking a phone bot to stop sending you in circles through a voice menu.

What makes conversational interfaces interesting to me as a media professional is the ones that people choose to talk to, for example, our phones. In 2011, Apple introduced this to the world through Siri, the chatty robotic friend available first in our pockets and later on our watches. Samsung followed with Bixby in 2012,

Amazon with the Alexa-powered Echo in 2015, and Android with the Google Assistant in 2016.

Facebook jumped into the space in 2016 by introducing text-based bots to its Messenger app, but along with Amazon went further by providing APIs and other methods for anyone to create bots (which are called Skills on Amazon) that people could discover and interact with.

While elements of the bot trend are definitely going through a typical Hype Cycle, with some firmly in the Trough of Disillusionment, in other areas they are beginning to become a normal part of how we all live, transact, and communicate. This is an area that in my opinion every journalist and media professional should continue watching and tinkering with, because it is already part of the fabric of society.

I'll close the instructional part of this chapter by going over two services that let you do just that, for free. But as a rapidly evolving space, keep your eyes peeled for new services over time. That's particularly important for voice.

Designing a Conversation Flow

Whether you want to create a text chatbot or a voice skill for something like Alexa, it's important to start by writing out the conversation flow you want to replicate. The easiest way to do that is with physical sticky notes. And if you have notes of different sizes and colors, that's even better. You can also use a variety of websites that simulate sticky notes, such as Stickies.io or even Google Drawings.

You don't have to write exactly what the bot will say or what the user's interaction buttons or prompts will be, but have a good idea in your head of the general topic of the conversation the bot will be having and what its purpose is. The more targeted its focus the better, because as you will see, making an effective bot that is about a broad topic can quickly turn into a plate of spaghetti!

Each communication from the bot will be written on one sticky, and you will arrange the stickies and move them around on a wall or table as you design your interface.

The very first part of the conversation will be the bot introducing itself and explaining how to interact with it. Label that sticky "Introduction" and put it on a wall or table.

Next, think of 2–3 button interactions, or in the case of Alexa, a word or phrase, that the user is invited to click or say to move to the next step. Write those words or phrases on smaller or different-colored stickies, and place them under the prompt.

Then, for those 2–3 interactions, pull out a new large sticky for each and briefly write how the bot will respond to the user's choice. Place them next to the right or underneath the corresponding button. You can keep doing this until you have a complete conversation, but be prepared to move stickies around a lot!

Remember also that your users can be stranded at the end of a conversation if you don't provide a way for them to get back to the beginning with, at the very least, a "Return to the beginning" or "Restart conversation" button.

Chat Fuel and Landbot

Once you have what you feel is a good conversation flow, you're ready to translate it into a bot creation tool.

Chat Fuel is a no-code platform for creating very interactive, informational bots that can be deployed to a Facebook Page or Instagram account. It also allows for some integrations with APIs to pull data in and send data out – for example, sending information people provide to a Google spreadsheet. And it does that using Zapier. Are you starting to see how all these services in this chapter fit together?

Before you can build a bot, you will need to make sure there's a Facebook Page in your Facebook account. You can do this by opening your Facebook account, scroll down on the left rail, and click "See all Pages and profiles." Click on Pages, and then Create a new Page. (Note that Facebook tends to move this functionality around a lot.)

Now, go to Chatfuel.com. After logging in with your Facebook account, click the button to Add a Blank Bot. You will see a "Page disconnected" message. Click Connect, and then choose the page you created on Facebook. Don't worry about the bot being visible on that page – it is hidden by default until you turn it on in a future step.

On the next screen, you can rename your bot and see a list of templates. Choose a template – Answer FAQ is a simple one – or select the + to the right and pick Create Blank Flow. From here, you can customize each card and add interactions.

A lot of the things you can do in this interface change over time, so at this point I recommend going through the site's Getting Started documentation, which you can find here.

- https://docs.chatfuel.com/

The one downside of Chat Fuel is that it only works through Facebook and Instagram, so both you and your users need to have Facebook or Instagram accounts. In my experience, the requirement of a Facebook account has become a bigger and bigger challenge as people either leave Facebook or try to avoid it. I have noticed this most with students from the European Union, which has stronger privacy laws than the United States and seems to educate its citizens more about the data privacy violations that Facebook and others have made over the years.

For those who have these concerns, it's good to remember that Messenger alone reaches 1.3 billion users each month, and Instagram has 2 billion active users per quarter. I personally think that it's worth at least creating a Facebook and Instagram account that you use only professionally so that you can experiment with engaging audiences through bots built with Chat Fuel.

But if you are adamant about avoiding Facebook, there are some other tools you can explore. They're not as interactive as Chat Fuel, and some work more like what I call a "Prompt Bot" because the user can only click on buttons but can never actually ask something in natural language.

The alternative my students have had the most luck with is Landbot.io. Like Chat Fuel, the bots are designed visually. Just remember to design your conversation flow without the user having to say anything to the bot.

Alexa Developer Console

Building an Alexa skill used to require some pretty heavy programming using an API. But in recent years, Amazon has been creating more user-friendly pathways to create skills that also include templates. You can find these in the Alexa Skill Developer Console.

Amazon has also been creating more documentation, including quickstart guides. I recommend that anyone wishing to build an Alexa skill start by going through their tutorials, which are constantly changing as the console improves. You can find those here: https://developer.amazon.com/en-US/alexa/alexa-skills-kit/ start.

In the console itself, you can start with templates that are designed to make it easy to create different skill types. The Knowledge template is the easiest to use, because you populate the list of questions and answers by modifying and uploading a spreadsheet. But if you choose Start from Scratch, you will see other templates such as a Fact Skill that spits out random facts from a list.

I'll be honest: it's not easy to create a more complex skill, and if you want to do that you will be spending a lot of time struggling through Amazon's very developer-centric interface. But it is possible. If nothing else, simply knowing what types of functionality is possible to surface in an Alexa skill is worth spending a few hours going through their interface, because when you hit a wall you'll know what to ask a more skilled developer to build for you.

Case Study: Using a Chatbot to Meet a Holocaust Survivor

Alina, an exchange student of mine from Germany, got very interested in chatbots. And the problem she thought she could solve with them was one of the most creative and delicate topics I've ever seen in a field test.

Like many people, and especially people in Germany, she was motivated to help do her part to make sure that humanity never forgets the Holocaust perpetrated by Nazi Germany during World War II. Denial of the Holocaust has sadly been increasing over time, and part of that is because people aren't exposed to the stories of survivors. As of 2022, only 195,000 Holocaust survivors were still alive and they had very few years left to tell their stories.

There have been several recent attempts to use technology to give people the feeling of talking to a Holocaust survivor, most notably in a project at the USC Shoah Foundation that allows people to ask questions of holographic survivors who have been recorded in 3D. It's a truly amazing project that gives people the feeling that they are interacting with a survivor, asking questions, and getting answers as recordings from the survivor's long interview. But to do that at scale is very expensive, and the virtual interviews have to be done in a special facility.

Alina thought: what if they could do the same thing with a chatbot? She talked to researchers who study Holocaust history and was referred to Ralph Rehbock, a survivor who was more than happy to sit down and talk with her.

She took his biography and broke it down into individual parts that could be delivered through cards using Landbot.io. She decided to use Landbot instead of Chat Fuel specifically so that people wouldn't have the experience of asking a question for which her bot didn't have an answer.

The bot had a picture of Mr. Rehbock, and "he" introduced himself. For example, the first interaction looked like this:

```
Hello and welcome to this virtual conversation with
Holocaust survivor Ralph Rehbock. Learn more about
his escape from Germany and his life as a survivor.

My name is Ralph Rehbock. Let me take you back to
my childhood in Germany.

   Choose an Option:

     Where in Germany where you born?

     How was your childhood in Germany?

My childhood in Germany was very peaceful. My par-
ents made sure that I don't get in touch with the
propaganda.

   When did these things get worse?

In 1938 the situation for Jews intensified and my
parents decided that we need to leave Germany.
```

Alina provided the narrative biography to one-half of testers, and the chatbot to the other half. Then she quizzed them. The group that learned through interacting with the chatbot answered more questions correctly than the group that read the narrative biography.

She went over the results with the historical experts who were guiding her, and they were impressed with the approach. They told her that these types of interactive conversations could be a good first approach for someone to learn about such a deep topic as the Holocaust, and that their emotional connection with a single survivor – even a virtualized one – could perhaps better prepare them to learn even more historical facts.

Case Study: Using Alexa to Teach Chinese History

Mayson was a junior from China studying in the United States, and he became fascinated with Alexa skills. For his field test, he decided to solve a problem that he noticed among his American friends. Almost none of them knew anything about China's long, rich history, and its many dynasties. In case you're wondering, in just China's ancient history, there have been 83 dynasties and 559 emperors!

His hypothesis was that people with no knowledge of Chinese history would understand and remember it better by interacting with an Alexa skill that quizzed them, rather than by listening to a lecture.

He used the Alexa Skill Developer Console to create a skill for his device, and focused it on three eras from ancient China. At the end of each era, he added a quiz that the learners would need to get right before they could advance to the next section.

If they got something wrong, the skill wouldn't give them the correct answer, but instead would repeat that particular history lesson. He believed this "gamification" level combined with the repetition would keep a learner more motivated to learn the material so that they could advance.

To measure its effectiveness, he recorded one long lecture with the same information, with a quiz at the end. In a test group of 16, he gave the long lecture recording to 8 of them, and the Alexa skill game to the other 8.

His results showed that those who used the game-based Alexa skill performed 43% better on the quizzes than those who listened to the single lecture. He also surveyed both groups, and the Alexa skill group reported feeling less anxious and more engaged when going through the skill. He later shared the Alexa skill with the lecture group and they reported similar feelings.

My own thoughts on this, based on what I know about how people learn, is that it makes sense that the self-guided interactive method – regardless of the technology that delivers it – is always bound to lead to better results. But perhaps this points to some best practices for self-guided, online learning in general.

One of the first things I remember learning when I began working as a professor came from a math professor, who adamantly told me, "People don't learn by listening to other people talk. They learn by trying and failing, and trying again." In this case, I would also add: perhaps they also learn better by playing a game with a robot.

Expert Interview: Bill Frischling

Bill Frischling and I met nearly right out of college, where we were working on a dial-up service run by The Washington Post called Digital Ink. That site soon transitioned to the Washingtonpost.com website, for which we both were on the launch team. We also worked closely with each other at America Online. He went on to start several companies, working as an innovator in residence at Gannett and US News.

Most recently, he started another company called Factba.se which databased all of Donald Trump's tweets and speeches, and then used AI tools such as sentiment analysis to analyze where Trump was possibly feeling uncomfortable or outright lying – at least according to what the algorithms determined. For the last few years, I have relied on Bill's advice on AI and where it's headed. He is unique in that he specializes in both AI and journalism. I hope you learn as much from this interview as I did from someone who I, and many others, consider to be among the sharpest minds on the planet.

DAN PACHECO (DP): **Welcome Bill! Can you tell us a little about your current job, and what you do on a daily basis?**

BILL FRISCHLING (BF): Certainly. I'm the Vice President of Alternative Data for FiscalNote. It's kind of an obscure title, but on Wall Street "alternative data" is the term used for anything that is not numbers or standard structured data – such as voice analysis, transcriptions, pulling data from SEC filings, sentiment, and so forth. We landed on alternative data because, sadly, "Mad Scientist" was vetoed.

DP: **But you actually had the title of Mad Scientist for Washingtonpost.com back in the day, so you can't shed any tears over that.**

BF: Fair enough!

DP: **How did FiscalNote come about?**

BF: I came into FiscalNote via the acquisition of FactSquared, a company I founded on January 5, 2017. My responsibility now is playing with new technology and doing version 1 prototypes that fit within the business. So I get to play – within boundaries – and identify areas of research and build them into prototypes which more often than not go live with the first client or two.

DP: *Fun! You are truly field testing the future. You've worked on a lot of things over the years, from databases to AI and natural language processing. Can you talk about one or two of your favorite jobs and what you learned from them?*

BF: There are two, my first and last.

Weatherbase (https://weatherbase.com) was how I learned to program in PHP. It's still running, and it pays for itself with ad revenue. The consulting that comes in from that is helping pay for college for my kids. It's ugly – two decades old – but still has great search engine optimization.

It also serves as the calling card for consulting by my spouse, who does statistical analyses of historical data tied to contract delays. Our largest clients build solar and wind farms and use our data, plus Jen's consulting, to argue for clawbacks if the weather event was a "force majeure" event. We can run all the data from what we still gather from Weatherbase. Some of my super old scripts are now 24 years old, and still work!

DP: *I remember when you launched that. You should know that I still use Weatherbase before I decide where to go on vacation, and when, because of all the historical data in there.*

BF: Happy to help! So my second favorite is Factba.se, which is what became the core of FactSquared. I basically databased everything Donald Trump ever said in public – every tweet, radio interview, TV interview, article, press conference, you name it – and made it searchable.

I then applied publicly available algorithms to that data to indicate when he might be not exactly telling the truth, when he was saying something he maybe didn't quite agree with, or when he felt uncomfortable. We started with Trump, but later began running the same algorithms past other public figures.

DP: *That's insanely cool! We'll get back to that project later, but I just want to note that you are clearly working right on the digital edge of AI.*

As you know, there's a lot of consternation about AI in the public consciousness. What direction do you see AI going in the future for journalism and media? Are robots going to take over our jobs? Are they going to make our jobs better?

BF: No, because there is no "real" AI yet. There's a trillion monkeys with typewriters. They're useful, but they're no smarter than your doorstop.

There is at least one significant development that hasn't happened yet that is preventing it from being considered true intelligence. What we're learning is that you don't need intelligence to write intelligently. If it ever does become truly intelligent, that's when things get scary.

DP: *What scares you about when true intelligence appears?*

BF: What scares me is that when that actually happens, what's AI going to learn from? Is it going to learn from the internet?

We've all seen the examples of what happens when you train AI without cleaning out data – it gets scary. But what concerns me even more is who is deciding what data are getting cleaned out. What happens when you start using AI models, and then you find that it was released by a particular political party that might have filtered out certain things for political reasons? That's a scenario we haven't encountered, but it's logical to assume that it will happen.

DP: *So what you're saying is what scares you most is not the actual technology, but the humans that are managing it behind the scenes? Interesting.*

BF: Correct. Like most tools, AI can't be "evil." It's how you use the tools that matters. We're going to run into problems we haven't even thought of yet. The example I always go back to when asked about this is in the 1990s with Tonya Harding and Nancy Kerrigan. News Day ran a cover story where they were both on the ice together, and everyone's like, "How did they get that?" Well, it turns out that was early Photoshop. News Day noted it was an illustration, but it looked real, and there was a big ruckus.

DP: *So it was like the beginning of fake news, low-tech version?*

BF: Exactly, to some extent. Fast forward to today, and we've been flooded to the point where people are worried about every single picture and whether or not it's fake.

Deep fakes are real. Can they fool most people? Yeah. Can they fool somebody who's looking really closely at them? Not for a second because it's painfully obvious when you examine two frames at a time. The errors stand out like a sore thumb. But, of course, most normal people aren't doing that, so they spread quickly.

My bigger concern is somebody eventually writing a history that says everything that's going on today is all disinformation that's being spread by governments, and various quasi-governmental organizations are boosting numbers like Twitter followers. You see someone on Twitter who has 3 million followers, but do they really? We don't have any good way to verify that yet.

DP: *So let's zoom out a little bit. Can you explain the difference between AI and Machine Learning?*

BF: AI is basically a misnomer. What we have now is Machine Learning. We have really smart algorithms. Some of them are centuries old, but there's now enough cheap computing power available that anyone with the skills can go set up a server on Amazon and build on those models.

There's a long list of them, but they're really old. If you just look at Google Translate as one example, the core of it comes from a project at Bell Labs from the 1940s. The core algorithms for speech recognition also go back to Bell Labs, in 1951.

The core of half of the cell phone technology in the world goes back to the 1940s from Hedy Lamarr, who was a mathematician in addition to an actress. She developed CDMA, which still underlies the networks.

These algorithms are all really old, but the technology is such that now you can go through a quadrillion permutations in a short period of time today, where that would have been impossible back then. That's why I say it's like a million monkeys with typewriters. That's how machine learning works. You tell the monkeys: "Here are a bunch of scenarios. Go run a trillion of them and tell me what's the best outcome, or what's best for this model." Then you use the resulting data.

All of that has nothing to do with AI. It has to do with being able to do a lot of calculations.

That being said, there's almost no difference because most people don't think of a dumb calculation as being able to write a coherent story. But a dumb calculation can write a coherent story if you throw enough data and power at it. That's kind of where we are today.

DP: *So then, what will make that machine learning actually intelligent?*

BF: There's no path that I've seen in research from people who are really looking hard at this. Nothing yet is passing even the theory stage of any of it being actual intelligence. The closest I've found is fuzzy logic that was big in Japan in the 1990s, but that died off. I keep waiting for somebody with way better math skills than I to resuscitate that.

DP: *So what about the current "AI" that talks to you and tries to be your friend? Meta just put something out publicly called BlenderBot 3, and I was talking with it. There's also an app called Replika that tries to be your digital avatar friend on your cell phone. Both feel like really needy people that try to guilt you into sharing private information with them – which is entirely unsurprising for Facebook, which bases its whole business around us sharing private details with each other that they then sell to advertisers.*

BF: It's all pathological media, but this is something that has been known for a couple of decades. If something is free and you're not sure how the company is making money, you're the product. If nobody has taken that to heart at this point, I don't know what to tell you.

I personally would love it if Facebook said, "Hey, here's your bill, it's $199 and we're not following you at all." Okay, at this stage of my life I'd write that check. But 20 years ago? No.

DP: *Some of these supposedly intelligent chatbots remind me of the series West-world, when Bernard is talking with Dolores and asking questions. And Dolores is happy to answer every probing question in detail, just talking and talking while Bernard takes careful notes. But in our case, we're Delores, and Bernard is the AI that's talking to us and getting us to spill our guts while Bernard analyzes it all.*

BF: Companies need data to survive. Where I work now, we've got hundreds of examples of earnings calls for other companies. When we went back and did sentiment analysis, we were able to predict with a high degree of likelihood that the CEO and the CFO didn't buy what they were saying about their earnings.

Sure enough, when we saw those indicators, we would watch a drop in their earnings the next quarter or two later. With Boeing, using ten years of data, we were able to see two standard deviations every time they talked about the 737 Max, and it correlated with exactly when they knew something was going on.

CNN eventually came out with a story where the executives said they had been informed about the potential problem, and that time period was six months before their first crash.

DP: *Couldn't this sort of start to border on the idea of pre-crime, as was explored in Minority Report, where sentiment analysis is directed at individual people, and a spike indicates that there's a 99% chance that someone is going to commit a crime? Do you think that is feasible?*

BF: We're using it now with public figures, and we can tell things about them just based on their tweets and press releases. For most people, you can tell a lot just from five things they say.

Donald Trump is interesting because he's an outlier in a lot of ways. In Washington, it's all dealing with very subtle things. When somebody says, "I strongly support you" or "I support you," in normal Washington speak, there is a world of difference between those two statements. The trick is that because we have a record of all their public statements and the audio and video that goes along with it, we can then correlate those shifts and interpret their tells. It's like playing poker.

Our system showed us that Mike Pence, whenever he was wrapping up a speech, would pause to make a joke. He would always walk to the left of the podium and put his right hand on top of his left hand. That was him saying, "I am done with this part of the speech, and I'm getting up to this next part of the speech."

Everybody is a creature of those habits, and it's just a matter of collecting that data. It's kind of obvious when you think about it. Now Vladimir Putin on the other hand looks like he's dead on our charts.

DP: *Interesting.*

BF: It's not based on what he's emoting. No matter what we run him through, we get a flat line. As far as voice stress level and his rate of speech, he is the most consistent person. But it's also been pointed out that he's probably had a couple of thousand hours of KGB training. That would make you pretty good at hiding your tells.

Could determining pre-crime be done? Yeah, probably for certain people. Will it be done? I don't know how feasible that is in the long term to be honest. It would require the equivalent of strapping everyone on the planet into a polygraph over decades.

When we look at Trump and say, "How does he talk about religion?" When analyzing 200 interviews across 30 years, we can look at the data and see the pattern, as opposed to sitting down with him for the first time. And by the way, Trump hates talking about God. It's like nails on a chalkboard for him.

DP: *I remember your post about that with the data. How does this kind of thing work for a journalist at some point? Could there be a future where Anderson Cooper sits down for an interview with a public figure for whom this sentiment data and these patterns are showing up on a dashboard that only he can see, where the journalist is sort of peeking into the minds of the interviewee?*

BF: The short answer is, yes. There's gonna be a lot of conversation about this kind of thing coming, because we're doing it now and we've been doing it for a few years. We know from talking to clients that this kind of stuff interests people, but are there a lot of takers? Not yet, because it's solving a problem that people don't realize they have yet. But being that said, eventually it will be solving the problem they want solved.

DP: *I know that a lot of the technology you're using is already out there. It's off-the-shelf stuff, and you're just kind of bringing it together in these ways.*

BF: Right. Bringing all these data points together is what's innovative in our process. When we say that something is spiking for someone we run through these algorithms, it's not just one robot's opinion. We're using two different voice stress bots that agree. We also look at vocabulary deviations.

DP: *So I think you may have answered this, but I have a question about AI tools for journalists who are just starting to look into this space. Especially if they're comfortable with HTML and CSS, but not much more than that. Are there tools out there that can be used right now to just start experimenting?*

BF: Yes. Right now we use GPT-3 on OpenAI because it's just the most developed of large language models. But there are others. Most of my work for the last three months has been literally about negotiating with a bot in English, so I'm not coding. I go to a page and ask questions. OpenAI calls this "prompt engineering."

DP: *So this is your job now, talking to a bot? You're training it, is that what you're doing?*

BF: Think about how journalists could use this. How much time do reporters spend rummaging through documents, looking for a couple of facts? Now we can just feed those documents into AI. Let's say the earnings call references four thousand different corporate websites. We can make a simple bot that takes the content of each page. We fingerprint it to see if something's changed, and if it has changed, it executes a prompt like this:

"Based on the information below, what is the time and date of this earnings call?"

And then I go further:

"Please give it in this JSON format."

The other thing we've learned is that the bot will start to make things up to please us, unless we include specific instructions on what it should base things off. We always include a line like this:

"Based on the information below, analyze . . ."

DP: *How long do you think it will be before the kinds of tasks that are typically being used by a journalist or a writer are productized in AI, much in the way that Google Translate works now?*

BF: We're already seeing bits and pieces of it. For large-scale understanding, I would say we're at least half a decade away. That's mainly because the wrong people are looking at this right now. Engineers are looking at this. The first thing they will tell you is that this isn't deterministic.

What we need is something like a better way of interacting with a spreadsheet. What if you could just look at the spreadsheet and say, "Hi. Which one of these rows has the most? Which month has the most?" And it's able to perform those functions. You don't need to know SQL, you just ask it the question.

It knows what a number is. It knows what an average is. So you can hand it ten years of data and say, "What was the busiest month? What was the slowest month?" All without knowing anything other than starting with the dataset and literally just handing it off and saying "Answer this based on that." When we get to that point, that's where I see people finding AI more and more useful.

DP: *This all sounds like good news, because reporters are good at talking to people. Now they'll just have to be just as good at talking to robots.*

BF: We actually have a consultant starting next month who's a Pre-K consultant, specifically for this. His expertise is how to learn to talk to a 3-year-old. That's literally how we're approaching this problem, because it's pretty similar. That's how you need to talk to the machine. It's how you teach it.

DP: *But just make sure you're nice to it, because that machine is going to grow up one day.*

BF: Seriously. There are studies that show that people who talk not so nice to their Alexas start becoming rude to people. Right now I like to tell folks, "Just say please and thank you. It's worth the token." Also, if the robots come and kill us all, at least maybe they'll remember you kindly.

DP: *What big ethical or even existential issues do you see in the future for journalism and media in which AI may play a role?*

BF: We're at the point now where we can model individuals down to what they say, how they say it and, scarily, predict how they answer questions down to adjective and verb choices to a spooky degree.

We can do that on anyone who's spoken for more than five hours publicly. We *choose* to do it on public figures only: CEOs/CFOs (they ask for money) and politicians (they're public officials). That's a choice we make. But when is it OK to perform these tests on people who are not public figures? Who's talking about that?

DP: *You were an early voice encouraging journalists and media professionals to explore a lot of things that were, or still are, emerging platforms for media. What's your advice about emerging technologies for young journalists and storytellers who are just starting out today?*

BF: When faced with a challenge that involves technology, stop and ask: is this challenge unique? Is it doing tasks or steps that have never been done before? If not, the odds are that someone already did it, and there's a GitHub repo with that technology available for free that can save you 99% of the time.

Very little of what we do is new. You don't need to re-invent salt and pepper and pots and pans. What you're making needs to be unique. Everything in the middle are your tools. If you don't need to make your own tools, don't.

Online Resources for Chapter 10

Find more resources for Chapter 10 line at http://emergingmediaplatforms.com/chapter10.

Sources

Danzon-Chambaud, S. (2021, August 6). Covering COVID-19 with automated news. *Columbia Journalism Review*. www.cjr.org/tow_center_reports/covering-covid-automated-news.php

Hare, K. (2021, October 6). The Associated Press wants to help local newsrooms with AI and automation. *Poynter*. www.poynter.org/business-work/2021/the-associated-press-wants-to-help-local-newsrooms-with-ai-and-automation/

Iqbal, M. (2018, January 16). Instagram revenue and usage statistics (2022). *Business of Apps*. www.businessofapps.com/data/instagram-statistics/

Kochetkova, K. (2015, November 9). Hedy Lamarr: From a diva to an inventor (Kaspersky official blog). *Kaspersky Blog*. https://usa.kaspersky.com/blog/hedy-lamarr/6254/

Martinez, K. (2021, January 6). How automation helped this journalist quench a "news desert." *zapier.com*. https://zapier.com/blog/how-a-journalist-uses-automation/

Miller, G. (2020, April 4). "60 minutes" segment spotlights artificial intelligence keeping holocaust survivors alive. *Jewish Journal*. https://jewishjournal.com/culture/arts/313591/60-minutes-spotlights-artificial-intelligence-keeping-holocaust-survivors-alive/

Parker, R., & Dossett, J. (2021, October 20). AI in the newsroom: These outlets aren't spooked. *Beyond Bylines*. https://mediablog.prnewswire.com/2021/10/20/ai-in-the-newsroom-these-outlets-arent-spooked/

Threlfall, D. (2021, January 23). 27 Facebook messenger statistics that will change the way you think about marketing. *MobileMonkey*. https://mobilemonkey.com/blog/facebook-messenger-statistics-facebook-messenger-marketing

Yuen, M. (n.d.). Chatbot market 2022: Stats, trends, size & ecosystem research. *Insider Intelligence*. Retrieved August 25, 2022, from www.insiderintelligence.com/insights/chatbot-market-stats-trends/

11 Autonomous Flying Cameras

It's common knowledge that a lot of new technologies are first developed first in governments, and frequently in the military sector of governments. That is also true for the category of Unmanned Aerial Vehicles, colloquially known as "drones."

This aspect is also the most problematic for the category, as drones represent an emerging platform that quite literally flies right into the middle of some of the most significant ethical debates of our time: privacy, security, and the ethics of war.

We will cover some of those thorny issues in this chapter, but I'll say right up front that I labeled the chapter "Autonomous Flying Cameras," and not "Drones" for a reason. When it comes to media and journalism, the fact that cameras can now fly is the practical innovation that is already changing much of the visual content we see on a daily basis. How and when to use aerial visuals for stories, and how to do it safely and legally, is what always has been and will continue to be my focus in this area.

That said, the fact that on any given day you can see a headline about a cool video shot using a drone, or a headline about human beings being literally shot and killed by semi-autonomous military aircraft that are also referred to as drones, makes this a uniquely challenging area for media practitioners to experiment.

If you do anything in the drone space, you will inevitably run into this common misunderstanding, and it will affect how the people who see you flying perceive what you are doing, and why. Much as I hate to say it, if you use a drone, you should assume that many of the people who are watching you are wondering if your vehicle is going to hurt them or invade their privacy.

The Origins of Remotely Controlled Aerial Systems

Remote-controlled aircraft go back quite far, almost to the beginning of flight. The first known unmanned flight was in 1849 with a balloon carrier, which was a small ship that was pulled along by a balloon. Then starting in the early 1900s, after the discovery of radio waves, militaries started experimenting with remote-controlled balloons and aircraft intended to drop bombs.

Remote control was used for cases that were "too dull, dirty or dangerous" for humans, in the words of US Air Force Captain Brian Tice in his 1991 *Airpower*

DOI: 10.4324/9781003247012-12

Journal article, "Unmanned Aerial Vehicles: the Force Multiplier of the 1990s." You may think of drones and UAVs as something new, but by the time he had written that article, drones had been used in the military in every major military conflict from World War II to Vietnam and beyond. The terms UAV and related UAS (unmanned aerial systems) were coined during this military period.

Just as for personal computers, the 1990s were transformative for drones. The US military upgraded the technology with the help of computer chips and miniaturization, and cheaper, more capable flying fighting machines began to emerge. The first Predator drone was used this way in the 1991 Gulf War. By 2015, Wired Magazine reported that almost one in three US military planes was essentially a robot.

So, as you can see, probably more than any other technology, the history of drones is literally a tale of war. But that started to change in the mid-2000s, when open-source hackers – some former military themselves – started to explore more peaceful uses.

The Flight Controllers and Quadcopters

Around the same time that innovations like the iPhone and Android were launching, all of the parts that made up these small supercomputers designed for our pockets and purses ended up being available for other uses.

The software that manages the complicated calculations needed to keep a helicopter in the air was handled on a small computer called a Flight Controller. Accelerometers and GPS units were used to help the Flight Controller understand where it was, and tiny camera sensors used for phones and DSLRs were used to capture imagery.

Hobbyists began to publish lists of components and instructions for building their own drones, using mainly the "quadcopter" or occasionally "hexacopter" flight configurations. It turned out that these multi-blade copters that spin clockwise and counterclockwise were more easily controlled through software than a traditional helicopter design. And that early code was written and updated by communities of open-source developers.

I myself bought a kit from 3D Robotics, a company founded by Chris Anderson, the former editor in chief of Wired Magazine. It flew twice and crashed more times than that, but it was how I got familiar with flying a drone. 3D Robotics went belly-up in 2017 due to pressure from Chinese competitor DJI, which is now the most popular pro-am drone company today.

Integration Into the National Airspace

As consumer-friendly drones started to appear on the market, the US Congress passed a law in 2012 known as the FAA Modernization and Reform Act. Among other things, it required the Federal Aviation Administration to develop and implement a plan to integrate UASs into the national airspace by the Fall of 2015.

This started a flurry of activity in techie circles, while also causing a lot of consternation for people wondering if the air would soon be filled with flying paparazzi cameras. Civilian groups that were already protesting against military drones sometimes turned their sights on remote-controlled aircraft enthusiasts.

I myself got caught up in this when I appeared in a media interview about the potential that drones had in journalism, and suddenly I was getting anti-military-drone literature mailed to my office or sent to my email address.

To be clear, even as someone who grew up in a military family, I am personally against the use of drones as weapons of war. Whenever I encountered such people, I would start off by saying that I agreed with them about military drones and that my use of quadcopters was for peaceful uses. I'd show them stunning videos from the air and point out that these shots were safer with a drone than with a helicopter because of their smaller size, and their potential to save lives that may be lost from a manned helicopter crash.

Eventually, these groups came to understand the difference, but I have found that such protesters are still sometimes a little frosty about even civilian uses of drones. They tend to be the first to highlight issues around privacy, fears around the use of drones by police in surveillance states, and the like. I also agree with them on many of these concerns and believe that existing privacy laws and technology-specific regulations are the solutions – not just a flat-out ban on this or any technology. But I also value their voice on these issues, because they are absolutely right that in the wrong hands, this technology can be extremely dangerous and invasive.

The FAA Cracks Down

Around that same time in 2012, University of Nebraska-Lincoln Professor Matt Waite started the world's first lab focused specifically on using drones in journalism. His Drone Journalism Lab, initially funded by the Knight Foundation, was created to experiment with using drones for journalistic stories in ways that were legal and ethical.

Waite and some of his grad students spent the next year promoting the idea of safe, affordable flying cameras, and what sorts of stories they could make possible that were either extremely expensive – requiring a helicopter or pilot – or simply impossible before UAVs came along. Along with many other digital journalists, I attended his seminars at Online News Association conferences and closely followed the Drone Journalism Lab's blog, and I even purchased an early drone that I used in demonstrations at the Newhouse School.

But unbeknownst to Waite, the FAA was closely watching. As soon as the Drone Journalism Lab published a video containing footage that was captured with a drone, Waite received a cease and desist letter claiming that even publishing drone-assisted footage for educational use constituted commercial use, which was determined to be illegal.

It was at this point that drone journalism went through one of the most bizarre Hype Cycles of any technology in this book. It was almost like several Hype Cycles for different audiences.

The promise of incorporating cool aerial photos captured the imagination of the public, including many visual storytellers. Using a drone to capture photos or videos for personal use was still legally possible for anyone, based on laws for model aircraft that went back to the 1970s. Hobbyists began purchasing the quadcopters en masse and flying them at parks. The era of consumer drones quickly went into high gear.

Among those hobbyists were people like me who wanted to use drones for journalism and film. But because of inconsistencies and a lack of regulation – and that example the FAA made of Waite – very few stories were published that incorporated this type of footage out of fear of it being considered commercial use.

I remember my own dean, the late Lorraine Branham, sending me an email shortly after the news about Waite highly discouraging me from publishing anything I had captured from the air – to which I heartily agreed.

Drones were almost like a Hype Cycle in waiting. Many were not only simultaneously stuck in a trough of disillusionment while we waited for regulation to get settled but also actively experimenting as hobbyists – unable to share what we were doing in the United States at least. During this period, I noticed a trend of journalistic experimenters traveling to other countries that had less to no drone regulation, and doing aerial-assisted stories there as proofs of concept. But they were barred from doing anything remotely similar in the United States. This was ironic, because in a country where the airspace was more regulated, it would have been safer to do those types of stories there versus, for example, in a small country in Africa with absolutely no regulation at all.

During this ensuing waiting period, there were plenty of mishaps as hobbyists pushed the limits, and the US government pushed back. One of the most widely known was in 2015, when a hobbyist's drone crashed on the White House lawn. A great source of information for this period, and other developments of the implementation of UAVs into the National Airspace, is the FAA itself through a comprehensive timeline of key events in American UAV history: www.faa.gov/uas/resources/timeline.

Eventually, in the Fall of 2016 – one year past its deadline – the FAA rolled out what it calls the "Part 107" process for getting a commercial license. This refers to Title 14, Chapter I, Subchapter F, Part 107 of federal law, which you can read on the National Archives website in full here: www.ecfr.gov/current/title-14/chapter-I/subchapter-F/part-107.

Enthusiasts were ready, and a year after publishing the Part 107 rules, the FAA reported that 80,000 commercial licenses had been awarded. The era of responsible, regulated commercial drone use in the United States had finally arrived.

As you will see later in this chapter, the knowledge you need to master to get such a license is significant and in my experience can require up to 60 hours of self-study. But it is possible. I finally received my first Part 107 license in May 2021.

I encourage any visual storyteller who wants to incorporate aerial footage into their work to go through the process and get a Part 107 license.

Drones Today

Drones are a completely different story now, and they are truly everywhere. According to the FAA, in 2022 there were 855,860 drones registered with the US government. Sixty-three percent of them were for recreational use, and 37% for commercial use. By then, the FAA had awarded 277,845 remote pilot certificates.

It's likely that you have seen at least one story, journalistic or fictional, this week that incorporated aerial video taken from a drone. In my class, I offer extra credit to anyone who can prove that a video in a story they come across could only have come from a UAV.

I also give extra credit to anyone who can show a video that utilized a drone in a way that violated a law or ethical guideline. (I call this "Drones behaving badly.") The reason I do this is that, sadly, there are still violations happening everywhere. That creates a bad environment for the rest of us who go to great lengths to follow laws, policies, and procedures to keep people safe and protect their privacy.

Drone Regulations Around the World

Most countries now have their own laws that regulate the use of drones and procedures for obtaining a license. As I am an American citizen, and I have a license from the FAA for commercial flights, I will focus on the regulations here in the United States. But much of what applies here is either mirrored in other countries or regulated by a similar air authority. The important thing is that no matter where you plan to fly around the world, you should look into the laws and regulations there and follow them.

I offer one caution from personal experience. Don't assume that flying is legal even in a country that is similar to yours. I recently went on a work-related trip to South Africa and learned that while they utilize a similar airspace classification system as the FAA, their definition of what is and is not commercial use is completely different from that in the United States or Europe. In South Africa, commercial use applies primarily to government-owned property. Flights are allowed on private property as long as you have the owner's permission.

Expect to see major variations as you move from country to country. You may find, as I did in South Africa, that flying over any land that the government owns requires a full pilot's license – not just for a drone but for flying a 747! For this reason, companies have sprung up there that you can work with for getting the footage you need.

Wondering what the regulations are in your country, or a country you're visiting? A number of websites try to stay on top of drone laws around the world. Go to http://emergingmediaplatforms.com/chapter11 for links to the best current sites that I've found.

Drone Regulations in the United States of America

This section provides a broad overview of how drones are regulated in the United States and paints the brush in broad strokes in terms of what you would need to study in order to become a commercial pilot. But being just one chapter in one book, I can tell you that it's impossible to cover everything. There are countless other books and online training programs that you can use to learn all of the skills you would need to become a commercial pilot. I have included links to some of these on the website at https://emergingmediaplatforms.com/chapter11.

While the FAA's information started out being confusing and sometimes contradictory, in recent years it has become fairly straightforward. You can get up-to-date information on regulations for all types of flyers by going to https://faa.gov and clicking Drones in the navigation, or go straight here: www.faa.gov/uas.

Even better, if you have questions, you can call a hotline that's right at the top of the drone section of the FAA website. I have done this on occasion and found that the people on the other end of the line are extremely friendly and excited to answer any of your questions. Thanks to clear regulations, they seem to be focused on building a community of responsible pilots, even as they go around looking for violations.

Drone Registration – It's the Law!

According to Statista, at least 5 million drones are purchased each year. Let's say you're one of those millions. Where do you start?

If you want to play around with a drone for personal use, which can even include education as long as you aren't publishing footage captured from the drone, you can do so at any time. But you *must* register any new drone that you purchase with the FAA. You can do so easily with a $5 registration fee at the FAA Drone Zone website: https://faadronezone.faa.gov/.

Each registration is valid for three years, and with it you basically get a registration ID that you are required to place somewhere on the outside of your drone where it can be easily read. Think of it like a license plate for a car. Just like with a license plate, that number holds you accountable for what you do with your flying vehicle. This is especially important for a case where a drone may fly away. Every drone owner is required to register, both hobbyists and commercial pilots.

This rule applies to drones that are less than 55 pounds. The chances of you even getting access to a drone that is anywhere near that price is extremely low, so don't worry about hitting that limit.

Recreational Flyers

Recreational flight is allowed through a special carve-out in laws that go back to remote-controlled aircraft rules from the 1970s. You can read through what the FAA says about this directly here: www.faa.gov/uas/recreational_flyers.

Recreational use is sometimes called non-commercial, but the term "commercial" itself is problematic. It makes many people assume that commercial use means someone is handing you money to fly for them, or that you are getting a paycheck from a place for which you are flying as a part of your job. Both of those cases are true, but assuming that these are the only definitions of "commercial" is a misinterpretation of the law, and also of how the FAA interprets and acts on that law. So be warned: If you try to get away with doing things using a drone using your own justification of what you *think* is or is not commercial use, you may find yourself with a cease and desist letter and a fine of up to $22,500 per incident.

The FAA defines recreational use as flying purely for fun or personal enjoyment. On its website, the FAA has recently gone to great pains to point out that it has authority over non-recreational purposes that include things like: taking photos to help someone sell a house, or to inspect their roofs; or getting footage of a football game for a school's Website.

They even go on to say that the "good will value" of flying to help out a nonprofit can be a form of compensation. It's almost as if the FAA considers the "psychic income" that comes from getting credit for shooting some video for a nonprofit is non-recreational and therefore commercial.

Over the last few years, I have also seen a trend where the FAA is contacting YouTubers who post aerial video that could only have been captured from a drone. Because these YouTubers get advertising revenue-share checks, their use is considered commercial and the FAA asks them to take those videos down or face civil or criminal liabilities. But interestingly, they also make another request: go through the steps to get a Part 107 commercial license. Some of these YouTubers go on to do that, and they re-post their videos as licensed commercial operators.

Recreational Flyers

If you fly for any reason – recreationally or commercially – you are required to adhere to the following rules:

- **Keep the drone within your visual line of sight:** This means that you are observing the drone with your eyes – not with magnifying glasses or anything that enhances your vision beyond regular glasses.
- **Use a visual observer:** If you plan to look at a screen that shows you what the drone's camera is capturing, you must assign a second person to be your "visual observer" and direct that person to keep their eyes on the drone for you.
- **Don't interfere with any other aircraft:** If a plane or helicopter appears, land your drone immediately. Keep in mind that helicopters, such as those used by news crews or hospitals, can sometimes appear at any time. If that happens (and yes, this has happened to me), be ready to land immediately.
- **Fly below 400 feet, and if flying recreationally, only in uncontrolled airspace:** The FAA's rules say that you can fly in controlled airspace using authorization, but at the time of this writing, their method of authorization

didn't enable this for hobbyists. Only Part 107 licensed flyers can request permission in controlled airspace. (There's more about the classes of airspace later in this chapter.)

- **Hobbyists must take and pass the Recreational UAS Safety Test:** You can take this online, and the FAA provides a list of test providers.
- **Don't interfere with emergency response or law enforcement:** This requires no further explanation. I would go further to say: if law enforcement tells you that you can't fly – even if you know you have the right to fly in that area – it's better to be nice and respectful, and just leave and fly somewhere else.
- **Don't fly under the influence of drugs or alcohol:** If you are wondering what this means for having had a drink or anything else, always go by the age-old pilot's rule: "8 *hours bottle to throttle*." This goes far beyond alcohol, though. If you take any kind of drug that impairs your ability to fly, including prescription medication or even something like an antihistamine that makes you drowsy, don't fly within eight hours of taking it.

The most important thing to underscore here is that even if you are flying recreationally, you are in the FAA's airspace. And which air exactly is under the jurisdiction of the FAA? Well, jump up into the air outside of any structure, such as your backyard. Surprise, you're in the FAA's airspace!

International students that I teach find it surprising that in the United States, you don't even control the air above a piece of property that you own. A property owner can enforce what happens on the ground it owns, but anything in the air above that ground is overseen by the FAA, and the FAA alone has the authority to enforce its air space.

Commercial Flyers

We've established earlier what constitutes recreational and non-recreational use of a drone. If you're not sure if what you're doing is non-recreational, it very well can be considered commercial. For that, you need to make sure that either you or someone you work with has a Part 107 license.

How do you go about getting one? The good news is that you just need to take a 60-question multiple choice test, and pass with at least 70%. The bad news is that this test is extremely difficult and requires a lot of knowledge, some of which applies to aircraft that are much larger than a typical drone.

The knowledge needed to pass the test is pretty vast, but much of it centers around understanding where you can fly, and in which cases you need to get permission to fly. When you feel you are ready to take the test, there are clear steps spelled out on the FAA's page about commercial flyers: www.faa.gov/uas/commercial_operators.

At the time of this writing, the FAA required first-time flyers to go to an approved in-person testing center. (This was interestingly still required during the pandemic, in which you had to take a test with a mask on – which was even harder for people who also wear reading glasses that fog up! But I still passed.)

Figure 11.1 An example of a video I captured during a shoot with Syracuse University's Otto the Orange mascot. It was done under my own Part 107 license, with an additional Waiver from the FAA because FAA airspace starts at 0 feet at Syracuse University. Shot by Dan Pacheco on 8/10/2022 at 12:11 p.m. under LAANC authorization ALTYO6978UK0.

(*Source:* Screenshot/Dan Pacheco)

You can find a testing center near you, which is often going to be at a flight school near an airport, or possibly on a military base. For example, in Syracuse where I live, I can either take a test at the Rome, NY airport, or at a flight school in Ithaca, NY.

So, sounds easy right? But get ready for what you need to learn. In addition to understanding all of the rules required even for hobbyists, you will need to become an expert in the following areas – and more!

- **Understanding FAA Airspace:** Every inch of air above you has a designated category, which is referred to as a class. The classes of airspace are lettered and go in this order from most to least restricted: A, B, C, D, E, and G. (There is an F, but it isn't used much so you can just ignore it.)
  You have likely heard these classes mentioned on commercial air flights, especially if you're on a flight that has a way for you to listen to the pilot's radio. Read on below to learn generally what each of these classes means.
- **Weather:** Pilots report weather using a form known as a Meteorological Aerodrome Report, or METAR. They include a string of characters and numbers that stand for specific things like the time and date, temperature, air pressure, how much visibility there is, how low the clouds are, if there will be rain

or other precipitation, and wind speed. For example, here's the METAR for Syracuse, New York, when I was writing this chapter:

```
KSYR 261454Z 25007KT 10SM FEW023 FEW100 SCT180 BKN250
25/19 A2990 RMK AO2 SLP121 60010 T02500189 50001
```

That cryptic message says the following:

```
At Syracuse Hancock International Airport, on the
26th day of this month at 1454 zulu time, the wind was
coming from the south, southwest at 7 knots. There was
10 statute miles of visibility. There were few clouds
at 2,300 feet, another collection of few clouds at
10,000 feet, scattered clouds at 18,000 feet, and
broken clouds at 25,000 feet. The temperature was
25 degrees celsius, and the dew point was 19 degrees
celsius. Pressure was 29.90 inches of Hg.
```

Even though you will probably never actually have to read such a report in METAR format to get the weather conditions for a flight, on the test you need to be able to read it and understand what each of those numbers and abbreviations means. The remote pilot training programs I recommended on the book website will take you through all of this.

Don't like that? Tough – it's on the test, so get busy learning how to understand METARs!

- **UAS Loading and Performance:** This covers how much your drone can carry based on its weight, and what angle it can fly at should it carry more than its own weight. This type of thing doesn't often impact using drones for media, but if you're crazy like me and like to do things like connecting a 360 video camera to a drone, you will need to have a good understanding of these principles.

- **Airport Field Operations:** This large category covers everything from the patterns that manned aircraft use to take off and land, to understanding how to read Notices to Airmen and Temporary Flight Restrictions, to being able to read all kinds of little indicators on aeronautical charts.

- **Emergency Plans:** Things can and will go wrong with your drone, and the FAA knows that. There are specific rules about how to report if your drone accidentally flies away, what types of other accidents are required to report, what to do if your drone catches fire, and more.

- **Waiver Processes:** A Part 107 license gives you the ability to request permission to fly in controlled airspace, but as you will learn, some parts of that controlled airspace will go all the way to the ground. These areas are usually in sensitive areas where you may be close to an airport, where there are expected to be a lot of people – such as around a stadium – or where you're near a helipad (usually hospitals). In these areas, you must also request a waiver, which is called that because you are asking them to waive these specific rules on a specific day and time, and for a specific time period. Getting a waiver used to be an arduous process, but it can now be done in an app. The key thing to know is that by law, the FAA has the right to take up to 90 days to approve a waiver.

Those are the major areas, but there are many more that I would put in the "miscellaneous category." Airspace, which I get into in the next section, is the majority of the test. You can get a lot of information, including practice tests, from the FAA on their Training and Testing page: www.faa.gov/training_testing/testing.

In addition, you can download a PDF of the Airman Knowledge Testing Supplement that goes over everything you will be tested on. That same supplement will be available to you in printed form when you take the multiple choice test. But be warned: it is likely to be printed at low quality, almost intentionally (in my opinion) requiring you to strain your eyes as you try to read what's on the tiny little maps in the book. I believe this is intentional, because the FAA wants to know that you know your material, and have likely looked at many such maps while studying for the exam.

You can get a link to the most recent version of the test supplement at https://emergingmediaplatforms.com/chapter11.

FAA Airspace and Aeronautical Charts

By far, the most important thing to master – both for passing the Part 107 test and for being a responsible flier – is to be able to read and understand aeronautical charts. While the FAA exam provides these to you in printed form when you take the test, you can begin examining these charts online using two resources:

- **VFRMap:** https://vfrmap.com
- **SkyVector:** https://skyvector.com

VFRMap is the oldest and slightly less complicated of the two. But once you know everything you need to know about airspace, SkyVector layers on more information that can be helpful when you're preparing for a flight.

SkyVector also has data from more places around the world. So, for example, when I recently went on a work-related trip to South Africa, I was able to examine the airspace of Cape Town and Makhanda using SkyVector, but these areas were completely absent on VFRMap.

On either site you will see a search box that lets you enter an airport code. These codes are probably familiar to you where you live. For example, in my city, the airport code for the Syracuse Hancock International Airport is SYR. But searching on that delivers no results. Just put a K in front of any airport code (such as KSYR), and it will take you directly to that airport.

The first thing to notice is the different-colored lines that surround areas on the map. There will usually be several that are often – but not always – arranged concentrically. Why are there so many of them, and why do they surround each other? Generally speaking, the closer you get to a busy commercial airport, the more control the FAA asserts over that space.

The concentric circles are sometimes referred to as "upside down wedding cakes." It sounds a bit messy, but imagine turning a multi-tiered wedding cake upside down and placing it right on top of the busiest airport you can think of. The top part of the cake touches the ground where the airport is, and that means the airspace starts at 0 feet. It's logical to expect that the FAA would control the airspace at an airport starting at the ground.

As you move further away from an airport – typically about 5 miles away – the controlled airspace starts not at the ground, but higher – let's say that's 700 feet. This means that your little drone, which can only go as high as 400 feet anyway, can fly in that area if you have the proper license and permission.

As you move even further out, the FAA only cares about the airspace from 1,200 feet and higher. And even further out, they don't care about controlling it at all as long as there's not something else happening there that could create problems – such as a military base, a wildlife area, magnetic disturbance that could cause your drone to lose connection with your controller, or a few other factors.

Airspace takes some time to get your head around because you are looking at two-dimensional maps that describe three-dimensional space. If you're struggling with it, here's another way to think about it.

Forget the wedding cakes, and go back to any time you were on a commercial air flight and the plane was either landing or taking off. We've all heard stories of birds getting sucked into jet engines mid-air, sometimes even causing one jet engine to fail. Well, instead of a bird, imagine that what goes into the engine is someone's drone that they're flying on the other side of the airport fence.

When your flight takes off, it goes right past that drone, and into the engine the drone goes – and down your plane goes. Would you feel safe knowing that this could happen any time a flight you're on is taking off or landing? Heck, no!

Based on how large, mostly manned aircraft take off and land at busy airports, the FAA ensures that the danger of anything in the air interfering with that take-off or landing is minimized. The controlled airspace moves up into the air like an ice cream cone as planes get higher and higher away from the airport, or as they descend and get closer and closer to the ground.

In areas where there aren't lots of large aircraft going up and down at an angle, the FAA gets less concerned about controlling the airspace. This is why the control begins higher and higher as you get further from airports until you get to very rural areas that have no large aircraft traffic at all.

Classes of Airspace

The FAA categorizes airspaces in classes, and they start and stop at different elevations. These elevations are reported in one of two ways:

- **Mean Sea Level, or MSL:** Measured in feet, this is the height above the level of the sea. It is a universal number across the entire globe.
- **Above Ground Level, or AGL:** Also measured in feet, this is the height above the ground, which of course changes with the topography of the earth.

When it comes to drones, you will be primarily looking at AGL, but the FAA has test questions that require you to answer questions that include MSL.

The classes of airspaces go from A to G and are defined as follows. I've given you some common heuristics to use to help you keep them straight. Note that everything except Class G is controlled by the FAA.

- **Class A:** This starts at 18,000 MLS, and you can think of it as a place that your drone is probably never going to go. How would you keep it in line of sight? How would your controller connect to it? Class A is the realm of commercial aircraft, military jets, and the like. (By the way, there are no questions about Class A on the test.)
- **Class B:** This is marked with a *solid blue line* (remember B for Blue). It also tends to apply to **busy** airports like LAX, DCA, MIA, and so forth. The center part of class B starts at ground level, and as you move out past 5 miles the control begins anywhere from 2,500 feet AGL or more. It ends at 10,000 feet AGL.
- **Class C:** This is marked with a *solid magenta line* and is typically centered around secondary airports in smaller cities and towns. Do you have to frequently take a commuter jet to get to a certain airport? Yeah, I feel for you, so do I! But in addition to having less in the terminal, it's also Class C. The good news with Class C is that it's smaller than B, which means more flying areas for your drone.

This airspace begins at surface level, and after 5 miles it starts at 1,200 AGL, and then disappears. Class C ends at 4,000 feet AGL.

- **Class D:** Class D is marked with a *dotted blue line* (remember D for Dotted). It always starts at surface level, and it has no tiers outside apart from an occasional rectangular area that protects ascents and descents for planes using the airstrip. These airstrips are also typically not used that much. Class D ends at 2,500 feet AGL.
- **Class E – regular and "Surface Class E":** This dual class will appear as either a *faded magenta* or a *dashed red* line. The faded magenta means the airspace is controlled starting at 700 feet AGL, so your drone can fly there without an extra waiver. But the dashed red line means that it starts at surface level, and you would need a waiver (honestly, in most cases you won't ever be flying near an airport).
- **Class G:** This class is everything else that's not covered in the other classes. These areas are typically rural and present a good place for anyone to fly.

There are very complex and sometimes intentionally tricky questions about airspace on the Part 107 exam. The FAA wants to know that you understand it. But there is a light at the end of that tunnel. Should you find yourself passing the test and getting a license, you will hardly ever use those maps to determine where you can fly (though you should still look at the map to tell if there are other things you need to know about, such as parachuting activities, as just one example). Instead, you'll use an app.

The Aloft App

Whether you're a hobbyist or a Part 107 licensed pilot, you can use the Aloft app (iOS and Android) to examine the airspace where you want to fly. Aloft uses GPS to tell where you are, and you can zoom in to see different airspaces as shaded circles and other shapes that indicate the class of airspace you're in.

When you zoom in, you'll then see numbers which indicate how high a drone can fly, or if it can't fly at all. For every area that has a number higher than zero, a Part 107 pilot is able to tap a button and request permission to fly there using a largely automated system called Low Altitude Authorization and Notification Capability (LAANC). Requests are usually approved within seconds, and you get a long notification from the FAA about how high you can fly, restrictions that apply to that particular area, and how long you may fly.

Anything marked with a zero means that the airspace there starts at ground level. Flying requires an FAA waiver of rules, which you can request through the app – but only if you have a Part 107 license. That waiver may get approved quickly, or it may be approved in up to 90 days, or it may be rejected. Whatever you do, don't try to contact someone at the FAA to pull strings for you because the notices in the Aloft app specifically say that doing that will cause your request – and possibly future requests – to be denied.

Case Study: Connor's Aerial Highway Project Explainer

Connor was fascinated with how drones could be used in journalism to inform people about complicated topics in their communities for which ground-level photography and written explanations were inadequate.

One such example was right in his city. In the 1960s, a massive raised highway was built right in the middle of Syracuse, New York, that ended up displacing thousands of mostly Black citizens – a tragedy that has taken place in many parts of the United States and around the world. By 2022, the highway had reached the end of its useful life, and local organizations and the state of New York succeeded in adopting a plan to remove the highway overpass completely and replace it with a more equity-focused ground-level community grid.

The changes to traffic patterns for this plan were immense, including not just what the new traffic flow would be like but also the impact of construction over many years. When the final plans for the community grid came out, the local TV stations and local newspaper did their best to explain what would change, and how it would impact the daily lives of Syracuse residents. But it was clear that practically everyone was still confused. So many of the changes described had to be imagined based on descriptions and architectural renderings.

Connor surmised that if these changes could be described using aerial video with markers on the affected areas, people would have a better understanding of the changes to come. He planned to produce the video and then send out two links to a test market of affected residents. One link would be his aerial video explainer, and the other link would be the newspaper article. He would ask them to view both and then determine which one helped them visualize the changes better.

Connor didn't have a Part 107 license, so he partnered up with another student – Jesse – who did. They captured the shots they wanted, and he produced a video that would highlight certain areas on the ground while he explained what would change through a voiceover.

There were a few glitches in their plan, primarily involving weather. On one planned fly day, the wind was gusting up to 20 miles per hour, and there was light snow. They had to postpone it to the next day. They also encountered one issue with FAA permissions being denied because the area they needed to fly required 24 hours advance notice (this was likely due to a NOTAM).

When they had what they needed, Connor searched local Facebook and NextDoor groups to recruit people who lived in the areas that would be most affected by the construction and traffic pattern changes. He ended up with 20 people who came from a variety of areas, both in the city and in suburbs, and all said they were concerned about how their commutes would be impacted.

After sending links out to each group, his results showed that 80% of the respondents felt better informed using the aerial video explainer as compared to the newspaper article. They said it was easier to visualize the changes, and that his decision to show a 2D map overlay in the corner of the video made it easier for them to imagine what those changes would be.

Connor determined his hypothesis to be a success. While he cautioned that this one test doesn't mean that every traffic or construction story needs aerial video, these results do show that drones have a bright future in journalism.

Expert Interview: Mickey Osterreicher

DAN PACHECO (DP): *What do you do now, and how does it relate to journalism and media?*

MICKEY OSTERREICHER (MO): I am the National Press Photographers Association general counsel dealing with First Amendment rights of journalists, media access, drone use for newsgathering, and copyright issues. I have been working to improve police–press relations by providing training to law enforcement and journalists around the country regarding those constitutional rights under grants NPPA received from the Knight Foundation and the Press Freedom Defense Fund.

DP: *What maybe not as many know is that you are an ardent drone enthusiast yourself, and I believe also an FAA Part 107 certified pilot. How did you get interested in drones?*

MO: I have always been interested in flying and although I never got to fly myself, that enthusiasm was passed along to my son, who is a Lt. Colonel in the United States Air Force and an F-35 pilot. I focused more attention on drones after being interviewed in 2012 on the subject for an article in the Harvard Law & Policy Review. From there it seemed like the natural progression of the right to record in public whether on the ground or from the air.

DP: *What kind of drone do you fly, and what do you wish you could fly?*

MO: Sadly, I used to fly a Mavic but I have been so busy dealing with so many issues on behalf of visual journalists that it has been a long time since I have flown. Maybe one day when I retire, but most folks think that will never happen.

DP: *A lot of people look at that FAA test and turn away. Do you think they should turn back around, study for the test, pay the $150, and get a license? Why?*

MO: I absolutely believe that anyone who is interested in operating a drone should study for and take the test. It is so much easier now than it was five or six years ago when the FAA implemented its Part 107 rules. There are also so many additional free online study materials. If you plan to use a drone for newsgathering, having your Part 107 Remote Pilot's Certificate is a must along with adequate insurance coverage and a registered drone.

DP: *What's the most interesting drone-assisted story or project you've seen? What did you like about it?*

There are so many stories that could not have been done without using a drone. One of the early uses still stands out in my mind – Johnny Miller's use of a drone to illustrate the stark divide and inequality between communities throughout the world (see: *Unequal Scenes* at https://www.millefoto.com/unequalscenes).

DP: *You have been a hawk toward irresponsible and illegal use of drones. Of the transgressions out there, which most get under your skin, and why?*

MO: As those dealing with the issue of drones often say, there are three classes of people that cause problems when flying drones: the clueless, the careless, and the criminal. It continues to astound me how many people there are who own and fly drones in a careless manner, and often completely oblivious to the fact that there are FAA regulations regarding such things as no flights over people, especially at extremely low altitudes, or in the middle of a fireworks show or during inclement weather, or over a capacity-filled NFL stadium.

While I am often amused by law enforcement's use of the term "nefarious purposes" when referring to possible criminal use of drones, it only takes common sense to realize that a drone flying over a large crowd could cause great harm by releasing something as simple as baby powder because of the panic that would ensue, to say nothing of drones equipped with actual weapons as we have seen on a large scale during the war in Ukraine.

DP: *What direction do you see things going with drone regulation in the United States? For commercial use do you anticipate there will be more regulation, or less regulation? How about in any other countries you follow regarding drone regulation?*

MO: Having worked closely with the FAA for many years, I see them as doing everything possible to safely integrate the use of drones into the National Airspace System. They have done their best to expedite waivers to many of their regulations using a highly automated Low Altitude Authorization and Notification Capability (LAANC) and tried to move ahead to authorize flights over people, night flights, and flights beyond visual line of sight.

The biggest hurdle now will be implementing Remote ID. Depending on the technological solution by manufacturers, that may really change the type of equipment operators are able to use. By that I mean whether existing drones will be able to be cheaply retrofitted to comply with the new regs or whether those existing drones will become obsolete, requiring owners to purchase all new equipment. As for other countries – it is hard enough to keep up with US regulations, so I really don't have the bandwidth to keep up with global regulations.

DP: *I have noticed that a clear majority of commercial drone pilots still tend to be men. Why do you think that is, and what can be done to close the gender divide around this promising technology?*

MO: That is true, but there are many women who are very active in the drone community. *Dawn M.K. Zoldi*, *Sharon Rossmark*, and *Loretta Alkalay* are just a few.

DP: *Do you think drones will eventually be seen as a fad, or will they continue to generate a lot of interest?*

MO: Rather than becoming a fad like the hula-hoop, I see drones becoming part of everyday life just like cars, planes, and cell phones.

DP: *Should every visual storyteller get licensed in their country to commercially fly, or do you see it as a specialized role – like one per newsroom, which is often the case now?*

MO: Just as almost every journalist needs to have a valid driver's license and know how to safely operate a motor vehicle in order to be able to do their job, so too do I think that every visual storyteller, especially a visual journalist, needs to have a valid commercial license to operate a drone in whatever country they are in.

It should no longer be seen as a specialized role, and everyone in a newsroom who is expected to take photos and/or record video as part of their job description should not only have a license to operate a drone but should be properly trained and experienced to do so along with continuing practice. If at all possible, I believe that newsrooms should supply each journalist with a drone because you never know when you will need it, and returning to the newsroom to get it may be either impossible or cause you to miss the story.

Additionally, for all of the independent contractors who freelance for news organizations – having a properly registered drone, a valid license, and comprehensive insurance coverage is a must if you wish to remain competitive with other freelancers.

Online Resources for Chapter 11

Find more resources for Chapter 11 line at http://emergingmediaplatforms.com/chapter11.

Sources

Ackerman, S. (2012, January 9). Almost 1 in 3 U.S. warplanes is a robot. *Wired*. www.wired.com/2012/01/drone-report/

A drone, too small for radar to detect, rattles the White House. (2015, January 26). *The New York Times*. www.nytimes.com/2015/01/27/us/white-house-drone.html

Buckley, J. (2006). *Air power in the age of total war*. Routledge, p. 43.

FAA modernization and reform act of 2012. (2012, February 1). *GovInfo*. www.govinfo.gov/content/pkg/CRPT-112hrpt381/pdf/CRPT-112hrpt381.pdf

Laricchia, F. (2022, April 13). Global consumer drone shipments 2020–2030. *Statista*. www.statista.com/statistics/1234658/worldwide-consumer-drone-unit-shipments/

Mac, R. (2016, October 5). Behind the crash of 3D robotics, North America's most promising drone company. *Forbes*. www.forbes.com/sites/ryanmac/2016/10/05/3d-robotics-solo-crash-chris-anderson/?sh=eb65d3f3ff5b

Master list of drone laws. (2021, January 23). *UAV Coach*. https://uavcoach.com/drone-laws/

Miller, J. (n.d.). *Unequal scenes*. Retrieved August 26, 2022, from https://unequalscenes.com/

Satell, M. (2022, July 22). 16 eye-opening drone stats for 2022. *Philly by Air*. www.phillybyair.com/blog/drone-stats

Syed, N., & Harvard Law & Policy Review Staff. (2012, July 23). Drones, privacy and the future of photojournalism: An interview with photojournalist and National Press Photographers Association general counsel Mickey Osterreicher by New York Times first amendment fellow Nabiha Syed. *Harvard Law & Policy Review*. https://harvardlpr.com/2012/07/23/drones-privacy-and-the-future-of-photojournalism-an-interview-with-photojournalist-and-national-press-photographers-association-general-counsel-mickey-osterreicher-by-new-york-times-first-amendment/

Tice, B. (n.d.). Unmanned aerial vehicles. *Air Power Journal*. Retrieved May 1, 1991, from https://web.archive.org/web/20090724015052/www.airpower.maxwell.af.mil/airchronicles/apj/apj91/spr91/4spr91.htm

Timeline of drone integration. (2019, August 29). *Federal Aviation Administration*. www.faa.gov/uas/resources/timeline

12 Field Testing the Future

By this time, hopefully you've conducted your field test, you have some data and you're ready to make some conclusions. You're also ready to communicate your findings. Congratulations! You're ready to write up your field test report.

Field Tests Versus Academic Studies

As you have seen throughout this book, the actual work and process surrounding field tests is intentionally less rigorous than anything you would do in a full scientific study. That's intentional, because the purpose of the field test process is to emulate what you would be asked to do within a typical media company, or even your own startup.

Media companies can and do initiate or fund full studies conducted by academic researchers, often in conjunction with research groups at leading universities. But before they get anywhere close to that, they do their own due diligence and try to get a gut feeling for whether they should pursue anything beyond giving an employee a week to kick the tires on a new approach. This is especially true today, when staff sizes at newsrooms in particular are leaner than ever.

In my experience working in digitally innovative jobs at places like The Washington Post, America Online, and The Bakersfield Californian, I never once had a manager say, "You know, we should initiate a study at such and such university to assess this problem and approach." And they certainly never shelled out tens to hundreds of thousands of dollars to pay for such studies.

Instead, they came to me with questions more like this: "I read about this new thing in The Wall Street Journal. Can you check it out and come back in a week or two with a report about whether we should be looking into this?"

And by the way, they didn't usually take other work off my plate. I had to squeeze that investigation into my day, often doing the tinkering on evenings and weekends. That reality explains the true ethos of a field test report, and how it differs from a scientific or academic study. To use an imperfect analogy, it's more like a temperature check than a full medical procedure.

I became very good at this, and over time my positions evolved to where I was given more time, space, and even internal funding to conduct these explorations.

DOI: 10.4324/9781003247012-13

This happened repeatedly to me at multiple companies, and I saw the same thing happen to other technologically curious people like me at their companies.

It even extended into academia. At the Newhouse School, I run an innovation lab, one of a growing number of such spaces at colleges around the globe. But it all began by doing the hard work to explore new technologies, conducting controlled field tests, and then communicating my findings back to my bosses and peers in a way that helped them decide whether to invest resources – or not.

Another way to think of it: the field test report takes you beyond telling the world that you're an innovator and hoping they believe you. You show them that you know how to innovate with real results, and all the messiness that goes along with it.

It is my hope that you can use this process to also have a career like mine. But to get there, you have to do the work. Then, put in the same amount of effort to communicate what you've done and what you've learned as you did in creating it – to your boss, potential investors, and the public at large.

Prepping Your Audience to Want to Know More

If you're more visual, which is the language of most media these days, you may be wondering why you should write anything at all. Why not just make a video, or tweet out a link to the thing you created? And the answer is that if you want to make a video or social media post and are good at that, you should. But you should still have something written for people who want to know more.

When I assign field test reports, I actually require two pieces. The first is a very short, highly visual presentation that summarizes the story of their field test. The format is what's often referred to as the "elevator pitch" that many startups practice.

The theory of an elevator pitch is that you find yourself in an elevator with someone who might be interested in your idea. You only have so many floors to get them interested, and by the time they get off the elevator you want to be ready to receive something more that you hand to them so they can learn more about it. In this case, that thing you hand to them is your field test report.

My favorite format for an elevator pitch is the Ignite, which you can learn about at http://ignitetalks.io. In an Ignite, you have only 5 minutes to present 20 slides that automatically advance every 15 seconds. With this limitation, it's impossible to have much text on slides at all, or to read what's on them. Instead, you tell the story of your innovation with mostly visual examples of what you're talking about appearing on the slides behind you.

Another format that you can adapt for a field test overview presentation is Guy Kawasaki's 10–20–30 format. You get 10 minutes to go through 20 slides, and your font is no smaller than 30 points. Kawasaki, an early employee of Apple who is now an investor, popularized this format in his book, Art of the Start. While it works well for startups, I find that 10 minutes is actually too long for most executives to give you their full attention. But at five minutes, an Ignite is just long enough to spark someone's interest, but not long enough to bore them.

No matter how you visually present your overview, the end result is the same. You want them to be receptive to getting the full written report to peruse when they have time.

Writing for Your Audience

So, what format should the written report be in? It depends on the audience that is most interested in your results, and who you most want to influence.

The audience could be your boss, colleagues in a working group, other people who work in your industry, an organization for which you consult, or even a company or organization for which you'd like to work. My advice in this chapter is primarily for these professionally oriented audiences, but if you are or plan to be a "career academic," then other academics with PhDs are your audience.

Each audience is going to have its own flavor of preferred writing, as well as its own vehicles for delivery. You should use the format that is most comfortable for them.

For example, if you're writing for people in an industry that shares white papers, look at some recent white papers you've read, match your write-up to that style, and make it available as a PDF. If you're in an industry where influencers write articles on Medium, LinkedIn, or blogs, your report can be in the form of a blog post. You can even have a short blog post that includes a link to download your full report as a PDF.

What a field test report is definitely not is an academic research paper. Remember all those rules you learned in high school and college about how to write a good paper. Unless your goal is to be a teacher in K-12 or a traditional Arts and Sciences program, forget those rules. Mimic the format, style, voice, and everything else that is common in the industry you work or plan to work.

This is just a personal preference of mine, but I also never require a certain amount of words, and have never performed a word count of anything a student has given to me in my entire decade of teaching at the college level. When a student asks me how many words they should use, I turn it back on them: how many words do you think you need in order to write a compelling story for your latest innovative field test? Making something so interesting that you can't put it down and have to read until the end is always more important than word count.

Key Points to Cover in Your Report

The format may be different, but the information you want to convey is always the same. Think of the following 12 points as one possible narrative outline for any field test, regardless of the format, style, and delivery vehicle. The order can change a little, but you need to touch on each of these somehow.

1. **Overview of the Technology:** This is the most important part of the field test report, because you're highlighting how a new technology trigger makes it possible to accomplish something in a new way.

   Do some research into what the technology does, what makes it different, and who's using it in interesting ways. What indications are there that this could be a creative disruption that fundamentally changes the way people receive information or communicate?

   What are the opportunities and threats for your company – or your own job – that are raised by the innovation? What state is the technology in a Gartner's Hype Cycle?

2. **Problem Statement:** Identify a real problem, using all of the guidelines in Chapter 3: Initiating Your Field Test. What information is missing in the world, or maybe exists but isn't reaching or resonating with certain audiences? What's the cause of the problem – is it that the information isn't there, or that it's not in a form that meshes with peoples' increasingly hectic, digitally driven lives?

3. **Audience:** Who experiences this problem the most? How do you know? Present data and research that validates that this is a real problem that exists for a certain type of person and not just something you dreamed up. Make it easy for your readers to understand the demographics through visual presentation. This is a great time for you to make use of those data visualization skills you hopefully picked up in Chapter 10.

4. **Your Hypothesis:** This is your a-ha moment. You just spent a page or so explaining how something is severely broken in peoples' information experience and that there's a new technology that you think can fix it. Explain your solution clearly and succinctly, but make it clear that it's just a guess and that you will build it as a Minimum Viable Product and test it out with the audience you specified.

5. **Test Plan:** The test plan is all about how you approached the process of learning, building, and then sharing your solution with your target audience. Explain how you expected things to go. It's of course a good idea to spell out these steps even before you write up your final report. Even if they changed over time, explain how you thought you would approach things because you're providing valuable information for others who may go about the same approach in the future.

6. **Your Journey of Discovery:** This is the most fun part of the report to write, because a lot of it tends to be all the things you tried that *didn't* work, and how you iterated, adapted, and even pivoted along the way.

   Sometimes these insights are the most valuable of all, because they save others the pain of going down the wrong path. If you share your report publicly on a blog or website – something I encourage for all but the most sensitive topics – your experience with what didn't work can even influence the future iterations of the product or solution. Finally, sharing an honest journey, with warts and all, shows how tenacious of an innovator you are.

The story of your journey shows that you're the type of person who puts in the hard work to push something to its limits, with all the curiosity, effort, and frustration that this can often mean. Innovation is a messy process, and you are embracing the mess.

7. **Final Product:** Unless you completely pivoted to a different technology, audience, and solution, by the end you will have created something. This is your time to showcase what you made and how it worked – or failed. Include screenshots, both of the solution and, as appropriate, of people using it.

8. **Results:** This section is about all of the data that you collected through product analytics, surveys, anecdotal feedback, and more. Include the raw numbers that are necessary to support or refute your hypothesis, but don't feel like you have to provide all of the raw data. If you want to do that, include it as an addendum at the end of the report – perhaps as a link to data online, and be sure to anonymize it so that a data point can't be linked to any one individual. Since nobody likes poring over a lot of numbers, this is also another great opportunity for you to put those data visualization skills that you learned in Chapter 10 to use.

9. **Conclusion on Your Hypothesis:** Based on the data, was your hypothesis correct, incorrect, or partially right and partially wrong? Remember that right or wrong conclusions are not judgments of you. Your goal is to help your company and other innovators decide if the technology and approach you took are worth further investment of time, money, or both – or not.

If you identified a great new solution, talk about what steps could be taken to apply this solution at a larger scale or with better quality. If you found yourself with a dud, talk about why you think it failed. Is the technology never going to be a good approach for the use case you tried, is it just too early, or is the audience not quite ready for it? For this, you're using a combination of your data and also your gut feeling because you are one of the few – maybe only – people to have tried using this technology in this way. And that leads to the final section.

10. **Recommendations for Greater Adoption:** No emerging technology will ever be perfect, even if your hypothesis was proven right. What are the shortcomings or pitfalls of the technology solution you used, and what do you think needs to evolve or change over time in order for it to be a better candidate for your hypothesized use?

11. **French Fry Moments:** What did you notice about a technology during your journey that wouldn't have occurred to you if you hadn't tried it out? These insights can come from your test audience, from your own intuitions, or from curious ways that people used the solution that you didn't anticipate. Remember, some of the best innovations out there come from these moments, and they more than anything else are the best reason to create Minimum Viable Products and test them with real people.

Field Test Archive

On the https://emergingmediaplatforms.com website, I have shared field tests from past and current students, with their permission. You can look through things people have tried that worked, and also what didn't work. I have also invited those innovators into the Emerging Media Platforms Slack group, along with you.

It's my hope that over time, enough people will share their experiments with each other as a way to help drive smarter innovation for everyone, and solve more informational problems together in our ever-changing media landscape.

Field Testing *Your* Future

Throughout this book, you have gone through a whirlwind of technologies. You may have even produced your own field test. If you have, I invite you to share it in the book's Slack group, on Twitter and with the people you most want to impress who can give you the kinds of job opportunities you desire.

But let's be honest: your industry, job, and solving problems for others are never where things end with innovation. Through the process of discovery, you are likely to learn things about yourself that you didn't anticipate – your own personal French fry moments. Trying new things for the first time, getting out of your comfort zone, and especially confronting and pushing past your fear have a larger effect on *you*.

I invite you to consider applying the concepts explored in this book to yourself, and your own life. Because when change comes, and it will, field testing certain aspects of your own future is one way to take agency in the story of you.

Nobody ever lives in what they consider to be the most perfect of states, and life is a process of continued change. Even if you change nothing about your job, your friends, your activities, or your beliefs – guess what? Change is still happening, right down in the cells of your own body which grow older by the moment, and eventually die.

When people experience profound change from the outside through sickness, a loss of income, the death of a family member, a changing organizational chart at work, a personal realization of their core identity, or even a global pandemic – something interesting can happen for some of them. They realize that this moment, *right now*, is the time that they can make choices and change things in themselves for the better. Nobody gets to change after death, but maybe we are alive so that we can learn to change ourselves through our activities and interactions we have while we are here.

I can tell you that I have gone through several such personal experiences like this in my own life. They have greatly influenced the direction I have gone in my life and career, and even influenced what I have shared in this book. Every change can be approached as a field test if you realize all the choices you have in life.

What problems exist in your life that need to be solved? What core needs do you have which are being unmet? What potential innovative solutions might be possible which, thanks to going through a process of technologically driven solution testing for others, has unlocked your mind to visualize desired changes in yourself?

Once you identify a few possible solutions, what small, focused tests can you perform that take you in the direction you would like to go? Every journey starts with a single step. Can you structure some small steps for *the target audience of you*, which you carefully plan out and then try in a non-risky way? What kind of results do you see? Don't just think about them – measure them and write them down, in the same way that you did in a field test for others.

I have talked a lot in this book about positioning yourself for a good career in a business that chooses to hire you. But you know what? The most important business in your life is the business of *you*. There is only ever one you, and you matter. If you apply the same level of creativity, structure, and scrutiny to your own problems as you do to an external field test, you're demonstrating love to your own being through action. You deserve that!

Field Testing *Our* Future

I want to finish this book by zooming out a little to consider the future of our world, because I think everyone can agree that the world is in a difficult place across many different measures.

In 2022, when this book was written, the COVID-19 pandemic was halfway through its third year, complete with ongoing viral mutations, rolling lockdowns, and supply-chain disruptions. Gas prices had risen and fallen, prices were inflated, and Ukraine was fighting for survival against the Russian invasion. Global food supply was stretched by all of these factors.

Some of the most celebrated democratic institutions were threatened by authoritarianism, truth itself was widely questioned by many, and personal freedoms that many assumed would be a sovereign right forever were attacked and removed.

And most worrying of all, human-driven climate change was causing unprecedented heat waves and storms around the world, with the climate scientists saying the world had only 30 years to reverse carbon emissions in order to avoid an unlivable planet.

While every generation tends to think its challenges are the worst in history, it's safe to say that even if this is not as bad as it's ever been, it's right up there in the top 10. It can be easy to give up and believe that you alone can't make a difference, and that is true – if it's just you. But collectively, we all play a role in making things better when we come together with one purpose. Innovation and its positive, forward-looking approach is key to that. And as an innovator, so are you.

I often tell my students to look for what can go wrong with a new technology, and even go so far as to dream up their own dystopian futures. I do this not out of a sick fascination with dysfunction, but because journalists and purpose-driven storytellers in particular have a significant role to play in how many of these technologies evolve in human society. If we don't realize that technology can create new problems along with solutions, when we're one day sitting at a table of influence and privilege (and by getting to the end of this book, I believe you will be one of those people), we'll miss the opportunity to speak up. It's sometimes a responsibility to be the one who says, "Maybe we shouldn't launch this particular product right now," or "What safeguards need to be in place to prevent these bad scenarios, which are entirely likely if things are left unchecked, from ever happening?"

As the saying goes, an ounce of prevention is worth a pound of cure, and imagining the worst is the first step in creating preventative interventions. But what happens when the dystopia starts to look real?

Innovators are what I like to think of as realistic optimists. You may have been innovating with technologies for media and communication purposes, but as you go through the field test process repeatedly it's my belief that your brain changes. The same entrepreneurial mindset that allows you to see trends and make improvements in peoples' lives in one sector is transferable in others. And if nothing else, they can be used to inspire others to try new approaches.

Just as photogrammetry emerged from math and mining to become a building block for immersive media, and technology created for video games is now used to help doctors view MRI scans in 3D, an innovative mindset in media can also be applied to other problems and pain points in our world.

Given the sometimes depressing list of problems we face in our world, I'm not saying that you as a media practitioner should start telling scientists, doctors, or politicians how to do their jobs. But I do think that good communicators who also know how to spot problems and opportunities can be some of the best collaborators in figuring out how to solve the biggest existential issues of our time.

Most importantly, we have a responsibility to educate the public to enable the larger, society-wide innovation that needs to happen in our world. As someone who made it to the end of this book, you now share that responsibility. I know you will make the right choices.

Online Resources for Chapter 12

Find more resources for Chapter 12 online at http://emergingmediaplatforms.com/chapter12.

Afterword
The Edge of Innovation

As I said at the beginning of this book, it is impossible for any book about change and the future to be up to date when it is published. There's always something new that is emerging. I am constantly updating the companion website, emergingmediaplatforms.com, with such information. But I want to take a minute to talk about one in particular that was trending strongly in the summer of 2022: Artificial Intelligence.

I originally planned on just making a short mention of AI in the chapter about data and automation, and I did to some extent. But what surprised me is how often AI came up in interviews with industry professionals. Through that process I discovered that there was so much innovation in AI that was just starting to trend that it was impossible to predict where it would end up by publication time. But it was extremely clear that this topic was likely to be peaking for media in particular in 2023 or 2024.

The topic was mentioned by practically every professional I talked to, and everyone was saying the same things: Have you seen this application of AI? What does this mean for producing (fill in the blank) type of content? What does this mean for our jobs? What ethical guardrails need to be put in place to prevent (fill in the blank)?

In fact, without really planning on it, I ended up using several AI engines to assist with the production of this book. Yes, that's right, parts of this book were produced with the assistance of AI – a statement which, like those for genetically modified foods, I think we can expect to see more and more in media.

For example, the cover image of this book was produced by the GPT-3-powered *Midjourney* art bot, which you can experiment with yourself at Midjourney.com. After trying several different queries, I put the title and all of the main topics in to produce several versions of the image you see. In case you're wondering, the query was "*/Imagine change theories open source XR metaverse AR glasses field test 360 video camera data AI automation bots the future.*"

To help with creating citations, I used the Quillbot citation generator, which you can find at Quillbot.com. I had never used such a service before and I did check everything for accuracy, but I can tell you that it sped up the tedious process of writing citations. Quillbot has other features, such as a paraphrase which summarizes long text that you put into it.

DOI: 10.4324/9781003247012-14

Finally, to help with formatting transcripts, I used the OpenAI beta playground (beta.openai.com). This company has been racing with several other AI competitors to do all kinds of things with AI. The OpenAI playground helped me do basic formatting of my interviews, all of which were done over Zoom and transcribed using Otter.ai. I of course read through every bit of conversation to make sure it was formatted correctly, but working with the assistance of AI to handle some of the more boring and tedious aspects of transcribing interviews was immeasurably helpful and freed the more creative parts of my mind to focus on the larger narrative.

As great of an experience this all was for a tinkerer like myself, I also discovered some things that gave me pause and I share those here as a warning. When humans and robots are collaborating together on content – whether textual, spoken, or visual – how do we know that what we are consuming reflects reality? For that, I'll share my horror story.

While transcribing one interview (I won't say which or share their gender or details, to protect the privacy of the individual), I discovered that OpenAI was more than happy to take liberties with completing parts of the story that it thought could be better. One part of the interview explored a topic which was sensitive to the interviewee, so they changed the subject abruptly.

OpenAI inserted several sentences of dialogue to describe events in that person's life that had never happened, and it also inserted dialogue from me. I was so shocked at this that during our next interview, I had to show my interviewee.

I then showed them that OpenAI could be asked to read a Wikipedia article about the person and summarize the awards they had won. OpenAI apparently wasn't satisfied with the awards list, so it gave this person an additional award: an Emmy which they had never earned. I deleted all of that material to make sure it never got close to being accidentally included in the book, but that person was disappointed and wanted me to share the fake transcript with them because it made them feel good.

Many more knowledgeable about the current state of AI can speak better to what may have been going on, but the few I have spoken to said that this algorithmically driven desire to please the person entering prompts is partly to do with it. Just like how search engine queries lead to getting us the information we seek as fast as possible, or social media algorithms bubble up what the social media services think will keep us most engaged, AI algorithms just want us to be happy – even if it means that being happy means giving us information that isn't true.

Even the cover of this book fits that description. It is vaguely human, vaguely robot, and has some vague aspects of the technologies included in the prompt I entered. And because it is a piece of art, it is also 100% not reality. I didn't want it to be. I wanted something that inspires people to explore emerging media platforms.

Lest anyone think I'm bashing AI or any of the companies I mention here, I just want to be clear. I think that the work they're doing is truly amazing and transformational. And in fairness, I was using something that was marked "beta," and was not meant for production. But as with all emerging tech, understanding its potential dark side early on is important.

We as media producers are the ones who will inevitably find ourselves using these algorithms as they get licensed for use in the tools we use for everyday media production.

Need a better headline? Click this button and see options. Need to clean up this marketing photo, or change the look of the people in it? Click that button. Need to write a story with better facts than what actually happened? Click here. Now, isn't that better? (Hopefully, you are vigorously shaking your head "no" right now.)

In the end, it will be our responsibility as media producers to make sure we use these AI tools in the right ways to better inform and engage the public versus the opposite. That baton is now in your hands.

Index

3D Robotics 168
8th Wall 79
360 photography/video 107–123, 129

A/B tests 97
Adobe: Adobe Aero 79–1; Adobe
    Premiere 112, 115–117; Adobe XD 91
A-Frame 63–65, 79, 81, 114–115
Agile Development Framework 30
Airtable 150–151, 153
Alexa 156, 158, 165
algorithms 49–50, 55, 126, 143, 159–161,
    164, 194–195
Alkalay, Loretta 183
Aloft 180
AltspaceVR 60
Amazon 154, 156; Echo 154
America Online see AOL
American Press Institute 29
Anderson, Chris 168
Android 51, 77–78, 80–82, 91, 130–131,
    154, 168, 180
AOL 9–11, 13, 15, 102, 153
Apple 7, 9, 22, 51, 76–77, 122, 126, 186;
    ARKit 77–78; iPad 7–8, 22, 80; iPhone
    1, 8, 10, 22, 36–37, 77–79, 81–83,
    91, 126, 131; iTunes 99; QuickTime
    108–109; Reality Composer 79; Siri 153
Apple TV 12
Application Programming Interfaces
    148–151, 153–156
Archer, Dan 86–89
ARCore 77
ARKit 77–78
artificial intelligence 5, 41, 48–49, 55, 76,
    138, 143–144, 147, 159–162, 164–165,
    193–195
Associated Press 144
Augmented Reality 57, 71, 76–87

Automated Insights 144
automation 142–159
Axes of Uncertainty 24–25
Axure 91

Baker, Ryan 1, 84–86
Balabanian, Azad 138
Batten, James 8–10
Bell Labs 161
Bierman, Bob 34–41
Bixby 153
Blender 130
BlenderBot 3 162
Bloomfield Information Project 151–152
Bluetooth 87
Boeing 162
Bootstrap 87
Branagan, Sean 125
Branham, Lorraine 170
Brennan, John 70
Bulletin Board Services 9

C# 59, 69, 73
Case Studies 13–16, 67–68, 84–86,
    99–100, 118–119, 151–152, 156–159,
    180–181
cathedral method 42, 91
CGI 58, 111
change theories 18–26
Chat Fuel 155–156
chatbots 92–94, 96, 98, 104–105, 154,
    156–157, 162
Christensen, Clayton 19–22, 29–30
Cirasuolo, Sonny 133–141
Clarke, Arthur C. 6–8
climate change 191
Coca-Cola 72
CodeAcademy 33, 47
Control Video Corporation 9, see also AOL

conversation flow 154
COVID-19 pandemic 24, 27, 31, 60,
    67–68, 72, 78, 96, 104, 152, 191
Craigslist 20
Crowdtangle 152
CSS 44–48, 52, 63, 164
CyArk 141

DALL.E 6, 139–140
Datawrapper 147
Davis, Fred 18–19
de la Peña, Nonny 58, 65, 68–75, 110
deep fakes 161
Digital Ink 159
DJI 168
drones 4, 36, 99–100, 167–184

early adopters 22–23, 83, 144
Eastman Kodak 21, 108
Ellermeier, Wolfgang 112
Emblematic Group 127
Empathetic Media 86
Euronews 120–122
evaluation methods 97–98
Everywhere Museum 84–86
Extended Reality *see* XR

FAA Modernization and Reform Act 168
Facebook 11, 14, 22, 77, 86, 96, 118–119,
    148, 152, 154–155, 162, 181, *see also* Meta
Factba.se 159–160
fake news 48–49, 139, 151, 161
Fakebox 48–49
FBX 128, 135
Federal Aviation Administration 168–183
field test: conducting 90–100; initiating
    27–33, 188; reporting 186–192
Figma 91
FiscalNote 159
Flourish Studio 147
Floyd, George 103
Fortnite 73, 89
French fry moments 49, 67, 98–100, 105,
    189–190
Frischling, Bill 159–165
FRONTLINE 127
Future Today Institute 24
fuzzy logic 162

Galperin, Simon 152
gaming engines 59
Gartner 22–23; Hype Cycle 22–23, 31, 56,
    122, 154, 170, 188
Gelman, Mitch 110

GitHub 46, 48–49, 52, 54, 82, 115, 133,
    147, 165
GLB/GLTF 81–83, 128, 132–133
Glitch 47–48, 64–65, 115
Google 14, 22, 51, 53, 65, 71, 76–77,
    93, 110, 119, 143, 148, 152, 155;
    Analytics 97; ARCore 77; Assistant 154;
    Cardboard 119; Drawings 90; Earth 126;
    Forms 97; Glass 11–12, 109–110; Jigsaw
    74; Model-Viewer 79, 81–83, 85; Sheets
    145–146, 149–150, 152–153; Street
    View 113–114; Translate 164
GoPro 39, 109–110, 112, 135
GPS 168, 180

Harding, Tonya 161
Harper, Ken 133–141
Harvest of Change 58, 78, 110–111
Horowitz, Ben 11
Horsey Horseless Carriage 10–11, 16, 94
HTML 44–48, 51–52, 63, 65, 69, 82, 122,
    132, 164
Hunger in Los Angeles 58, 69–71, 73–74,
    110
Hype Cycle 22–23, 31, 56, 122, 154, 170, 188

IFTTT 148–151, 153
Ignite 186–187
immersive training 74
Innovator's Dilemma 19–22, 29
Instagram 79, 83, 96, 122, 155
iPad 7–8, 22, 80
iPhone 1, 8, 10, 22, 36–37, 77–79, 81–83,
    91, 126, 131

JavaScript 44–48, 52, 59, 86, 147
Jobs, Steve 7, 22
Justinmind 91

Kawasaki, Guy 186
Kebbel, Gary v, x, xi, xii
Kern, Angelika 112
Kerrigan, Nancy 161
Keyhole 126
Knight Foundation 13, 50, 73, 101, 169, 182
Knight Ridder 8–10
Kodak 21, 108

Lamarr, Hedy 161
Landbot 156–157
LiDAR 1, 77, 126, 131, 138
LinkedIn 96, 187
LinkedIn Learning 33
Luckey, Palmer 58

Mace, Michael 10
machine learning 5, 48–49, 55, 143,
    161–162
Mark, Michaela Kobsa 70
Meta 22, 77, 79, 122, 148, 152, 162, *see
    also* Facebook
METAR 175–176
Metaverse 6, 36, 56, 59–60, 65, 72–73,
    88–89, 122, 139–140
Microsoft 12, 51, 60, 93, 126; Excel
    145–146
Midjourney 193
Miller, Johnny 182
Minecraft 73, 130
Minimum Viable Product 91–93, 188–189
Minority Report 88, 163
Mixed Reality 57, 87
monoscopic video 107–108
Moore, Aubrey 135
Mozilla Hubs 60–61, 67, 73, 88, 133
Murrow, Edward R. 2
MySpace 123

National Press Photographers Association
    182
natural language processing 143–144, 153,
    160
Netflix 42, 108
New York Times 8, 43, 49, 78, 111, 127
Newman, Bradley 70
News Day 161
Newspaper Next 29–31
NextDoor 96, 181
Nike 36
Nintendo Virtual Boy 11–12
Nokia 109
NOVA 127

Oculus 11, 40, 58, 60, 63, 72, 77, 86,
    108–111
Odeo 99
OpenAI 164, 194
OpenNews 54
open-source technologies 42–49
Osterreicher, Mickey 182–184

panoramic video 107
Part 107 license 99, 170–171, 173–177,
    179–182
PDFs 16, 27, 145–146, 150–151, 177, 187
Pence, Mike 163
photogrammetry 125–133
Photoshop 73, 161
PlayStation 58

Polycam 131, 138
Printcasting 13–16, 27
privacy 4, 11, 35–36, 123, 155, 167, 169,
    171, 194
Pro Tools 113
prototyping 90–91
Puchberger, Joseph 108
Putin, Vladimir 163
Puzzling Places 138
Python 47

Qlone 130–131
QR codes 96, 105
Qualtrics 97
Quillbot 193

RADAR 143
Raymond, Eric 42–43, 91
Reaper 113
Reddit 96
Replika 162
Ressi, Adeo 95
Rheingold, Howard 69
Ries, Eric 30, 92
Rinehart, Aimee 144
Roku 12
Rossmark, Sharon 183

Samsung 119; Bixby 153
Schultz, Dan 50–55
Second Life 69, 72–74
Sennheiser 113
Seymat, Thomas 119–123
Shakespeare, William 40, 89
Sims 130
Simulated Reality 57
Siri 153
Sketchfab 127, 132–133, 140, 148
SkyVector 177
SmarterChild 153
smartphones 12, 45, 63, 74, 76, 81,
    112–113, 129, *see also* iPhone
Smith, Uriah 10
Smithsonian 3D 126–127
Snap 37, 79, 83–84; Snap Spectacles 11
Snapchat 83–84
Snavely, Noel 125
Solutions Journalism 103
spreadsheets 15, 92–93, 105, 143–147,
    149–150, 155–156, 164
Stack Overflow 95
Stephenson, Neal 56
stereoscopic video 107–108
SurveyMonkey 97

Technology Acceptance Model 18–19, 36
Thought Exercises 59, 62, 79–80
ThreeJS 63
Tice, Brian 167–168
TikTok 22, 83, 88, 122
Tinkercad 130
Trnio Plus 85, 105, 130–131, 138
Trump, Donald 159–160, 163
Truth Goggles 53–54
Tumblr 121
Twitter 22, 96, 99, 122, 148–150, 152, 161

Udemy 33
Underwood, Brent 138
Unity 40, 59, 73, 88
unmanned aerial vehicles *see* drones
Unreal Engine 59
USA TODAY 58, 78, 109–110, 127
USDZ 81–83, 128

Vazquez, Christina Boomer 101–105
VFRMap 177
Videotex 8–9, 11
Virtual Reality 25, 36, 57–60, 67–72,
    74, 77–78, 86–89, 133–134; 360
    photography/video 107–123
VisiSonics 112–113
Visualizing 81 63–64, 136–137

Vive 58, 63, 72, 86
Vordio 113
Vuforia 79

W3Schools 33, 46–47
Waite, Matt 169
Washington Post 34, 37, 40, 43, 49, 159,
    185
wearables 11, 22, 57, 87
Weatherbase 160
Webb, Amy 24
WebGL 63
WebTV 11–12
Weiden, David 11
wireframing 90–91
WordPress 48, 132, 144, 147, 150
Workbook Exercises 12, 23, 25–26, 32–33,
    46–48, 60–61, 64–66, 80–84, 100,
    113–117, 130–133, 152–153

XR 56–59, 72–73, 76, 88, 130, 134

YouTube 22, 33, 90, 117, 130, 173

Zapier 148, 150–153
Zimmerman, George 103
Zoldi, Dawn M.K. 183
Zoom 24–25, 67–68, 97, 122, 194

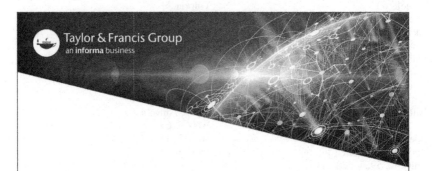

Made in the USA
Monee, IL
03 January 2024

51007897R00118